COGS IN THE
CLASSROOM FACTORY

COGS IN THE CLASSROOM FACTORY

The Changing Identity of Academic Labor

Edited by
Deborah M. Herman
and Julie M. Schmid

Foreword by David Montgomery

Westport, Connecticut
London

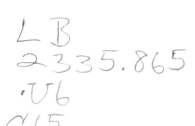

Library of Congress Cataloging-in-Publication Data

Cogs in the classroom factory : the changing identity of academic labor / edited by
Deborah M. Herman and Julie M. Schmid ; foreword by David Montgomery.
    p.   cm.
  Includes bibliographical references and index.
  ISBN 0-89789-814-1 (alk. paper)
  1. Universities and colleges—Employees—Labor unions—Organizing—United
States.   2. College teachers' unions—United States.   3. College teachers—
Tenure—United States.   4. College teachers, Part-time—Salaries, etc.—United
States.   5. Graduate teaching assistants—Salaries, etc.—United States.   6. Group
identity—Political aspects—United States.   I. Herman, Deborah M.,
1963–   II. Schmid, Julie M., 1968–

LB2335.865.U6 C65   2003
378.1'2—dc21   2002068611

British Library Cataloguing in Publication Data is available.

Library of Congress Catalog Card Number: 2002068611
ISBN: 0-89789-814-1

First published in 2003

Praeger Publishers, 88 Post Road West, Westport, CT 06881
An imprint of Greenwood Publishing Group, Inc.
www.praeger.com

Printed in the United States of America

Copyright Acknowledgments

The editors and publisher gratefully acknowledge permission to use excerpts from the
following materials:

Dennis Deslippe oral history, State Historical Society of Iowa, Iowa City.

Lyrics quoted in the Foreword are from "You Gotta Go Down and Join the Union,"
words and new music adapted by Woody Guthrie. TRO—© Copyright 1963
(Renewed) Ludlow Music, Inc., New York, NY. Used by permission.

Contents

Acronyms   *vii*

Acknowledgments   *xi*

Foreword: Preserving Our Independence, Acting Together   *xiii*
David Montgomery

Introduction: The Changing Identity of Academic Labor   *1*
Julie M. Schmid and Deborah M. Herman

PART I. A WIDENING DIVIDE: FACULTY AND OTHERS   *19*

1. Above and Below: Mapping Social Positions within
   the Academy   *21*
   Wesley Shumar and Jonathan T. Church

2. Dueling Identities and Faculty Unions:
   A Canadian Case Study   *41*
   Mike Burke and Joanne Naiman

3. In a Leftover Office in Chicago   *59*
   Joe Berry

PART II. THE NEXT GENERATION: CHARTING NEW WATERS   *69*

4. More than Academic: Labor Consciousness and the Rise
   of UE Local 896-COGS   *71*
   Susan Roth Breitzer

5. Pyrrhic Victory at UC Santa Barbara: The Struggle
    for Labor's New Identity   91
    Richard Sullivan

6. Unfinished Chapters: Institutional Alliances and Changing
    Identities in a Graduate Employee Union   117
    James Thompson

PART III. NEW TACTICS, OLD BATTLEGROUNDS   137

7. Shutting Down the Academic Factory: Developing Worker
    Identity in Graduate Employee Unions   139
    Eric Dirnbach and Susan Chimonas

8. Are You Now or Have You Ever Been an Employee?:
    Contesting Graduate Labor in the Academy   153
    William Vaughn

9. The Politics of Constructing Dissent: The Rhetorical
    Construction of Faculty Union Membership   171
    Darla S. Williams

    Afterword: Classroom, Lab, Factory Floor:
    Common Labor Struggles   191
    Carl Rosen

    Index   201

    About the Contributors   205

Acronyms

AAUP	American Association of University Professors
AFL-CIO	American Federation of Labor-Congress of Industrial Organizations
AFSCME	American Federation of State, County, and Municipal Employees
AFT	American Federation of Teachers
AHOC	Ad hoc Organizing Committee (UC-Santa Barbara)
APSCUF	Association of Pennsylvania State College & University Faculties
ASE	Associated Student Employees (UC-Santa Barbara)
BOR	Board of Regents (University of Florida)
CAUSE	California Alliance of Unionized Student Employees (alliance of UC campuses)
CAUT	Canadian Association of University Teachers
CC	Community College Bargaining Council, United Faculty of Florida
CGEU	Coalition of Graduate Employee Unions
CIO	Congress of Industrial Organizations
COGS	Campaign to Organize Graduate Students (University of Iowa)
CUE	Coalition of University Employees (University of California clerical union)
CUNY	City University of New York
CUPE	Canadian Union of Public Employees
CWA	Communication Workers of America
FAMU	Florida Agricultural and Mechanical University
FAPUQ	Fédération des associations québecoise de professeures et professeurs d'université
FAT	Frente Auténtico de Trabajo/Authentic Workers' Front
FEA	Florida Education Association
FNEEQ	Fédération nationale des enseignantes et des enseignants du Québec

FTE	Full Time Equivalent
FTP	Florida Teaching Profession
GA	Graduate Assistant (inclusive of both research and teaching assistants)
GAU	Graduate Assistants United (Florida)
GEO	Graduate Employees Organization (Michigan and Illinois)
GESO	Graduate Employees and Students Organization (Yale)
GPSS	Graduate and Professional Student Senate (Iowa)
GSI	Graduate Student Instructor
GSSA	Graduate Student Staff Assistant
HEERA	Higher Education Employee Relations Act (California)
IEA	Illinois Education Association
IELRA	Illinois Educational Labor Relations Act
IELRB	Illinois Educational Labor Relations Board
ILWU	International Longshore and Warehouse Union
IUP	Iowa United Professionals
NEA	National Education Association
NLRA	National Labor Relations Act
NLRB	National Labor Relations Board
NOW	National Organization for Women
PERB	Public Employee Relations Board (California or Iowa)
PERC	Public Employee Relations Committee (Florida)
Pfac	Part-Time Faculty Association at Columbia College (Chicago)
PSU	Pennsylvania State University
RA	Research Assistant
RAFO	Roosevelt University Adjct Faculty Organization (Chicago)
RFA	Ryerson Faculty Association (Toronto)
SAC	Students Against COGS (Iowa)
SEIU	Service Employees International Union
SM	Special Master (Florida)
SSHE	State System of Higher Education (Pennsylvania)
STOP	Students Tired of Propaganda (Iowa)
SUS	State University System (Florida)
TA	Teaching Assistant
TAA	Teaching Assistants Association (Wisconsin)
TOP	Technical and Office Professionals (Division of the UAW)
UAW	United Automobile Workers
UC	University of California
UCSB	University of California, Santa Barbara
UE	United Electrical, Radio and Machine Workers of America
UF	University of Florida
UFF	United Faculty of Florida
UF-GAU	University of Florida chapter of Graduate Assistants United

UFW	United Farm Workers
UIUC	University of Illinois, Urbana-Champaign
UPS	United Parcel Service
USF	University of South Florida
USL	United Student Labor (UC Santa Barbara)

Acknowledgments

This volume would not have been possible without the kind and generous assistance of many colleagues and friends. We would especially like to thank Cinda Coggins, Ryan Downing, Jane Garry, David Montgomery, Christine Ogren, Terry Osborn, Carl Rosen, Jennifer Sherer, and Elliott Vanskike for providing information, support, and editorial assistance. We would also like to thank the many activists and founders of UE Local 896-COGS, whose dedication and sacrifices for the principles of fair compensation, respectful treatment, and collective representation allowed us, and many other graduate employees, the means to complete our graduate studies.

We dedicate this book to all faculty and researchers who labor in the best traditions of teaching, scholarship, and inquiry.

Foreword: Preserving Our Independence, Acting Together

David Montgomery

Graduate student employees at forty universities and university systems in the United States and Canada had won union contracts by the summer of 2001, while those at more than a dozen others had affiliated with unions in organizing drives.[1] The aspirations that brought them into the labor movement are summed up by Richard Sullivan of the University of California at Santa Barbara: "A voice in the decisions that affected them, respect for the contribution they made to the university, decreased workloads, better pay, and benefits," and improvement in the quality of education, which winning those objectives would help bring about. The graduate employees, adjunct faculty, and full-time faculty whose experiences are discussed in this book make themselves part of a worldwide struggle for democracy. Men and women demanding a voice in shaping their own conditions of life and work have taken to the streets outside the formidably guarded halls where business and government officials decide the future ("uniting teamsters and turtles," as demonstrators said in Seattle) and for good reason: Representative institutions of government, which should offer their constituents such a voice, have ceded control of economic and social life to corporate enterprise through gutted budgets, deregulation, privatization, contracting out, and international trade agreements. Political leaders and the dominant voices in public discourse assure us that the best decisions for society are those made by "the market."

Colleges and universities have become a prominent arena in the current struggle to revitalize democracy. In the United States, they employ more than two and a half million workers, not counting those in firms to which the institutions have subcontracted work.[2] They have been subjected to relentless pressure from their chief executives, trustees, donors, and budget-cutting legislatures to refashion their own governance in the corporate image. Administrative salaries and personnel (assistant deans, development officers, public relations officers, and presidential speech writers) have swollen even while teaching budgets have been trimmed, driven by what Barbara Bergman of the American Association of University Professors has analyzed as "the desire of each administration for more underlings, and a governance problem—weak curbs on administrative growth."[3] To use current managerial jargon, administrators "unbundle" the many functions needed to sustain teaching and research and then contract out as many operations as possible to prove their devotion to "cost saving." They denounce faculty claims to tenure and to shared governance in the name of "flexibility," while pressing for ever greater "productivity" in teaching and research and transferring teaching responsibility to adjunct faculty and to graduate employees. Consequently graduate students are not only employed to perform much, if not most, of their universities' classroom teaching, but also face the prospect that after they have earned their degrees, they may well end up teaching for years at various colleges on a contingent or even part-time basis. Such positions, as Wesley Shumar and Jonathan Church argue, relegate these faculty to perpetual outsider status. The tenured professor, they argue, gains both autonomy for himself or herself and authority over others. The adjunct gains neither. Moreover, as poignantly elucidated by Shumar and Church, academic freedom has little purchase for someone whom administrators can dismiss at will, simply by failing to renew a contract.

In a word, much academic employment has been converted into casual labor. Over the course of the 1980s and 1990s, the percentage of college and university teaching done by part-time and adjunct faculty has risen to about 45 percent.[4] At public and private research universities offering graduate training, however, graduate students employed as teaching assistants and part-time instructors staff a comparable or even larger proportion of the teaching hours. As Joe Berry ponders gloomily on this trend, he remembers the large groups of contingent workers who had subdued the brutally arbitrary nature of the markets in which they sought work and dramatically improved their own conditions of life through democratic social movements: longshoremen, construction workers, parcel service workers. If they could do so, he wonders, "why can't we?"

The chapters in this book recount the discussions in which graduate employees, adjuncts, and tenure-line faculty in the United States and Canada have been engaged when they considered unionization, the strategies used by organizing committees to win collective bargaining, the pitfalls lurking in the path of their efforts, and the relations between organized graduate students and other workers, both on and off campus. The reader will learn from Susan Roth Breitzer how graduate employees at the University of Iowa formed their own organization to deal with the growing need for fair employment conditions to sustain themselves and their families. Two attempts to win recognition and a contract were defeated by a barrage of "informational" letters from the administration warning that collegiality and the mentoring relationship between students and faculty would be undermined by collective bargaining, supplemented by a well-orchestrated campaign by antiunion students echoing the same themes. The experience graduate employees had gained during these unsuccessful efforts informed the careful discussions by which they planned new strategies and evaluated various unions, before deciding to affiliate with the United Electrical, Radio and Machine Workers of America (UE). Their solid certification election victory in 1996 made the Iowa local one of the five largest unions to be certified in the United States that year. It did not, however, end the need for serious collective discussion about the strategy, goals, and primary identity of the organization. Hard decisions made during subsequent contract negotiations and interaction with other UE locals, during struggles that reached far beyond the boundaries of the campus, kept debate about who they were and what they were doing vigorous over the years that followed certification. Democracy turned out to be not a singular accomplishment but a process without end.[5]

The unrelenting discussion of who we are and what we want in life echoes through all the contributions to this collection. It provides the counterpoint to the submission of the academy to "market forces." University administrators, eminent faculty members, and antiunion students celebrate the academy's legacy of collegiality, mentoring, and individual distinction, which, they allege, makes higher education an island of intellectual privilege in a harsh world and warn that the interposition of a third party and formal agreements between the aspiring student and the institution threatens to destroy that precious heritage. Graduate employees and adjunct faculty reply that their daily work experience has taught them that the business practice that has reshaped the academy during recent decades has made a mockery of that vaunted legacy and transformed it into a set of advertising slogans designed to lure student customers and wealthy donors. They envisage forming unions as a necessary step in reconstructing collegiality from below.

To reach that conclusion, however, faculty of all varieties have been obliged not only to combine their forces in collective efforts to improve the terms of their employment (and even to establish those terms clearly), but also to reconsider personally the relationships linking their commitment to scholarship to their careers as workers and to the millions of other men and women who work for a living. Thoughts about identity loom large in the following chapters. This emphasis may well be as much a reflection of current themes in academic writing and instruction as it is of the peculiar circumstances of academic employment. Nevertheless, it does underscore both the nature of the attacks leveled against unions by administrations (and also by eminent professors in the disciplines within which graduate students and adjunct faculty plan their careers) and the questions union members and potential members must answer for themselves as they respond to those attacks. Discussions of identity lend new meaning to the words of the old union song:

Nobody here can join it for you
You gotta go down and join the union by yourself.[6][©]

STRATEGIES

For those involved in building unions these chapters offer strategic and tacti-cal lessons in abundance. Susan Roth Breitzer and William Vaughn both stress the importance of concerted action on behalf of members' economic demands when and where collective strength can be mobilized without waiting for a cer-tification election or contract negotiations. They also note the peculiarity of unions whose members carry on their work in many locations scattered over the campus (just as is the case with a university's clerical and technical workers) and some of whom (for example, in sciences or engineering) confront very different circumstances than others (for example, English or history). High annual turnover of members lends special importance to the stabilizing role of elected departmental representatives both before recognition and after. International unions can offer indispensable funding and advice, but the decisive initiative, understanding, and staying power can only come from those who have con-sciously, and often at considerable personal sacrifice, undertaken to organize their colleagues.

Federal and state labor relations laws provide at best cumbersome and un-trustworthy support for unionization of adjunct and graduate employees, but these laws cannot be simply ignored. During the 1960s and 1970s, many states enacted statutes authorizing public employees to unionize, but often circum-scribed that authorization with prohibition against going on strike, bargaining over specified issues, or negotiating compulsory membership or contributions. Although the state's law permitted a relatively expeditious election at the University of Iowa and made provision for arbitration that helped the union win concessions at the table, graduate employees at the University of Illinois (Champaign-Urbana), as William Vaughn details, found their state's legislation a nightmare of obscurity and obstruction. In sharp contrast to Illinois, rulings by the labor boards of Pennsylvania and Michigan opened the way to bargain-ing elections and clear victories for graduate student teachers' unions affiliated with the American Federation of Teachers at Temple University and Michigan State University.[7]

Adjunct faculty have also made effective use of state labor boards, especially when substantial numbers of part-timers are concentrated in a single institution and can mobilize the support of existing unions. At the University of Massa-chusetts, Boston, the Faculty Staff Union/NEA successfully organized in 1998 a campaign of part-time faculty members in the continuing education division for a salary increase and access to the university's health plan. The NEA then filed with the state labor board for a representation election, and in July 2001, it won recognition as the agent for 180 part-time instructors in the division. Both campaigns enjoyed effective support from the Boston chapter of the Coalition of Contingent Labor. Success in Boston inspired the graduate employees at the Amherst campus of the University of Massachusetts, which employs most of the three hundred part-time instructors in continuing education, to petition for an election for representation by the campus Graduate Employees Organization/UAW). After a full year of hotly contested hearings, the union also engaged in picketing and sit-ins demanding immediate recognition.[8]

Employees of private colleges and universities are under the jurisdiction of the National Labor Relations Board (NLRB). In 1970, the board reversed a twenty-year-old decision that had previously assigned such workers to state labor boards. Cornell and Syracuse universities had asked the board to assume jurisdiction over disputes they faced with their nonacademic employees. Cornell's position was vigorously seconded by Yale University, whose maintenance workers were then on strike, because the federal Taft-Hartley Act allowed unfair labor practice charges to be brought against unions, while Connecticut's law did not. Yale got what it wanted. The NLRB assumed jurisdiction over employees of private universities; a year later, the NLRB decided that its ruling applied to professional personnel as well as maintenance workers. Recent events have now cast that decision by President Richard Nixon's NLRB in an ironic light. When the general counsel of the NLRB ruled in 1995 that graduate student teachers were professional employees, he opened the way to an election victory for the United Auto Workers as the representative of those teachers at New York University in 2000—and breathed new vigor into the organizing campaign at Yale.[9]

Nevertheless, seeking certification from the NLRB, or even protection of union activists from university sanctions, has proven to be a tortuous and highly unreliable route for graduate employees and adjuncts at private universities to follow. The board can take years to decide which employees are eligible to vote and which are not, and administrators can then appeal through various levels of courts any decisions they dislike. When an election is authorized, the campaign becomes the occasion for intimidation of union supporters, public and private meetings organized by administrators, and a barrage of newsletters designed to dissuade graduate employees from voting for the union. NLRB sanctions against threats and intimidation have proven to be as ineffective today on campuses as they are in industry. Consequently, the Graduate Employees and Students Organization at Yale (GESO) has taken the approach now used in its many campaigns around the land by the Hotel Employees and Restaurant Employees, with which it is affiliated. GESO has called on the Yale administration to recognize its employees' constitutional rights to associate by refraining from intimidation and sanctions against union supporters and to recognize and negotiate with the union if and when it presents membership cards representing a majority of the graduate student teachers. The local unions representing other workers at Yale have decided to support GESO's demands during their own 2001–02 negotiations for contract renewals.

Union demands for recognition by card count and for a pledge by management to remain neutral during organizing campaigns have become increasingly common, especially in those service occupations where organizing is now most vigorous. The practice represents a return to the early years of the Wagner Act, when the legal right to organize and bargain collectively was interpreted by the NLRB to protect debates among workers over the merits of unionization, not debates between workers and their employers, as they came under "employer free speech" provisions of the 1947 Taft-Hartley Act. Moreover, the board has always had authority to certify a union without an election (even under Taft-Hartley), and it does so routinely with construction workers. During 1938 and 1939, the first full years of NLRB operation, fully one-third of its certifications were based on card counts.[10] Unions in the forefront of new organizing today have revived that practice. Organizations of adjuncts and of graduate employees that face hostile administrations and dilatory labor boards, but that also enjoy the active local support of other unions, may in the future pursue paths to contract negotiations that do not involve the hearings and election procedures of state and federal labor boards.

AFTER RECOGNITION

Bringing the administration to the bargaining table, however, is not the end of the story, but only the first step. As Eric Dirnbach and Susan Chimonas illustrate, the experience of the Graduate Employees Organization (American Federation of Teachers Local 3550) provides especially instructive lessons because it has been bargaining with the University of Michigan since 1974. Graduate employees learned that the administration treated bargaining sessions as occasions simply to exchange views, not to change conditions of employment. Although the union had initially fought to open negotiations to public view, it found in 1998 that the main problem its negotiators faced was not a lack of openness, but rather the need to speed up the pace of talks with an eye on the academic calendar. Demonstrations that rallied the membership and one-day stoppages that promised other later and larger strikes provided effective ways to improve what the administration put on the table. Whether graduate employees or full-time faculty, the lessons are often the same. Darla Williams shows that the faculty union in the Pennsylvania State College System learned, as had Michigan activists, how carefully and thoroughly a strike must be prepared.

Generally speaking, unions formed by full-time faculty members have provided inspiration and (sometimes) assistance to organizing efforts of graduate employees, but their relationship to adjunct faculty has been especially important and contentious. Faculty unions spread rapidly in both the United States and Canada during the early 1970s in both two-year and public four-year colleges. By 1995, there were 422 faculty bargaining agents on campuses in the United States, most of them affiliated with the American Federation of Teachers (AFT), the American Association of University Professors (AAUP), or the National Education Association (NEA). All told, they represent about one-quarter of the full-time faculty and non-supervisory staffs of U.S. higher education. About fifty thousand faculty members are represented by local mergers of unions, which are distinct and even rivals elsewhere, like those at the universities of Rhode Island and Massachusetts—an unusual and very healthy development in the history of American labor. The rapid growth of faculty unionism at a time when unions have been shrinking in manufacturing and mining has resulted in the astounding development that, in 2001, a college teacher was more likely to be a union member than was someone mining coal.[11] That development becomes easier to fathom when we remember that the graduate employee unions at Iowa and in the California system are among the largest bargaining units certified in the last decade.

In Canada, where the population is little more than one-tenth that of the United States and almost all postsecondary institutions are publicly funded, over half the faculty members are unionized. In recent years, bitter strikes on many Canadian campuses have revolved around the most fundamental issues of the purposes, funding, and structure of academic life. In Quebec, most faculty members are members of unions affiliated with the Fédération des associations québecoise de professeures et professeurs d'université (FAPUQ), though the graduate students employed at McGill University bargain through the Fédération nationale des enseignantes et des enseignants du Québec (FNEEQ).[12] Other unions play the crucial roles in English-speaking Canada. The Canadian Association of University Teachers (CAUT) was transformed by its members into a collective bargaining agency during the early 1970s with much the same hesitation, then increasing determination, evident in the American Association of University Professors (AAUP) at roughly the same time.[13] It has joined the Canadian Union of Public Employees (CUPE) as a leading force in faculty unionization, though CUPE has played by far the more important role in unionizing graduate employees.

Burke and Naiman show that the CAUT local at Ryerson Polytechnic, faced with a change to full university status and also with serious cuts in government funding, accepted in 1991 the introduction of a two-tiered salary structure, coupled with an intensification of work loads and minimal prospects of tenure for newer members of the faculty. The impact of that agreement seriously undermined the solidarity and the expectations of union members in subsequent negotiations. Concession bargaining throughout North American industry during the 1980s had induced many unions to safeguard the established members at the expense of new hires, only to find that the commitment of both groups of workers to the union cause deteriorated as result. Burke and Naiman issue a warning that even when teachers have a union, administration strategies can intensify the difference between the ways tenured faculty and adjuncts envisage themselves and their needs at a time when both groups stand in need of forging a common front.

Richard Sullivan issues a different type of warning. He argues that, even as the United Auto Workers (UAW) secured a contract covering ten thousand graduate employees in the University of California system, the leadership given by the international union undermined the local activists who had built the union at the Santa Barbara campus and, ultimately, most members' participation in and support for contract struggles after the union had been recognized. Serious differences in perspective and goals between graduate employee activists and organizers representing international unions are an all too common experience, but the case study of Santa Barbara and the testimony its disgruntled pioneer activists express are especially grim and thought provoking.

The victories of the UAW in bargaining elections at the University of California and later at New York University raised the hopes of local activists facing intransigent university administrations elsewhere in the land and won their admiration for the UAW as a union that stays with the battle and wins. Any effort encompassing several campuses requires a coordinated leadership council to devise strategies and to oversee the execution of those strategies (as the experience of the Pennsylvania State College System makes clear). Nevertheless, the relationship between local activists and the members they have recruited and mobilized is of decisive importance, not only to the success of an organizing drive, but also to the subsequent achievement of the goals for which graduate employees took up the union cause. The experience at Iowa and at Michigan has underscored the crucial role of elected departmental representatives in both organizing a union, many of whose members change each year, and in maintaining its vitality after recognition. Effective coordination or organized struggle encompassing eight widely scattered campuses requires the creation of an authoritative body made of representatives from each locality, supported and advised by the international union. But it also requires recognition by all concerned that graduate employees at different localities may produce quite different styles of operation and that members on every campus must have ready and effective access to making the decisions that affect that campus.

The reader of Sullivan's chapter may wish for the testimony of activists on other campuses of the University of California system who, he writes, "with a few exceptions ... tended to support the UAW program and consistently joined them in opposing USCB initiatives." There are, however, other conclusions of a quite different nature to be drawn from his account. The strategy pursued by the union leaders in California hinged on winning over the Public Employees Relations Board, the courts, and state legislators to the position that graduate employees were entitled to coverage under the state's Higher Education Employee Relations Act. We have already learned from the harsh experience of academic unionists facing labor boards in other states, as well as the National Labor Relations Board, why university administrations hostile to unionization appeal to such boards with considerable confidence. The decision of the Illinois board, which excluded from the bargaining unit every student who taught a course related to his or her field of study, is especially ominous, and it has already provided the basis for arguments used by attorneys for recalcitrant university administrations before federal boards and courts. One way to circumvent such legal roadblocks to representation, while also keeping the struggle for recognition directly in the hands of members, is to demand recognition on the basis of a card count, instead of a labor board election, and to mount public campaigns in support of that demand.

Women and men who engage in the struggle for democracy at the institutions where they study and earn a living can learn three important lessons from the experiences recounted in this book. First, they must think and act together with those in the same circumstances as themselves, but also with other working people in their country and in the world who also confront lean and mean management and the cult of the free market. Second, all activists must be prepared to face disagreement, dissention, and even betrayal within the circles of people closest to them and on whom they most depend for support. Think of the ups and downs union militants active in the United States from the 1920s through the 1950s experienced over the course of their lives. Time and time again, in constantly changing circumstances, they had to regroup their workmates around the unchanging goal of democratic control of their own lives and fortunes.

Third, the struggle of adjunct faculty and graduate employees, the casual laborers of corporatized higher education, for a decent income, medical care, respect, and a voice will bring a change not only in their own lives, but also in the contemporary culture of teaching and research. University administrations have mimicked corporate management while cloaking their opposition to graduate employees' unions in the archaic and hollow rhetoric of "collegiality" and "mentorship." It is left up to the students and faculty, using all forums at their disposal, to open their own serious discussion about the true meaning of collegiality and about the nature and mission of higher education in society today. Unionization is but one step in this process—an indispensable step, for it can give collective voice and power to counteract the pressures of the bottom line and business needs that are felt today. But we also study, debate, and teach in order to find answers to the problems facing our society and its environment. The fight for a democratic voice within the academy reopens questions not only about our own identities, but also about the social purposes of higher education.[14]

NOTES

1. CGEU Contact List, <http://www.cgeu.org/contacts.html>.

2. Robin D.G. Kelley, "The proletariat goes to college," in *Will teach for food: Academic labor in crisis,* ed. Cary Nelson, 146. Minneapolis, MN: University of Minnesota Press, 1997.

3. Barbara Bergman, "Bloated administration, blighted campuses," *Academe* 77 (Nov-Dec, 1993), 13.

4. Carey Nelson, ed., *Will teach for food,* 146.

5. A similar process of protracted debate and accumulated experience characterized the pioneering 1971 union victory at the University of Rhode Island. See Gordon B. Arnold, *The politics of faculty unionization: The experience of three New England universities,* 55–76. Westport, CT: Bergin & Garvey, 2000.

6. Woody Guthrie, "You gotta go down," in *People's song book,* ed. Waldemar Hille, 93. New York: Boni and Gaer, 1948.

7. Scott Smallwood, "TA's at Temple U vote to unionize," *Chronicle of Higher Education,* March 1, 2001, <chronicle.com/daily/2001/03/3001032902n.htm>; message of Joseph E. Slater, <H-LABOR@H-NET>MSU.EDU>, July 23, 2001.

8. *Boston Globe,* July 13, 2000, 1.

9. Robert K. Carr and Daniel K. Van Eyck, *Collective bargaining comes to the campus,* 20-30. Washington, D.C.: American Council on Education, 1973; Ronald L. Johnstone, *The scope of faculty collective bargaining: An analysis of faculty union agreements at four-year institutions of higher learning,* 11. Westport, CT: Greenwood Press, 1981; C. Leatherman, "NLRB ruling may demolish the barriers to TA unions at private universities," *Chronicle of Higher Education,* April 14, 2000.

10. David Brody, "Criminalizing the rights of labor," *Dissent,* 42 (Sum 1995), 363–367.

11. Philo A. Hutcheson, *A professional professoriate: Unionization, bureaucratization, and the AAUP,* 180. Nashville, TN: Vanderbilt University Press, 2000; Johnstone, *Scope.*

12. I am grateful to professors Jacques Rouillard and Nelson Ouellet for the information about faculty unions in Quebec.

13. On the protracted controversy within the AAUP over collective bargaining, see Hutcheson, *A professional professoriate.*

14. That question is posed well by Cary Nelson in *Will teach for food,* 23–25.

Introduction:
The Changing Identity of Academic Labor

Julie M. Schmid and Deborah M. Herman

I consider it important, indeed, urgently necessary, for university workers to get together, both to protect their own economic status and, also, generally speaking, to secure their influence in the political field.

—Albert Einstein

As our epigraph suggests, the phenomenon of academics adopting a worker consciousness is not new. Excerpted from Einstein's essay "For an Organization of Intellectual Workers" (1950) these words are perennial favorites among higher education union organizers—undoubtedly as much for the stature of the speaker as for the sentiment expressed. This excerpt makes it clear that the need for an academic worker consciousness and a strong higher-education labor movement is not the result of the vicissitudes of the academic job market over the past two decades. Nor is it the result of the erosion of tenure and the increasing dependence on adjunct and graduate-employee labor. Written over fifty years ago, these words indicate that the development of a worker consciousness among faculty has been a long time in coming.

This quotation, with its emphasis on academics as workers and on the importance of collective action as a means to protect economic status and increase political influence, could lead one to intuit that little has changed in higher education in the past five decades. In fact, the nature of higher education in North America has evolved significantly, and as a result, the context in which we ask questions about the identity and the role of faculty has changed as well. The division between tenured and nontenured faculty at four-year colleges and universities has widened into a gaping divide that threatens old concepts of "faculty" and, consequently, the nature of teaching, scholarship, and academic freedom. What does academic freedom mean when, for example, 60 percent of

an institution's teaching faculty are permanently "temporary"?[1] Have research
agendas been influenced by corporate monies and, if so, how? Can academic departments continue scholarly development when, year after year, tenure lines
disappear from the budget? These are the issues facing virtually every college
and university today. The participation of growing numbers of contingent faculty—that is, those working in adjunct or fixed-term, nontenurable positions—
and graduate employees in unions is creating a new generation of academics
who are struggling with these issues. They, along with their tenure-line colleagues (both union and nonunion), continue to struggle with reconciling their
collective identity as "academics" with that of "mind workers" in this new corporatized context.[2] While it has long been assumed that these issues only affect
scholars in the humanities and social sciences, scholars in the hard sciences today
face the same problems, as pointed out in a recent *New York Times* article:

> What used to be two or three years of career development often becomes five or more
> years in one [temporary postdoc] after another. Many of the postdocs are almost 50 be-
> fore they start their first permanent positions and begin saving for retirement.... With
> research appointments starting to feel more like long-term commitments, postdocs are
> starting to organize on dozens of campuses and demanding higher pay and benefits like
> health care and parental leave. On a few campuses, they have even begun talking to
> unions. (Lee 2001)

As this passage makes clear, and as the contributors to this volume eloquently
argue, for an increasing number of scholars the five to ten years spent on a doc-
torate no longer results in a tenure-track job. Rather, the best that many newly
minted PhDs can hope for is an "academic career" comprising a series of temporary positions. This increased reliance on temporary, nontenurable faculty at
colleges and universities around North America has resulted in a workforce that
has more in common with other temporary workers than with tenured and
tenure-track faculty. Like other temporary workers in the new global economy,
many contingent academic workers are paid poverty-level wages, receive little
or no health or retirement benefits, and have no job security.[3] As Cary Nelson
and Jeremy Smith point out, the experiences of these exploited workers are a
bellwether; things will undoubtedly get worse for all sectors of the academic job
system before they get better (Nelson 1997a; Smith 1998).

THE ROOTS OF THE ACADEMIC UNION MOVEMENT

While some elements of the current battles in higher education are new, the
tension between professional and worker identity in the professoriat is not. Neither is the phenomenon of academic unions. In fact, the histories of identity tension and unionization in academia are closely intertwined. The first major push
in the United States for teacher unionization was coincident with the expansion
of K-12 education at the turn of the twentieth century.[4] Between 1890 and 1920,

the United States began development of a mass education system intended to involve virtually all children throughout adolescence, not just a privileged few. With this came large and increasingly bureaucratized forms of organization. Layers of hierarchy, inherently entangled with class, race, and gender issues, developed, especially in the large cities. The early teachers unions fought not only for better pay and better working conditions, but for respect as professional experts and for a say in the governance of the school district. Impatient with the "study and report" mode of the National Education Association (NEA), Chicago teachers who wanted the right to control their own curricula and to reconnect the school with the local community formed a local union in 1897. By 1915, this Chicago-based local evolved into the American Federation of Teachers (AFT). By affiliating with the American Federation of Labor (AFL) in 1916, the AFT became the first "brain workers" (as they were called by AFL founder Samuel Gompers) to try to apply the model of industrial unionism to educational institutions. (For reviews of the development of mass education systems, the history of K-12 teacher unions, and current issues in K-12 teacher unions in the United States, see Wesley 1957; Eaton 1975; West 1980; Urban 1982, 2000; Murphy 1990; Kerchner, Koppich and Weeres 1997.)

While there was some interest in these developments among college and university faculty, the unionization movement did not take hold in higher education during the early decades of the twentieth century. Although under pressure to conform to the same business models of efficiency, productivity, and accountability that were being applied to K-12 systems, colleges and universities were in most cases able to fend off those practices that they deemed incompatible with academic life. It is probably no coincidence, however, that the American Association of University Professors (AAUP) was founded in 1915, around the same time as the AFT. For the first years of its existence, its primary goal was the protection of academic freedom. Political conservatives—many of whom were newly affluent business elites who gave generous donations to colleges and universities—were not always friendly to independent research and scholarship, particularly if such work led to professors espousing unpopular opinions in the classroom or other public venues. Despite the perceived need for protection against such outside influence, the founders maintained the group's identity as a professional organization rather than a union and stated in its call to organize:

Believing that a society, comparable to the American Bar Association and the American Medical Association in kindred professions, could be of substantial service to the ends for which universities exist, members of the faculties of a number of institutions have undertaken to bring about the formation of a national Association of University Professors. (Hutcheson 2000, 7)

The assumption among academics and nonacademics alike that the AAUP was a union continued, however, and in the February 1938 *Bulletin of the AAUP*, its former general secretary H.W. Tyler again clarified:

The Association is not a "Professors Union." The epithet, many times thoughtlessly rather than ignorantly applied, might be fitting if the Association had devoted itself to protecting the economic rights and increasing the monetary rewards of its own members, or perhaps of restricting their performance. (Hutcheson 2000, 14)

Tyler's linkage of "performance restriction" to unionism is a telling one: It presumes a style of unionism that is in direct opposition with meritocratic ideals and the concept of individual scholarship. Nevertheless, the AAUP spent decades pushing for salary improvement, due process, and other issues clearly parallel to the types of workplace issues addressed in union collective action and, later, in union contracts. It would not be until the late 1960s that the AAUP formally embraced collective bargaining as a means to those ends. While a little more than half of all AAUP members in the United States now are in collective bargaining chapters, the association's dual identity as a professional organization and a union emphasizes the double-consciousness that typifies the academic union movement. This dual identity is complicated by the AAUP's recent forays into organizing among contingent faculty. Although the AAUP is often thought of as a union for the tenured, many of the faculty currently represented by the association are in nontenure-line positions. The changing identity of AAUP membership can partially be attributed to the changing demographics in the academic workplace; it is also the result of the organization's recent focus on organizing this sector of the academic workforce.

The lower levels of bureaucratic pressure experienced by faculty in higher education made it easier for the AAUP to reject the union label prior to the late 1960s. However, there were other factors. First, college and university professors certainly wanted to embrace the professional ideal, so much a part of the development of the modern culture of the twentieth century, and separate themselves from their less-educated teaching colleagues in the K-12 system. Gender and class also played into the desire for distance. As K-12 teaching became a feminized—and thereby more closely monitored and controlled— "semi-profession" (as Ladd and Lipset termed public school teaching in 1973) that drew heavily from the up-and-coming children of the laboring immigrant classes, the predominantly male, Anglo, middle- and upper-class college professors had every reason to look for ways to differentiate themselves. Although unionized K-12 teachers fought valiantly for increased respect as professionals and for shared governance, they essentially lost that fight and, like their industrial labor counterparts, "settled" for better pay, improved benefits, and better working conditions (see, for example, Tyack 1974 and Apple 1986 for discussions of the bureaucratization and the feminization of teaching in the K-12 school system). Professors, especially at the more elite colleges and universities, could still legitimately claim a great deal of genuine control over the policies and practices of their institutions; this was particularly true at those institutions that had imitated the German university structure of strong professorial control.

The watershed in higher education unionism came, as it had for K-12 teachers, with a dramatic expansion of higher education systems. In 1904, the president of the University of Wisconsin, Charles Van Hise, had proposed the university as a center of research and service to the public; its duty was not only to educate, but also to spur economic growth, solve social problems, and serve the national defense. After the end of World War II, implementation of the "Wisconsin Idea" accelerated dramatically. Spurred on by the G.I. Bill, billions in federal monies, and demand for research during the cold war, by the late 1960s higher education had reached levels of development unimaginable just twenty years earlier. Enrollments doubled between 1940 and 1960, and then doubled again by 1970, with the overwhelming majority of growth coming in the public sector. A college education was no longer restricted to the privileged few; increasingly, it was seen as a middle-class right and a means of upward class and economic mobility for the masses (Lazerson 1987). As enrollments grew, so too did the number of faculty (from 354,000 full-time faculty in 1965 to over 623,000 in 1978) and the size of budgets (from $5.6 billion in 1959 to $42.6 billion in 1976–77, a more than eight-fold increase) (Johnstone 1981, 5).

The phenomenal expansion of higher education as a system after World War II inevitably meant that the academy would experience an equally dramatic expansion in the complexity of administrative tasks. Like K-12 education in an earlier era, higher education developed its own hierarchy of bureaucracy and, eventually, a growing class of educational bureaucratic specialists. While not the only factor in the sudden burst of unionization among faculty in the late 1960s and early 1970s, this organizational complexity and its attendant distancing of faculty from administration and governance laid the groundwork. As numerous authors writing on the topic during this period concluded, there were multiple factors at play in the widespread trend of faculty unionization. Economic stress on campuses and a serious decline in real earning power among professors was central, as was the advent of new legislation enabling public employees to unionize, the general anti-authoritarian and egalitarian climate of the 1960s, and faculty concern over the erosion of their decision-making power from administrators above and student movements below. Moreover, the general growth in white-collar public employee unionism during this period provided academics with examples of unionized professionals (see Ladd and Lipset 1973; Kemerer and Baldridge 1975; Johnstone 1981; see also Drescher and Polishook 1985; Arnold 2000).

The arguments made during this period by faculty opposed to unionization often echoed Tyler's earlier assertion that faculty were individual scholars, not a collective of workers; that higher education was best served by a competitive, meritocratic system, which was not compatible with a union model; and that, plainly put, unions were not needed by educated professionals capable of rational and respectful—not adversarial—discussions with their administrative peers (see, for example, Lipset 1975; Skorpen 1978; Devinatz 2001). The arguments of those faculty who were in favor of unionization bear striking resemblance to those that would be made twenty years later by graduate employee and contingent faculty unionization proponents.[5] Those who supported faculty unions argued that academic freedom was being imperiled by the breakdown in shared governance, that an overproduction of PhDs left new professors at the mercy of the market, that good teachers and scholars were being sold to the lowest bidder. A University of California professor, Donald Wollett, a strong advocate of faculty collective bargaining, stated in 1973:

From the standpoint of simple humanity and decency, the situation which exists at such places as the University of California where a faculty member can work his tail off for five years, receive no adverse evaluations and no indication of dissatisfaction with his work, and then be placed on one-year terminal appointment at the beginning of his sixth year of service, has nothing to commend it other that the fact than, given the present labor market, money can be saved and a superior replacement obtained (perhaps). (Ladd and Lipset 1973, 79)

In 1966 there were eleven recognized faculty bargaining units on college and university campuses in the United States; by 1973 there were 330 such units (Kemerer and Baldridge 1975, 1). Referring more narrowly to four-year colleges and universities, Ladd and Lipset reported 205 such units in 1973 at 304 institutions, representing almost eighty thousand professors—approximately one-sixth of the professoriat. These numbers included the multicampus systems of the City University of New York and the State University of New York; an additional twenty-six thousand faculty were represented through "negotiating councils" in the California community college system (Ladd and Lipset 1973, 1–2). By 1981 there were 422 bargaining units at 136 four-year institutions and 286 at two-year colleges (Hutcheson 2000).

By the early 1980s, campus organizing had slowed considerably. The primary reason for this ebb in academic unionization was the 1980 U.S. Supreme Court ruling in *National Labor Relations Board v. Yeshiva University*. In this decision, the Supreme Court ruled that professors at private colleges were "management," not employees, and therefore not covered by the 1935 National Labor Relations Act (NLRA). Although the ruling did not apply to public colleges and universities and although faculty at private institutions retained the right to organize outside of the NLRA, the *Yeshiva* decision had a chilling effect on academic union organizing. Undoubtedly the conservative ideological climate, and the re-embracing of the old conviction that "the business of America is business," played a part in this slowdown.

How did the faculty involved in unionization answer the critics who charged that unionization would destroy collegiality, professional standards, and individual scholarship? An analysis of the patterns of faculty unionization makes it clear that, in some ways, the professoriat as a body was able to sidestep some of these issues, since unionization was most frequently adopted at two-year (community) colleges and "lower-tier" four-year institutions. The expansion of higher education had led to a large-scale stratification by institutional type in which

"lower-tier" schools offered a supposedly lower quality education to undergraduate students as compared to Ivy League and first-tier schools. It was also
assumed—oftentimes correctly so—that professors at these institutions would
produce less research and fewer publications; this in a profession that increasingly valued research and publications over teaching. Both opponents and
proponents of faculty unionization pointed out that at institutions of lesser prestige, faculty were expressing many of the same complaints voiced sixty years
earlier by K-12 teachers: loss of autonomy, lack of policy and decision-making
power, low pay, and poor working conditions. A parallel was drawn between
K-12 academic labor and "lower tier" postsecondary academic labor (see Ladd
and Lipset 1973; Arnold 2000). A direct confrontation between a professional,
scholarly identity and worker identity was thus delayed.

THE INFORMATION ECONOMY, THE "NEW" ACADEMY, AND THE EROSION OF TENURE

More than twenty years later, globalization, the information economy, and
the coming knowledge society have brought issues of scholarly work and identity back to the fore. The educational bureaucracy is now larger and far more
sophisticated than before. What's more, corporatization has proceeded at a pace
unimagined in the 1960s and has reached deeply into the oldest and most prestigious of institutions: the Ivy League is now deeply tied to corporate research
agendas and funding.[6]

For newly graduated PhDs and those who are already part of the contingent
academic labor force, the corporatization and "casualization" of higher education—that is, the conversion of what were tenure-track, full-time positions
into temporary, adjunct, and/or otherwise unstable jobs—are concretely obvious in their daily lives. For faculty who are already tenured, the implications
may have seemed until recently more remote. The dismissal of a third of the
faculty at Bennington College in 1995 makes it clear, however, that "presump-
tive tenure" does not provide faculty with the same level of academic freedom
and job security as formal tenure does. And even formal tenure has come under
direct attacks. The Board of Regents' attempt to dismantle tenure at the University of Minnesota in 1996 indicates that tenure is no longer considered integral to the mission of that institution.

The largest attack on tenure—and therefore on academic freedom—has been
subtler, however. Contingent faculty lack the job security and protections af-
forded their tenure-line colleagues, and without job security and the right to
due process, academic freedom is compromised. In 1993, for example, the Iowa
State Board of Regents implemented an "Unusual and Unexpected Classroom
Materials Policy" in response to a student's complaint after an in-class screen-
ing of a video that included electronically altered depictions of male-on-male
oral sex. Although this policy attempted to define what qualified as appropriate

classroom materials and outlined punishments for faculty of all ranks who failed to adhere to it, the overwhelming weight of this policy fell on the university's most vulnerable instructional ranks. Many tenure-line faculty members actively opposed this policy and refused to follow it in the classroom, but the only university employees to be punished under it—which included having letters of reprimand placed in personnel files, being publicly censured at Board of Regents meetings, and being removed from the classroom—were graduate teaching assistants who, by the nature of their job appointments, lacked job security (Fallow, Peltier and Smith, n.d.). The "Unusual and Unexpected Classroom Materials Policy" was quietly removed from the University of Iowa's College of Liberal Arts Handbook in January 1996, but the impact of this policy on graduate instructors at Iowa was profound. The vigor of the Campaign to Organize Graduate Students (COGS), the graduate employee unionization drive that followed on the heels of campus-wide organized resistance to the "Unusual and Unexpected Classroom Materials Policy," suggests that this policy helped convince graduate employees at the University of Iowa of their status as a marginalized workforce and impressed upon them the connection between their workplace struggle and campuswide issues of academic freedom.

While most institutions continue to pay lip service to tenure and the protection of academic freedom, tenure is being slowly eroded via "golden parachute" retirement packages for older tenured faculty, the freezing of tenure lines, and the growth among the contingent faculty ranks. Moreover, recent U.S. Supreme Court and circuit court decisions that rule that tenure inheres in the institution rather than to the individual faculty member have the potential of curtailing research and pedagogy nationwide (see Rabban 2001). How academic workers respond to the ongoing challenges to tenure and to academic freedom remains to be seen. The increase in academic organizing over the past decade suggests that many faculty—especially graduate instructors and adjuncts—believe that unionization will provide the means for addressing these challenges. Most faculty-union contracts, however, are silent on such issues as the ratio of tenure-line to nontenure-line faculty, job security for adjuncts, or the preservation of tenure lines, and thus leave their bargaining units vulnerable to the effects of the casualization of the higher education workforce.[7]

THE CHANGING FACE OF THE ACADEMY AND THE REBIRTH OF THE ACADEMIC LABOR MOVEMENT

One of the results of the casualization of the academic workforce has been a renaissance in labor activism on university campuses. Graduate research and teaching assistants, adjunct instructors, and full-time faculty are organizing and affiliating with international unions as a means to address workplace issues such as wages, benefits, and workloads. While organizing among the tenure-line faculty ranks is proceeding at a less-than-ideal pace, the rapid increase in graduate employee and adjunct unions over the past decade establishes that the academy is one of the fastest growing sectors of the North American labor movement. Clearly, higher pay, health insurance, decreased work hours, and legally binding grievance procedures have been important fruits of this unionization movement.

As contributors to this volume make clear, many graduate employee locals have been successful in addressing social justice issues as well as "bread and butter" issues through collective bargaining. But perhaps an equally important result of the academic unionization movement for faculty as well as graduate employees is the development of a worker identity and the resulting solidarity between the academic workforce and other workers. Cary Nelson describes the emergence of this academic worker identity and the resultant cross-campus solidarity in his introduction to *Will Teach for Food* (1997a). He writes:

Faculty members have long assumed a great gulf in status separates them from campus blue-collar laborers. But part-time faculty and cafeteria workers have a good deal in common. Moreover, even full-time faculty and workers lose relative authority when their numbers are reduced and their jobs outsourced or given to part-timers. Permanent faculty, adjunct faculty, graduate students, secretaries, and maintenance workers suddenly acquire common interests and reasons to build working alliances. Improbably enough, the academy has become a place to build workplace solidarity that crosses class lines. (6)

Grassroots movements such as the nationwide Students Against Sweatshops movement and the recent living wage campaign at Harvard indicate that worker solidarity movements are experiencing a resurgence on college campuses. Moreover, the current spate of graduate employee organizing by traditionally blue-collar unions such as the Hotel and Restaurant Employees (HERE), the United Electrical, Radio, and Machine Workers of America (UE) and the United Auto Workers (UAW) suggests that, at least among the graduate employee ranks, solidarity with workers from other sectors of the economy and an attentiveness to what Carl Rosen in his afterword to this volume calls "common labor struggles" are foregone conclusions.

THE STRUGGLES OF REBIRTH

The impetus for *Cogs in the Classroom Factory* comes from our personal experiences with UE Local 896-COGS and with the academic labor movement in general. It had been our experience while serving as officers in our local that, as is often the case with organizations that are run by a transient, volunteer workforce and are subject to high turnover among the rank and file, institutional memory was spotty and important events in the history of the local were forgotten as the activists involved in these events moved on. As a result, we originally conceived of this volume as a means for collecting and preserving that history. Many of the proposals that came to us, however, echoed the struggles with issues of identity and class politics that we had experienced within our union local and helped us refine the focus of this volume. We began to ask ourselves, which of the fundamental differences that once existed between knowledge workers (or "mind workers" as Kerchner, Koppich & Weeres (1997) call us) are still relevant? How have these shifting identities in academic labor played out in the different regions and on different campuses throughout North America? How has the higher education union movement shaped the debate over identity and workplace solidarity in the academy? Can academic labor truly merge with industrial labor over shared goals? The contributors to this volume all struggle with these questions, and through their discussions and analyses of the state of the academic job system on their campuses, they suggest some alternatives for responding to the higher education job crisis and the reshaping of the academic workplace.

The chapters included in Part One, "A Widening Divide: Faculty and Others," explore the terrain now navigated by the academy's "others"—those faculty living on the casualized margins of academic life—and the difficulties faced by all faculty once a two-tiered system becomes the norm. In "Above and Below: Mapping Social Positions within the Academy," Wesley Shumar and Jonathan T. Church write from the positions of "participant observers" and explore the effects of this two-tiered system on the adjunct workforce as well as the tenure-line faculty at their institutions. Through this chapter's dialogic structure, the authors map a bifurcated academic labor force in which the privileged class of the tenure-line faculty is not only oblivious to the existence of the adjunct underclass, they are complicit in its creation. In "Dueling Identities and Faculty Unions: A Canadian Case Study," Mike Burke and Joanne Naiman describe the tenure-line faculty's complicity in the creation of an academic underclass as it played out in their union local, the Ryerson Faculty Association (RFA). They look at the union's role in the imposition of a two-tiered faculty system on the bargaining unit and analyze the effects that the development of this system has had on faculty salaries, workload, and morale. Joe Berry's "In a Leftover Office in Chicago" uses the trope of the archaeological dig to describe the experiences of the adjunct faculty members who have replaced the vanishing ranks of tenured faculty. Looking at the San Francisco General Strike of 1934 and the 1997 UPS strike, Berry goes on to draw parallels between these blue-collar unions and current organizing efforts among adjunct faculty on numerous campuses in Chicago.

The next generation of academics—graduate students—is painfully aware of this divide. Underlying the surge in graduate employee unionization over the past ten years is the growing realization that tenure-track positions—or full-time positions of any sort—are simply not going to be there upon graduation for many doctoral candidates, regardless of their teaching qualifications or scholarship potential. The essays in Part Two of this volume, "The Next Generation: Charting New Waters," document the ways in which this new generation of academics is addressing this dilemma. In "More than Academic: Labor Consciousness and the Rise of UE Local 896-COGS," Susan Roth Breitzer looks at the two COGS union certification campaigns and the negotiation of the first contract and examines the development of a labor consciousness within the University of Iowa's graduate employee union. As Breitzer makes clear, COGS's success is due, in part, to the local's ability to integrate itself into the Iowa City labor movement and build connections between its mission and that of other UE locals. While Breitzer focuses on the successes of the union movement at the University of Iowa, she also acknowledges the difficulties faced by this young local—most notably the struggle between a larger vision of the union as a social justice movement and a more traditional view of the union as an organization concerned primarily with "bread and butter" issues such as wages and benefits.

Richard Sullivan's chapter, "Pyrrhic Victory at UC Santa Barbara: The Struggle for Labor's New Identity" analyzes the culture clash between the United Auto Workers (UAW), the international union that represents the graduate employees in the University of California system, and the union activists at the Santa Barbara campus. Focusing on two events—the campaign leading up to the union certification vote in spring 1999 and the negotiation of the first contract—Sullivan documents the challenges that the Santa Barbara activists faced when they struggled to preserve their vision of a grassroots local within the context of the larger, more bureaucratic UAW. Particularly troubling for Sullivan was the UAW's insistence that the Santa Barbara local forego their locally developed organizing techniques in favor of the UAW's methods. James Thompson also looks at the difficulties inherent in organizing a strong graduate employee union in "Unfinished Chapters: Institutional Alliances and Changing Identities in a Graduate Employee Union." Thompson examines the recent successful efforts to rebuild the faltering Graduate Assistants United (GAU), the collective bargaining agent for the graduate employees at the University of Florida (UF), and argues that the development of a worker consciousness among graduate employees at UF is complicated by Florida's prohibitive labor laws and by the intricate relationship between the GAU and the United Faculty of Florida, the NEA-AFT affiliate that is the parent union for GAU. Unlike Sullivan and Breitzer, who focus on the union's role in creating an academic worker identity among graduate employees, Thompson emphasizes the union's role as a social organization as well as a labor organization. As he points out, the GAU's recent organizing success is due, in part, to the fact that the union is the best means for meeting graduate students from other departments and for learning about university life. While little has been written about this aspect of graduate-employee unionism thus far, Thompson's analysis of the union as a social community as well as a labor organization deserves note. Certainly the success of this sector of the academic union movement will depend on the ability of these union locals to serve as the social center of graduate student life on organized campuses. How to balance this social function with union business—contract negotiations, grievances, contract maintenance and (at public institutions) effective lobbying efforts—is a challenge that must be faced.

Alongside contingent faculty, graduate employees now constitute the backbone of the postsecondary education system. Undergraduate education at many institutions could not function without contingent faculty and graduate instructors; research projects would, in many cases, be crippled without the day-to-day work put in by research assistants. Like the postdocs and adjuncts described earlier, many graduate employees are paid a per-course "stipend" that amounts to less than minimum wage, don't have access to affordable health insurance, and have no job security. Even if one can make the argument that tenured faculty are not "workers" in the blue-collar sense (and, as Carl Rosen's afterword makes clear, that argument today is not without serious flaws), certainly, contingent faculty and graduate employees are.

The old apprenticeship model under which graduate students did relatively small amounts of teaching and research as a part of their professional training is disconnected from current realities, and it cannot be mended by calls for collegiality or a disdain for solutions that associate academic employees with blue-collar models. Once the possibility of a decent-paying job and the hope for meaningful work grow dim, there is no longer an implicit exchange of current sacrifice for future reward. If, at the end of six to eight years of teaching or researching at a graduate employee salary that barely pays the rent, there is only a slim chance of finding a full-time position and earning enough to repay student loans, then the climate for unionization is created. The perceived need for unionization is accentuated by a national health-care crisis that leaves those in the United States without employer-sponsored health-care benefits more than out in the cold: It can leave them bankrupt, desperately ill, or worse. Compared to generations past, today's graduate students are older and more of them have families. They cannot afford to ignore this state of affairs. The case studies of California, Iowa, and Florida unions in Part Two explore the ways in which graduate employees are embracing an identity as academic workers, with varying degrees of success.

While the members of the graduate employee unions described in Part Two experienced difficulties and roadblocks, the chapters that constitute Part Three, "New Tactics, Old Battlegrounds," present detailed descriptions of a different set of roadblocks and the ways around them. How do you unionize if the law says you don't work at the university where you teach or do research? What do you do if the collective bargaining process becomes an obstacle to getting a contract? How do you seize the moment and turn it to your advantage when the administration sets out to corner your union with two equally disagreeable choices— a bad contract or an unpopular strike? Eric Dirnbach and Susan Chimonas address some of these questions in "Shutting Down the Academic Factory: Developing Worker Identity in Graduate Employee Unions." In this chapter, the authors draw upon the 1995–96 and 1998–99 contract negotiations between the Graduate Employees Organization (GEO), the graduate employee union at the University of Michigan, and the university and analyze how the union developed a worker consciousness among its members and prepared for an effective strike. As Dirnbach and Chimonas indicate, developing this worker consciousness among academic union members is difficult; the majority of graduate instructors—like other faculty—identify as professionals and feel a certain obligation to their students and their classes. In order to become strike-ready, Dirnbach and Chimonas argue, the union local must "facilitate [an] 'identity shift' by creating and sustaining a serious union culture that discursively focuses on graduate students' role as workers." In the GEO-University of Michigan contract negotiations, the union implemented a number of strategies to effect this identity shift, including a living wage campaign, and demanded open negotiation sessions.

In "Are You Now or Have You Ever Been an Employee? Contesting Graduate Labor in the Academy," William Vaughn looks at how the process of legal recognition and the vagaries of labor law can derail a successful organizing campaign. Vaughn analyzes the six-year legal battle between the University of Illinois and the Graduate Employee's Organization (GEO), the American Federation of Teacher's affiliate that represents the graduate employees at the university, looking specifically at how some rather poorly worded statutory language left the graduate employees without legal recognition under the Illinois Educational Labor Relations Act. Only recently this struggle for recognition has resulted in the university and the union reaching an agreement on the composition of the bargaining unit. This agreement represents a major victory for the GEO. Perhaps the more important victory, however, is the development of a worker consciousness among the graduate employees at UIUC. In spite of the history of litigation, the graduate employees at Illinois have been able to effectively make the "identity shift from students to workers, as is evidenced by their effective union-card drive and third party-monitored union certification election."

Like Dirnbach's and Chimonas's chapter, the final chapter in this section, "The Politics of Constructing Dissent: The Rhetorical Construction of Faculty Union Membership," looks at how unions construct an activist identity during the build-up to a strike authorization vote. In this chapter, author Darla Williams analyzes the literature produced by the Association of Pennsylvania State College and University Faculties (APSCUF), the statewide union that represents full-time and part-time faculty on the fourteen State System of Higher Education campuses. Examining such documents as letters from the union's president and newsletter articles, Williams shows that the APSCUF leadership was able to effectively develop a high level of support for the strike. Rather than forcing faculty to chose between their professional and union allegiances, the union leadership was able to portray the strike as "an act of institutional patriot, one that underscored the faculty's commitment to quality education.

In each of the cases reported in the various chapters, the union's strategy involved effecting a shift in both the self-perception of individual bargaining unit members and the public's perception of the professoriat. Their success in making such shifts was an integral part of achieving concrete gains. The ability of academics of all types to make such shifts, to adapt in the face of new structural realities in higher education, may be a crucial element in the survival of such old concepts as academic freedom, shared governance, and independent scholarship. Moreover, if, as many of the authors included in this volume argue, higher education is part of the pending structural revolution—call it globalization, the technology revolution, or the knowledge revolution—then it is not illogical to think that, as blue-collar unionism followed on the Industrial Revolution, the current upswing in organizing on campuses may be the harbinger of a wave of white-collar unionism. Since we sent out the call for contributions for this volume, there has been an increase in unionization in all sectors of the academic job system. Just as the *Yeshiva* decision resulted in a slowing in faculty unionization in the 1980s, the *NYU* decision issued by the National Labor Relations Board in 2000 has provided further impetus to the already strong graduate employee unionization movement by ensuring graduate employees at private institutions the right to organize under the NLRA. Indeed, the NEA, AFT, and AAUP are all now busily analyzing how to reinvigorate faculty unions and meet new challenges (see, for example, Rhoades 1998; Rhoades 2000; Laiacona 2000). Events such as Campus Equity Week underscore the important role that adjuncts and graduate instructors play in educating the faculty ranks and the public at large about the changing face of academic labor. This week-long event, which was cosponsored by the AAUP, AFT, NEA, and the Canadian Association of University Teachers (CAUT), consisted of rallies, guerilla theater, and informational pickets devoted to consciousness raising around the increased use of contingent faculty on North American campuses.

Moreover, as the numerous panels at academic conferences devoted to the topic and the publication of such volumes as *Will Teach for Food* (Nelson 1997c), *Chalk Lines* (Martin 1998), *The Employment of English* (Bérubé 1998), *Manifesto of a Tenured Radical* (Nelson 1997b), and *Managed Professionals* (Rhoades 1998) indicate, the rapid rise in unionization among graduate employee and contingent ranks has resulted in the development of a new area of academic study, usually referred to as academic labor studies or critical higher education studies. This new area of inquiry has its roots in English, composition, foreign language, and history departments, undoubtedly due to the fact that the now decades-long "job crisis" in the humanities and the pernicious exploitation of the graduate instructors and adjuncts in these fields make questions about the nature of academic work and the shifting identity of academic workers urgently necessary—to borrow a phrase from the epigraph at the beginning of this chapter. Indeed, the continuing popularity of *Workplace*, the web-based journal founded by members of the Graduate Student Caucus of the Modern Language Association in 1998, emphasizes how central the concepts of academic worker consciousness and the shifting nature of university work have become in recent years.

This volume asserts that if this revolution in academic worker consciousness continues, it will be because faculty of all types have decided that the university no longer stands apart in any significant way from corporate practice,
and that, within this new context, they and their interests are threatened. The
history of higher education unionization suggests "teachers" unions such as
the AFT and the NEA may offer a more palatable model for academics because
of the "professional" status of their members—indeed the majority of academic unions discussed in this volume are affiliated with teachers unions. The
increasing balkanization of the academic workforce suggests that in order for
the higher education union movement to flourish, these unions must develop
an integrated collective identity—one that is inclusive of all sectors of the academic workforce. Blue-collar unions, many of which focus on organizing a
variety of workers, regardless of job classification, into factorywide locals
("wall-to-wall organizing"), may provide a model for how to create a thriv-
ing union local from a disparate workforce.

Faculty of all ranks and titles face a crucial decision, one that will be fundamental to the future of the academic labor movement. Can the "mind workers"
of the classroom, the library, and the lab make the identity shift—from privileged and sheltered members of an elite with no collective interests, to workers
whose economic survival and standards of professional excellence depend upon
collective action? Whether or not they make this shift will shape the course of
academic life, scholarly and scientific research, academic freedom, and the quality of education for both undergraduate and graduate students in the future.

NOTES

1. "Casual Nation," the Coalition of Graduate Employee Unions' 2000 report on the
increased use of adjunct and nontenure-track faculty in higher education, places rate of
nontenure-line faculty at 41 percent. This figure, which is based on data collected in 1995,
is nearly double the 1971 rate of 22 percent. Many other studies, however, suggest that
this number is conservative. The Modern Language Association's "Survey of Staffing in
English and Foreign Language Departments, Fall 1999" includes data on hiring practices
from 1,986 departments in the United States and Canada. This study represents a range
of hiring practices. However, for Research I institutions the rate of nontenure-line faculty hovers at 60 percent, and in some notorious instances, it is as high as 79 percent.

2. The 1999 joint convention of the AAUP and the Newspaper Guild—the branch of
the Communication Workers of America (CWA) that represents journalists—is a fine
example of faculty acknowledging that they share a collective identity with other "mind
workers." At this convention, the AAUP and the Newspaper Guild issued joint statements addressing such common issues as the "unbundling" of intellectual work and the
corporatization of the academic and journalistic industries and the resultant incursions
on freedom of speech.

3. Cross-disciplinary information on salary and benefits for adjuncts is hard to find,
thus making it difficult to draw any hard and fast rules about salary and benefits for

adjunct faculty. The Modern Language Association's "Survey of Staffing in English and Foreign Language Departments, Fall 1999" is, to date, the most comprehensive survey of adjunct faculty salaries and benefits and on departmental hiring practices. This survey includes information on adjunct salaries and benefits for English and foreign language departments in the United States and Canada. Based on a sample of the information reported in the MLA survey, salaries for adjunct faculty at Research I institutions ranged between $2,729 and $7,200 per course. While a few of these institutions offered health insurance and retirement benefits to adjunct faculty, eligibility was often contingent upon working .5 FTE ("half-time") or more. Adjunct salaries at two-year institutions were much lower than those at Research I universities, ranging between $500 and $3008 per course, with no benefits. Although four-year colleges reported using adjunct faculty to teach courses, many of those institutions did not include salary or benefits information.

4. The history presented here references developments in the United States. While there are many parallels with developments in Canadian higher education, this brief recounting does not claim to be inclusive of Canadian history.

5. The parallels between contemporary and historical arguments over the supposed dichotomy between professionalism and unionization are especially striking when reading the letters to the editor regarding Ellen Willis's *New York Times* article, "Why Professors Turn to Organized Labor" (May 28, 2001, p. A15). The responding letters to the editor can be found in the *New York Times* of June 3, 2001, Sec. 4, p. 16. See also Anthony Kronman, "Are Graduate Students Workers?" (*New York Times*, May 19, 2001, p. A23); responding letters to the editor were printed May 22, 2001.

6. For discussions of the influence of corporate culture on campus governance, and the influence of corporate funding on university research and academic freedom, see Birecree 1988; Jacoby 1991; McLaughlin 1996; Lazerson 1997; Ginsburg and Wion 1998; Press and Washburn 2000; Rhoades 2000; Slaughter and Rhoades 2000; White 2000.

7. There are a few notable exceptions among current faculty union contracts. For example, Article 20 of the 1999–2002 "WMU-AAUP-Western Michigan University Collective Bargaining Agreement" ensures that nontenurable full-time faculty (referred to in this article as "Academic Career Specialists") receive all the rights that other instructional faculty receive, except tenure. Moreover, the "continuous appointment" language in the article ensures job security and the right to due process. Finally, Article 20 of the agreement also includes language that establishes a cap of not more than 10 percent of the bargaining unit for these positions. The *Agreement 1999–2002 between Rider University and the Rider Chapter of the American Association of University Professors* addresses the issue of job security for contingent faculty by establishing a seniority system for adjunct faculty.

REFERENCES

Agreement 1999–2002 between Rider University and the Rider chapter of the American Association of University Professors. Available online at <http://sabrina.rider.edu/aaup/current_contract/index.html>.

Apple, M.W. 1986. *Teachers and texts: A political economy of class and gender relations in education.* New York: Routledge.

Arnold, G.B. 2000. *The politics of faculty unionization: The experience of three New England universities.* Westport, CT: Bergin & Garvey.

Bérubé, M. 1998. *The employment of English: Theory, jobs, and the future of literary studies.* New York: New York University Press.

Birecree, A.M. 1988. Academic freedom in the academic factory. *Challenge* 3(4): 53–56.

Coalition of Graduate Employee Unions. 2000. Casual Nation. Available online at <http://www.cgeu.org/Casual_Nation.pdf>.

Devinatz, V.G. 2001. Unions, faculty, and the culture of competition. *Thought & Action: The NEA Journal of Higher Education* (Summer): 87–98.

Drescher, N.M., and I.H. Polishook. 1985. Perspectives on the development of faculty unions in the United States. *Journal of Tertiary Educational Administration* 7: 5–19.

Eaton, W.E. 1975. *The American Federation of Teachers, 1916–1961.* Carbondale: Southern Illinois University Press.

Einstein, A. 1950. *Out of my later years.* New York: Philosophical Library.

Fallow, J., J. Peltier, and B. Smith. n.d. Timeline: University of Iowa classroom materials policy. Unpublished material produced by the Campaign for Academic Freedom, circa 1994. Photocopy.

Ginsburg, M.B., and P.K. Wion. 1998. Organizing university faculty for collective action in the U.S.: Corporatization, a divided professoriate, and the possibility of community. *Contemporary Education* 69: 191–195.

Hutcheson, P.A. 2000. *A professional professoriate: Unionization, bureaucratization, and the AAUP.* Nashville, TN: Vanderbilt University Press.

Jacoby, R. 1991. The greening of the university: From ivory tower to industrial park. *Dissent* 38(2): 286–92.

Johnstone, R.L. 1981. *The scope of collective bargaining: An analysis of faculty union agreements at four-year institutions of higher education.* Westport, CT: Greenwood.

Kemerer, F.R., and J.V. Baldridge. 1975. *Unions on campus.* San Francisco: Jossey-Bass Publishers.

Kerchner, C.T., J.E. Koppich, and J.G. Weeres. 1997. *United mind workers: Unions and teaching in the knowledge society.* San Francisco: Jossey-Bass Publishers.

Ladd, E.C., and S.M. Lipset. 1973. *Professors unions and American higher education.* Washington, D.C.: Carnegie Commission on Higher Education.

Laiacona, J. 2000. Unionizing in Chicago: Big gains for part-timers. *Thought & Action: The NEA Higher Education Journal* (Summer): 99–106.

Lazerson, M. (ed.). 1987. *American education in the twentieth century: A documentary history.* New York: Teachers College Press.

———. 1997. Who owns higher education? The changing face of governance. *Change* 29(2): 10–15.

Lee, J.S. 2001. Postdoc trail: Long and filled with pitfalls. *New York Times* (21 August) F3.

Lipset, S.M. 1975. Faculty unions and collegiality. *Change* (March): 39–41.

Martin, R. 1998. *Chalk lines: The politics of work in the managed university.* Durham, NC: Duke University Press.

McLaughlin, J.B. 1996. The perilous presidency. *Educational Record* 77(2–3), 13–17.

Modern Language Association. 1999. Survey of staffing in English and foreign language departments, Fall 1999. Available online at <http://www.mla.org/>.

Murphy, M. 1990. *Blackboard unions: The AFT and the NEA, 1900–1980.* Ithaca, NY: Cornell University Press.

Nelson, C. 1997a. Between crisis and opportunity. In *Will teach for food,* ed. C. Nelson, 3–31. Minneapolis: University of Minnesota Press.

———. 1997b. *Manifesto of a tenured radical.* New York: New York University Press.

———(ed.). 1997c. *Will teach for food.* Minneapolis: University of Minnesota Press.

Press, E., and J. Washburn. 2000. The kept university. *The Atlantic Monthly* (March): 39–54.

Rabban, D. 2001. Academic freedom, individual or institutional? *Academe* (November– December): 16–20.

Rhoades, G. 1998. *Managed professionals: Unionized faculty and restructuring academic labor.* Philadelphia, PA: Temple University Press.

———. 2000. New unionism and over-managed professors. *Thought & Action: The NEA Higher Education Journal* (Summer): 83–98.

Skorpen, E. 1978. The professoriate and faculty unions. *Educational Forum* (May): 395–410.

Slaughter, S., and G. Rhoades. 2000. The neo-liberal university. *New Labor Forum* (Spring/Summer): 73–79.

Smith, J. 1998. Faculty, students, and political engagement. In *Chalk lines: The politics of work in the managed university,* ed. R. Martin, 249–263. Durham, NC: Duke University Press.

Tyack, D.B. 1974. *The one best system: A history of American urban education.* Cambridge: Harvard University Press.

Urban, W.J. 1982. *Why teachers organized.* Detroit, MI: Wayne State University Press.

———. 2000. *Gender, race, and the National Education Association: Professionalism and its limitations.* New York: Routledge Falmer.

Wesley, E.B. 1957. *NEA: The first hundred years: The building of the teaching profession.* New York: Harper.

West, A.M. 1980. *The National Education Association: The power base for education.* New York: The Free Press.

White, G.D., ed. 2000. *Campus, Inc.: Corporate power in the ivory tower.* New York: Prometheus Books.

WMU-AAUP/Western Michigan University Collective Bargaining Agreement. 1999. Available online at <http://www.wmich.edu/aaup/9902con.pdf>.

Part I

A Widening Divide: Faculty and Others

Chapter 1

Above and Below:
Mapping Social Positions within the Academy

Wesley Shumar and Jonathan T. Church

In this chapter, we attempt to describe the social geography of specific aspects of the new economy of academic labor. We are particularly interested in the development of a dual labor market where a privileged tenured class has access to more stable employment, high social status, and prestige, and an academic underclass is marginalized in temporary and part-time work, part of a developing flexible workforce within the recent transformations in global capitalism. Further, we are interested in the gross symbolic differences and access to a public voice that each position entails: the traditional faculty as the intellectual conscience of the nation and the flexible workforce as a silenced group within the new sweatshops of academic labor.

Our interests are not merely academic but part of our political practice as well. We are part of this social world that we describe, and so our participant observation becomes a critical participation (Rigby 1985) in the social world. For us, one central goal of ethnographic practice is to use ethnography and participant observation to investigate, as Rosaldo (1989, 217) states, "an interdependent late-twentieth-century world marked by borrowing and lending across porous national and cultural boundaries that are saturated with inequality, power and domination."

In anthropology it has become popular to discuss marginal groups and the ways they are constituted through marginalizing discourses from centers of power. It has also become popular to talk about how these margins do not constitute whole cultures and whole identities but fragmented and contradictory identities and cultures. These discursively constituted lines of force and the ways they mark out distinct groups make groups invisible, or, ironically, both marked and invisible; they have attracted the intent interest of much recent ethnographic work (Tsing 1994; Rosaldo 1989; Giroux 1992). While this work is very important, there is a danger of falling into a "false ontological objectivity." The new others are fragmentary and contradictorily constituted products of global transnational economic forces, but others nonetheless. Yet these new others still play the traditional role of the other. They are temporally and spatially removed from us (Fabian 1990) and serve as a foil for the definition of intellectuals and society at the center. They can be the symptom of our crisis of identity. In other words, we—the intellectuals, the speakers, the creators of social groups—remain invisible in the analysis (Rosaldo 1989, 206–207). What is not recognized is the operation of power by Western institutions and systems and the internal fissures and contradictions of these institutions and systems.

The dual labor market in higher education is a particularly interesting example of the complex ways in which ideologies work. One of our colleagues recently stated that she did not think that tenured faculty wanted to take on "the adjunct issue" because they fear that the administration might say, "Well let's get rid of tenure all together." In other words, the flexible, temporary worker among us is a symptom of the weakness and political ineffectiveness of all university intellectuals. If this is the case, how much academic freedom is there anyway?

Anthropology is particularly well suited to deal with this crisis on at least two fronts. We are one of the disciplines, along with literature, that has the worst job situation. Many very qualified anthropologists are working in marginalized situations. Also, the goals of participant observation and ethnographic writing—to give a picture of the "native's" situation—is uniquely suited to describing the ironies of being part of the same structural forces dislocating thousands of people worldwide, the people who are the traditional subjects of ethnographic writing.

We have pursued these ironies with a particular style of presentation, one that involves a dialogic interpenetration of the voices of informant and ethnographer. In our work on academic labor, we have spoken in both of these voices and have participated in the different speech genres entailed in being informant and ethnographer. Likewise, we have felt the irony of being fragmented in this particular way, as a professional self confronts a marginalized, dislocated worker self. To give a sense of the splits and ironies of these fragmentary identities, we have rendered this chapter into two voices: the voice of the authorial (playing on both authority and author) ethnographer and the voice of the informant, the marginalized academic. Toward a gesture of distinguishing, conjoining, and spatializing the many ways these voices interpenetrate each other, we have placed the voice of the ethnographer as that of the dominant body of the text. The italicized sections of text are the voice of the informant, the flexible worker. This voice seeps through the cracks of the dominant discourse and yet is incorporated as the mortar that holds that discourse together. However, even as that discourse speaks the need of liberation, the subaltern is quieted,

but not silent within that speaking, as there is a constant refiguring of authorial narrative tropes.

THE DISCOURSE OF ACADEMIC FREEDOM

On March 22, 1996, *The Chronicle of Higher Education* published an article
on Louis Menand, English Professor at The City University of New York
(CUNY) and contributing editor to the *New York Review of Books* and the *New
Republic,* discussing his ideas about the professoriat and its relationship to the
larger public discourse. The article quotes Menand saying: "They [college cam-
puses] are amazingly cloistered communities.... There is no reality check. Most
academics are protected from having to confront the real-world consequences
of their ideas" (Wilson 1996, A: 16).

The article goes on to discuss some of Menand's ideas on higher education. He
is very critical of conservatives who see gender studies and multiculturalism as
subverting or undermining the public culture. From his perspective, these conservative theorists are out of touch with the real-world culture in that academics have much less of an impact on the young and the public than does the mass
media and popular culture. But on the other hand, Menand feels that professors
of literature and social science on the left are doing their students a disservice by
focusing on such esoteric and specialized subjects as queer theory and multiculturalism. He suggests that students' lives have no connection to these issues, and
they would be better off if professors taught them how to write a will.

The article in *The Chronicle* was not front-page news, although it did get into
the "Quote, Unquote" column. In many respects, it is not an unusual or significant article. However, for the purposes of this paper it stands as a very interesting document in its formulation of the problems of higher education. Menand
is another professor calling for higher education to relinquish the "ivory tower"
and engage with the real world. What is interesting in this call is that it comes
from across the political spectrum—right, center and left, though perhaps with
different emphases. If the most hysterical critics on the right see universities as
corrupting the young, then many on the left see the focus on more specialized
academic subjects—such as postmodernism, multiculturalism, and queer theory—as a sign that the right has won the culture war. After a decade of attacks
by the right wing, professors have been unsuccessful in their responses, leaving
them vulnerable to cutbacks and criticisms of irrelevance or worse. By turning
inward and becoming more specialized and esoteric, left university professors
have avoided real political confrontation. These new and often fashionable areas
of study are a symptom of political ineffectiveness and the power of the political right (Said 1983, 1989; Sartre 1974; Jacoby 1987, 1994).

This chapter is in no way a refutation of the fears of political domination and
the forms that political domination has taken. However, I do want to read the

self-critique on the left as another kind of symptom. It is both a symptom of political ineffectiveness and a symptom of the ways the reorganization of the workforce in transnational capitalism has made it more difficult for intellectuals to think about class, culture, ideology, and their own positions within a globalizing economy. The central thesis of this chapter is that global infrastructural shifts have had significant impact on the university and the structure of the professoriat. Further, university professors have thus far been able to imagine themselves as less affected by transnationalism (or only in some ways) because the flexible workforce (part-time and temporary faculty) have made it possible for universities to maintain the traditional system of tenure and low teaching loads. These shifts have not been assessed by the academy because the part of the professoriat that has been most affected—the flexible workforce—remains largely stigmatized and/or invisible.

Every morning brings us the news of the globe, and yet, we are poor in noteworthy stories. This is because no event any longer comes to us without already being shot through with explanation. In other words, by now almost nothing that happens benefits storytelling; almost everything benefits information. Actually, it is half the art of storytelling to keep a story free from explanation as one reproduces it. (Benjamin 1968, 89)

I find that I keep getting explained, and I find that I keep vanishing. Here's an example that I told the anthropologist. I was attending a graduation ceremony at a small comprehensive college in the middle-Atlantic. My rented academic attire was completely ill-fitting. The robe was very short, and the sleeves only reached the midsection of my forearm. Embarrassed and chagrined, I fretted about how inappropriate my attire looked to my colleagues. One of them responded in utmost seriousness and with great sympathy in explanation: "Perhaps, the sleeves are meant to be so short. I mean, you don't have a PhD, so perhaps that's the way it's meant to look."

Stunned, I sputtered, "No, no, I have a PhD," but he had already moved on to another conversation. I had been cut off at the sleeves, and the length of my arms had become a set of phantom limbs.

Yet there was also that disquieting sense that if I protested too much, too loudly, a decisive act or proclamation would be itself dishonoring, and I would be disrobed in a completely different sense. I couldn't proclaim this type of innocence. Perhaps his explanation was fitting. My position at the college was stitched together in the most precarious way. I had a three-year contract as a full-time faculty member, but I didn't have the visibility of those jockeying for tenure. Involved in the ceremonial etiquette of academic labor in a different way (not having to proffer deference or offer up a particular demeanor within the political crucible of promotion and tenure), my awkward visibility could be easily maintained, and so I had vanished, as my stigma had been explained.

As Goffman (1963) pointed out, the management of impressions of stigma is invariably done by those whose identities are spoiled. It is the stigmatized who tell the jokes that put the nonstigmatized at ease. For the stigmatized, this acknowledgment of their realization and corroboration of stigma is a formal commitment to the system of social honor. To "own" one's stigma, so to speak, is to provide the convenience of explanation that allows for the toleration of one's presence and the public vanishing of one's story. The stigmatized become present as "other."

Stemming from the transformation of the university over the last three decades, and with increasing rapidity within the last decade and a half, the social relations within the professoriat have undergone discursive transformation with the concomitant structural shift and segmentation of professoriat labor markets. Recognition of the tremendous symbolic violence that has accompanied this shift is most easily seen in the constant reportage of the "culture wars" that reaches the pages of The Atlantic, Harper's, *and the* New York Times, *as well as in the pages of* Lingua Franca, The Chronicle of Higher Education, *and* Academe. *But these explanations are only informative, like baseball scores or stock market reports. They only reflect the situation.*

ADMINISTRATING OLIVER

Beginning to unmask this labor force shows that issues of gender, multiculturalism, queer theory, postmodernism, and more are, in fact, often very much to the point of people's experiences in the world. The following story is one example of such connections. Oliver Kontopulos is a European émigré. He came to the United States over twenty years ago. A son of a very modest working-class family, Oliver found himself working in the United States with some success in international banking and attending university at night. He was the only manager in his firm without a university degree. Oliver not only finished his undergraduate degree, but his experience with employment inequities in the bank as well as the contradictions of finance capital drove him to leave the bank. Later, he decided to study for a PhD in sociology. When he received his PhD, Oliver, who is a very talented sociologist, tried to find academic employment. He has held a number of temporary jobs and part-time jobs but has not landed a tenure-track job in sociology. Oliver thinks it may be his age or his politics that has limited his success. He feels that he is incapable of compromising with the middle-class duplicity that he sees rampant in the academy. Oliver is stigmatized. On the one hand, he is a mature, graying man with European dignity and style, very intelligent, highly educated, and articulate. On the other hand, he is a man in his fifties, from another country, who is marginally employed. Many of his students see his sociological analysis as an attack on their values. They suggest to him that if he doesn't like it here he should go home. Many of his colleagues see his talent but feel that if he could just learn to "play the game" he might do better with academic employment.

Oliver has had more than his share of conflicts within the various university departments where he works. While his older, tenured European colleagues are often seen as different, their differences are tolerated as idiosyncrasies. They are charming. Oliver, however, is seen as a problem, someone who doesn't know how to be invisible, to suck up, be humble, so he is a pariah.

Recently, Oliver has been caught up in a controversy. He said "fuck" in class. He's used the term several times. According to Oliver's interpretation, he has used the term within a context and never as an epithet. His students either don't understand that the contextualized usage of a term might be different than saying "fuck" to someone, or they disagree with its use in the classroom under any circumstances because they complained to the department chair about his use of obscene language. The chair indicated that there was a procedure for dealing with the problem. The students must first approach the professor. If they are not satisfied with how he handles their concerns, they can return to the chair for another meeting with the professor and the chair will be the mediator. The students felt the chair was ignoring their issues. Instead of returning to Oliver they went directly to the president of the university.

Going directly to the top administration had the effect of making the controversy public. People around the university began to say that this professor always uses "fuck" in his class. The president delegated the problem to the provost and the dean. When they learned that the professor was adjunct, the administration contacted the department and indicated to the department that his contract might not be renewed. Because of Oliver's status, the administration realized that the problem could be just made to go away. Concerned for Oliver's welfare, the chair asked a tenured member of the faculty who was a friend of Oliver's to informally call him at home. The tenured friend was to tell Oliver the story and to coerce an apology out of him, getting his assurances that he would never use "fuck" in the class again.

Oliver was quite shocked by the experience and thanked his friend and in fact did give the needed assurances. But, he pointed out to the friend that the political implications of this situation were not good. Oliver was told by his friend that while this was true and the story had implications for academic freedom, he should "pick his battles." Interestingly, beyond the initial student complaints that are part of a public record (as well as a rumor mill), the entire administrative response—conversation with the chair, call to Oliver by a tenured friend, exacting of confession and atonement—are all unofficial, off the record. They can be used to justify retaining Oliver and disciplining his voice, or they can be ignored, denied to have ever existed, and Oliver can be dismissed through the simple act of not being rehired for future terms. He can be cooled-out and hired again later or never called again. Invisibility and marginality are very much about not having a voice and a presence, not existing within the arena of everyday politics from not having an office or phone to never participating in one's own conflicts with students and the university. Further, by sanctioning Oliver, the administration sent a disciplinary message to the department chair: bring your faculty into line or suffer the consequences.

The department chair, in another context, indicated that Oliver's story was not an isolated incident. Students have also come to him at other times referring to other faculty and said that they don't like what this professor is teaching, their values are offended, and they want him to stop teaching these things. It might be easy to dismiss these stories on a case-by-case basis, but, when looked at more broadly, the picture is not a good one. Students, who come from many different backgrounds and possess many different agendas, meet at the university to achieve their educational goals. This meeting ground has become a highly charged one where differing values, ethics and even knowledges compete for authorization and legitimacy.

As Benjamin (1968, 90) suggested, "the value of information does not survive the moment in which it was new. It lives only at that moment; it has to surrender to it completely and explain itself to it without losing any time. A story is different. It does not expend itself. It preserves and concentrates its strength and is capable of releasing it even after a long time." So the stories of this shift, the distillation of symbolic violence within them, seem so different from reportage. As aspects of what Stewart (1991) has termed "contaminated theorizing," they don't reflect a situation; they are the situation.

Let me give you an example. Recently a colleague emailed a list of jokes to me. The colleague who sent them is also part of this new professoriat and has constantly negotiated her own spoiled identity. These were PhD jokes following from the hackneyed standard of what "PhD" really stands for: Piled Higher and Deeper—the inherent humor of disciplinary specialization. These jokes had been forwarded to her by another marginally employed academic and apparently had been circulated widely along the university interstices of the internet.

What I want to note is that there are two senses of loss apparent in these jokes: of promised self (what Goffman [1963] referred to as the virtual) marked by psychic disturbance, and of promised place marked by a slide or descent. The following is the list of promised self: pour him (or her) a drink; probably headed for divorce; pathetically hopeless dweeb; parents have doubts; professors have doubts; potentially heavy drinker; pretty heavily depressed; prozac handouts desired; and then, as if in summary, pathetic homeless dreamer. Notice how this series internalizes the deservedness of a spoiled identity just as it points to a material reality that is so difficult to bear.

The second set clarifies the story. "PhD" stands for: professorship? hah! dream on!; please hire. desperate; patiently headed downhill; professional hamburger dispenser ... "would you like fries with that?"; and, again as if in summary, pizza hut driver. In this series, the finality of the story is set: The pathetically hopeless dreamer drives through the dark night delivering pizzas. It is as if the protagonist has fallen from the ivory tower, plummeting down the class system, and is now marked by the inability to fit—even as a pizza hut driver—into the bowels of the cursed new service economy, but an impatient sensibility of deservedness makes him or her unable to accept his or her lot. Perhaps the story is more like Orpheus, who confronts hell with an artful intelligence (both poetry and music) only to watch Eurydice returned there by a single miscalculation. Driven to despair by his constant recollection, Orpheus is finally killed by the Thracian maidens who can't stand his moroseness or his lack of sexual appetite. Simply, he has complained too much and desired too little to have any social position.

Complaining is not possible for those who have such shaky positions within the university, except, as with Orpheus, as the recollection of a loss. But this must be done with a certain sense of never complaining too much or too loudly, lest one be deemed an "alterity without appeal." Therefore, the very rhetorical strategy of complaining that requires an acknowledgment of position lost creates the phantasm—the academy (Ivy 1995).

DOWNSIZING AND COLLECTIVE IDENTITIES

Unlike Menand, I would argue that much current theory directly addresses the world students and certainly adjunct professors live in. The issue is that it may not much address the world of the intellectual elite, editors for *The New Yorker,* or privileged tenured faculty. (Ironically, while the theories may address the fragmented and contested worlds of the everyday, they are often the symbolic capital of the elite and, as such, are best conveyed in an esoteric crypt that preserves the commodity function of the sign of the new and hip over the explanatory or liberating potential of their ideas.) The face-to-face public has largely disappeared and been replaced by an electronically mediated simulation of the public, except in educational institutions. These institutions are some of the few places where we still meet and struggle over our collective identities. But the university has become a very specific kind of meeting ground. In an era of government fiscal crisis and economic downsizing, the university is under pressure to seek its funding through elaborate fundraising techniques and by treating every student as a valuable consumer. In the world of consumer economics, the customer is always right. In some universities, the faculty are given a notice that says "the students are our customers, and they are the ones we serve." The remainder of the flyer goes on to enumerate the consumers' bill of rights. The dilemma is how to reconcile the notion that a university is a place where scholars freely exchange ideas and profess their philosophies (whether those philosophies are the teaching of evolutionary theory or the reportage of vulgar street language) with the desire to micromanage a product for the consumers of that product, especially in an era when those consumers come from many different religious, ethnic, class, and even taste groupings. Fashion and identity politics struggle in a contradictory arena that demands fiscal exigency and social relevance. The flexible workforce not only meets the demands of a business that contracts and expands very rapidly, it is also a workforce that is more directly responsive to discipline.

Suppression and expulsion can be the tools of a professional technical managerial class of university administrators trying to negotiate these forces of a strong state reducing educational revenue and the demands for public relevance in an era when we are nostalgic for a face-to-face public we are sure we have lost to a previous more innocent era. The adjunct faculty, temporary, and part-time laborers become the most important element in a new managerial labor strategy as they are invisible to their colleagues and each other. But at other moments the invisibility is rather more a specter. They are a sign to both the tenured faculty and the administration of a new future imagination of the university; an imagination that a few years ago would not be spoken but is now erupting from its silence. It is a university rationalized to market forces, which has moved beyond the medieval notion of community and toward a solution to social problems as well as staffing problems with the logic of the marketplace. In this new world, there is no room for outmoded institutions such as tenure.

Now I mean something both very allegorical and yet literal about this social imaginary—the academy as a phantasm. In the everyday working of the restructuring university maintenance of profit margins, program flexibility and the privileges associated with "academic freedom" require a tremendous amount of flexible labor. So that at the same institution in which I find myself to be ill-fitting and solitary, memorandums predominately displayed in copy rooms throughout the campus inform me that there are approximately two hundred adjunct faculty and about eighty full-time faculty. Yet, out of these full-timers, about 10 percent are on temporary full-time contracts like myself. Rough calculations suggest that more than 50 percent of classes are taught by temporary and adjunct labor.

But adjunct labor is strategically made invisible; they are not allowed to perform committee work, usually are dissuaded from attending department meetings, and are without voice or vote at faculty meetings. Outside of the particular department in which they work, adjunct faculty members rarely know of each other's existence. Appearing within the classroom via semester-by-semester contracts, they must vanish with a startling immediacy upon leaving the classroom. In this sense, they are considered to be adjunct to the faculty, but not actual faculty themselves.

Let me give you an example. A colleague of mine has taught for the last twenty-eight years in an MBA program at a medium-sized technical university. The first twenty-five years he was an adjunct. During the last three, he has had a one-year renewable contract as temporary full-time faculty. Recently, senior members of the business school decided that a banquet was in order for those members of the school who had served for five or more years. My friend was not invited, as it was explained to him, because he is considered rather new. In other words, he has only been visible at the school for the past three years; the prior quarter century merely evaporated into another's story.

Conversely, full-time faculty members encounter each other constantly in committee meetings, at AAUP (American Association of University Professors) functions, faculty meetings and within their daily lives in the library, gym, and dining commons. Full-time faculty appear to each other as having a tremendous solidity and as members of the academy. At the same time, they have an eerie sense that the academy is dissolving. On one hand, they are surrounded by ghosts, constantly changing apparitions one sees teaching students. On the other hand, they watch as growing administrations formulate strategic plans that dictate the actual terms of their daily teaching and research.

For full-timers, the two, administration and adjuncts, are conjoined. Looking at the university as a whole, adjuncts are emblematic of the declining standards forced by administrative fiat. Adjuncts become portrayed as the cause of university change, not part of the overall effect. Looking within their own departments, these adjuncts are perceived as special exceptions to the rest of the university. Often, these adjuncts are perceived as "young scholars" gaining "valuable teaching experience." They are held as being eternally young, no matter their actual age or years of service, as in the example cited above. So it is quite common to hear a full-time faculty member with relatively few publications speak to a well-published adjunct in tones of friendly infantilization: "How's that dissertation coming?" Also it is quite common for the well-published adjunct to not inform full-time scholars within their department of their accomplishments.

Deference requires adjuncts to deny their accomplishments as a form of denying their difference. Within the tones of infantilized conversation, both parties speak in the murmuring discourse of the vanishing academy. The creation of a homogenous identity of fellow academicians is traded on the displacement of their laboring difference (Ivy 1995, 22). The daily performances of this shared identity requires an explanation of declining entitlements for one (the constant murmuring from left and right about their disengagement from public life), and from the other the routine management of their stigma.

Several state legislatures have used fiscal exigency to argue for the limitation or elimination of tenure. At the University of Minnesota, the situation is very interesting in that the Board of Regents would like not only to rewrite the tenure rules to fire tenured faculty due to fiscal exigency, but they also seek to restructure, which may include reassigning, retraining, or firing a faculty member without the direct evidence of a financial crisis. A lawyer hired by the university stated, "We are in a downward spiral on funding for our university from the taxpayers ... and we're in the midst of selecting a new president here. We think that down the line, our president might need some tools to react to these funding problems" (Magner 1996, A12).

It seems very clear that what the regents are seeking is greater flexibility in the workforce. In the new global economy of highly flexible institutions that move labor and services at a rapid rate, the older models of tenure don't fit. In a climate of downsized workforces and streamlined businesses, the state sees its tax revenue for education shrinking, requiring a more streamlined university. State institutions are pressured to be like economic institutions, and thus the regents are making their move. While Minnesota is a groundbreaking case, it is not a lone example. In Pennsylvania several members of the legislature have begun to talk with the State System of Higher Education board about changing tenure rules at the state's universities to gain greater flexibility. There are cases in other states as well. The City University of New York system has been pushing the requirement of fiscal exigency by firing a large number of tenured faculty even after the fiscal crisis abated. The faculty took the board to court, and the university's response was to attempt another firing before the first case was settled.

TENURED FACULTY RESPONSES

Faculty responses to these new pressures coming from the state and boards of regents are revealing. One University of Minnesota faculty member quoted on National Public Radio stated that if the regents go through with these changes, it may be a school but it won't be a university anymore. I am struck by this notion that the system of tenure and control over hiring and firing is the sign of a university. In the *Yeshiva* decision, the Supreme Court more or less agreed. But a large portion of the teaching force that works in most universities has not been part of the system of tenure. The tenured faculty are right; universities should not be disciplining faculty through elimination of tenure. But there has been a general failure to recognize their own collusion with university administrations. For years, universities have been disciplining the full-time faculty with the strategic employment of adjuncts and temporary faculty, leaving the tenured with the illusion of autonomy and academic freedom. Another faculty member in the same radio interview lamented the situation but suggested that many young faculty members have never known tenure and will never know it. He waxed nostalgic and suggested that what his generation experienced was perhaps an aberration and something that was passing from the scene. So we have another way in which the politics of labor discipline is misrecognized now as the transience of all things.

Tenured faculty see assaults on all fronts. There are the direct assaults of university systems trying to get rid of tenure as just discussed, but there are actions being taken by university administrations, influenced by a new culture of corporate management, to limit unilaterally the power and even legitimacy of tenure. Another example of such a situation occurred in Philadelphia at Temple University. David Bradley, a prominent and tenured member of the English department, was fired for not agreeing to an across-the-board increase in teaching loads for tenured faculty. Bradley's contract is for four courses a year, and when the university decided that everyone's load would increase, Bradley refused the speed-up. He said he had a contract, and the university could not just change it. The university response was to fire him. The dean said that by his refusal to increase his teaching load he had resigned his position.

The stories at the University of Minnesota and Temple University and many other universities are interesting for many reasons. For us, the denial of the adjunct labor market (through its relative invisibility) has allowed the tenured faculty to be taken by surprise. Most younger faculty see these overt exercises of bureaucratic power as common, but for the tenured, some of whom have labored under the illusion that *they* are the university, the recent movements on the part of state legislatures and university administrations are a shocking new development. In this new landscape, the adjunct is pointed to as both part of the problem and as the image of the future. As teachers, part-time faculty are not often seen as part of the university community. Perhaps they are not as good as the tenured. They are imagined as perpetually younger and professionally unaccomplished. In other words, they are inferior labor being used by administrations that care only for managing the universities and nothing for the quality of an education. The part-time teachers are also pointed to with resignation as the wave of the future. This is the generation that has not known tenure and probably never will. They are permanently disenfranchised. Further, they are a sign of the university's future.

SYMBOLIC STRUGGLES

Yet, two questions confront us: first, why does a discourse of infantilization take place so routinely? Second, why is it that those who are so frequently infantilized must in other moments manage stigma beyond the fact of being of junior status?

As Louis Menand has recently pointed out, academic freedom is the key "legitimizing concept of the entire enterprise. Virtually every practice of academic life that we take for granted—from the practice of allowing departments to hire and fire their own members to the practice of not allowing the football coach to influence the quarterback's grade in math class—derives from it" (1996, 4). Admittedly, this notion is double-edged: For those who are credentialized, gainfully employed, and working within their specialization, academic freedom grants the protection of the professional group. Academic freedom is the emblem of the group's self-interest to self-regulation. For those who fall out of this circle of protection, academic freedom is the very condition of their exclusion.

The concept of academic freedom operates in a similarly double-edged way in the case of graduate students, junior professors, and other untenured members of the profession. The doctoral student and the assistant professor are free to write what they choose, but what they write had better accord with their senior colleagues' idea of what counts as acceptable scholarship in the field. It is expected that those senior colleagues will make judgments in a disinterested spirit—in the spirit, indeed, of academic freedom. But they perform a judgment, not a measurement—the dissertation is read, not weighed—and no one who is an assistant professor coming up for tenure is likely to feel a strong association between the experience and the concept of academic freedom. Again, in being free to regulate itself, the profession is free to reject what does not intellectually suit and essentially to compel, by withholding professional rewards (including monetary ones such as promotions and merit increases), the production of work that does (Menand 1996, 9).

Now regardless of the whole slew of objections that might be made regarding this characterization of academic freedom, it is precisely within the formal mythologizing of this characterization that the phantasm academy appears.

First, academic freedom becomes the boundary condition by which a community of affinity may appear. As the mechanism of both protection and self-regulation, academic freedom is the condition of community. But the conditions of self-regulation are not spelled out. While Menand does trenchantly point out that conditions of self-regulations are, often, protective reactions against the potential threat of regulatory mechanism imposed from without, he fails to see that mechanisms of self-regulation are at best always a compromise with this threat of regulation. Instead of regulation being realized as such, regulation becomes internalized as part of a disciplinary stance. This is why when the anthropologist interviewed adjuncts, they remarked that their tenured colleagues seem completely coerced and cowed by administrative gambits to change the curriculum as part of university marketing efforts, cost reduction, or facilities coordination. These tenured faculty members remark that their decisions are based on internal changes within their departments and disciplines and are part of a larger strategy to make sure that administrations don't force compliance by further budget cutting. Therefore, these decisions are not coerced but sensibly correspond to a changing world.

Second, implied within academic freedom is a hierarchy of statuses that correspond to a greater proportion of professional entitlement and responsibility for professional surveillance. As one climbs the rungs through tenure, promotion, and merit, one gains greater and greater professional autonomy at the very same time that one is called to patrol the borders of these entitlements to ensure that they go to those who are deserving candidates. In this sense, academic freedom as the "key legitimizing process of the whole enterprise" takes place with an imaginary field of work where there is full employment and a constant movement of juniors through to senior status.

One of the ways the labor contradictions are smoothed over in higher education is by the denial of the symbolic struggle at the heart of academic labor. This denial has at least two major components. As Bourdieu suggests (1977, 168), all doxa deny their arbitrary character by creating a sense of the naturalness of a point of view. In the academy, imaginings of community, rules of governance, and systems of academic freedom and tenure are all self-presented as rational and fair. Even the critiques of Menand (1996) and Said (1994, 1996) form a kind of orthodoxy by suggesting that the elect had better respect their gifts and use them to encourage diversity and tolerance, to teach about what is practical in order for these gifts to be best used. Their critique underscores the naturalness of the arena.

Bourdieu suggests that this is true of all symbolic universes and that the larger critique of that symbolic order is silenced by its falling outside of the domain of what is considered natural. Moments of rupture, however, come when the crises of a symbolic universe force a reconsideration of the basic tenets. Such a crisis for higher education might be the declining state support for higher education and the fiscal crisis experienced by so many schools, leading them to discipline labor so much that the orthodox positions are being threatened. This decline of state revenue is itself the product of contradictory forces. On the one hand, neo-liberal economic ideas about the role of the state in public financing are increasingly more popular. This worldview suggests that all institutions should pay their own way and not be a drain on the capital necessary to the "health" of the economy (Block 1996). On the other hand, corporations and politicians have worked over the last twenty years to make it easier for state-funded research to be used for private gain. Central to this move were the changes in patent law in the 1980s where universities could hold the patents to research produced with federal grants. Ironically this change led to decreased revenues as many corporation made their matching funds contingent upon universities exclusively leasing any patent to grow out of the research to them. These corporations also tended to stipulate that funds could not be used for operational expenses (Press and Washburn 2000, Shumar 1997, Soley 1995). These threats open up a symbolic moment where tenured and older faculty might see that the system has been compromised for some time, but thus far they have avoided this truth, electing rather to stigmatize a whole generation of scholars.

The flurry of conferences and recognition of the labor problem in higher education might be the sign of such a moment. It could also be the sign of the need to draw the lines more tightly and secure the positions of those who are privileged in the system. Already the labor problem is being represented by prominent left intellectuals who are gaining notoriety for the issue though they themselves have not been directly part of the labor crisis. This kind of notoriety establishes the sense that they are the scholars who write and have authority, and speak for the marginalized laborers. While scholars on the right suggest we open the university to market forces, scholars on the left secure notoriety and publication by criticizing the system. To some extent, this is an example of what Bourdieu (1990b, 380) has called the "Scholastic view." As senior and elite scholars make hay out of the current set of labor relations, they misrecognize a set of relationships that they have been in now for over a decade, sometimes two. They have the time to sit back and look at the situation of part-time and temporary academic labor, "to play with these issues seriously" (Bourdieu 1990b, 381). But, ironically, in their play they see the part-time and temporary labor as Other. The relationships they have had with these part-time colleagues who have made their leave time possible, kept their teaching loads lighter, and saved their grants money have gone unrecognized. Sometimes these trade-offs between cheap labor to save a budget and exploiting a colleague are brought to consciousness but then forgotten. Forgotten because their part-time colleague has no official place; they are officially forgotten, no phone numbers, office numbers, fax numbers, no place at the faculty meeting or on committees. Many part-time colleagues have held up a department's teaching load only to be told they didn't cut it when it came time for a permanent hire; they were not seen as part of the scholarly community.

Furthermore, the current crisis is being misrecognized as a crisis of the young and the graduate students. We would not suggest that the current state of academic labor is not a crisis for upcoming graduate students, but it has been one for many years, it is nothing new. One of the further social ruptures, and the reason for current attention to the problems of academic labor, is that the crisis in academic labor has penetrated even the most elite and privileged graduate schools. When Yale and Stanford have trouble placing their graduate students, then a crisis of academic labor can be legitimated as real. We are clearly already in a moment when the elite institutions and their spokespersons, occasionally co-opted graduate students who momentarily become the spokespersons for a generation, and prominent faculty on the left and right are speaking for the dispossessed—can the subaltern speak? James Scott (1985, 317–35) argues in *Weapons of the Weak* that the marginalized and subordinate classes are often misrecognized by the elite. We could make a similar argument for the academic dispossessed. They clearly see the ways in which they have been exploited as part of a system that maintains the illusion of a scholarly community and academic privilege. At points, they are required to obscure their own exploitation. However, it is not due to ignorance, but rather because of what must be done. Further, the marginalized intellectual doesn't seek to change the system, only to fit in, and in the effort to do that will appear as if he/she accepts the conditions of his/her exploitation.

The phantasm of the academy imagined through this discourse of freedom confronts a present labor situation in which this phantasm haunts all those professing within it. The routinization of a discourse of infantilization found within daily interactions between tenured and adjunct faculty stabilizes the conditions of the present emergency in the short term. However, the ambivalence and tension found within these interactions are haunting for all parties. Symbolic juniors become spectres of these conditions as they age through the system. Through their aging, they destabilize the orthodoxy of academic freedom. Their aging bodies become the markers of promises of the past that can never be regained and the sense that all promising futures have already been betrayed. The only alternative left for those who are structurally imagined as perpetually young is to be imagined as failures—those who haven't fulfilled their promise. Many of us have become professionalized as failures.

When graduate employees strike for collective bargaining rights, as has happened recently in the University of California system, they rally together (outside of the confines of specialized disciplines where debates over academic freedom are voiced) and confront the university as an overall corporate employer. Most administrations and some tenured members within particular departments voice their opposition to this process; it is a hallmark of the dissolution of the

academy and an abrogation of academic freedom. Upsetting the administra-
tions of tenured imaginations of hierarchy, these graduate students are trad-
ing their apprenticeship, promising professional freedoms at a later date, for
mere benefits of common labor. In this sense, labor outside the imagination of
academic freedom is beyond the domain of one's professional status; by default
it is stigmatized because it is amateurish. For those who are well-placed and
sympathetic to these students' plight, the call for collective bargaining is cur-
rent news that marks a most recent commodification of education. Yet, listen-
ing to the stories told by adjuncts, moving past the information of today's news,
this most recent crisis has been a story unfolding for perhaps three decades.

For so many of us who labor within the university system, who only appear
visible as permanent children of the academy, who vanish as flexible labor of
the transforming university, who bear the stigma of being professional failures,
the phantasm of the academy is a ghostly apparition that haunts our own de-
sires and coerces our daily commitment to a form of academic freedom that ex-
cludes, confines, and discounts our daily conditions and stories.

While it is clear that marginalized university faculty are not part of the subordinate classes in a more global sense, they are part of a large set of structural
processes in which intellectuals are seeing themselves declining in class position
and voice. A globalizing capitalist system increasingly rewards a professional
technical managerial class and less a more traditional notion of the liberal intellectual. In this way, our essay is a continuation of an argument begun by
Gouldner (1979) and Sartre (1974), when each in his own way talked about the
declining symbolic power of intellectuals in advanced capitalism. Further, while
these are conditions that all academic intellectuals are facing in their universities, sometimes disguised as the need to be more applicable, provide a practical
life skill (read marketable trade) to students, boost enrollments, and so on, it is
often the marginalized who understand these process and the relations of power
in the university. Again following Bourdieu (1984, 1985, 1988, 1990a), there is
an isomorphism between position and disposition. It is in the interests of tenured
faculty to see academic freedom as having meaning and their role as an important one for the future intellectual life of the society. Ironically, it is the elite
who can be mystified by the ideology of their own institutions and their roles
in those institutions leading prominent intellectuals such as Edward Said (1996,
227) to wax romantic and idealistic, stating:

Our model for academic freedom should therefore be the migrant or traveler: for if, in
the real world outside of the academy we must needs be ourselves and only ourselves,
inside the academy we should be able to discover and travel among other selves, other
identities, other variety of the human adventure.

and again,

It comes, finally, to two images for inhabiting the academic and cultural space provided
by school and university. On the one hand, we can be there in order to reign and hold

sway.... The other model is considerably more mobile, more playful, although no less serious. The image of traveler depends not on power, but on motion, on a willingness to go into different worlds, use different idioms, and understand a variety of disguises, masks and rhetorics. (1996:227)

Two things are important to note in Said's vision. There is the internal homogeneity of those inside the academy. The academy is posed as a fortress set off from the real world, which creates the illusion of an internally homogeneous space. It is also a denial of real world global labor processes in the academy; the subaltern is invisible. Relating to the first point, there is a denial of power, of the lines of force that have made it possible for the tenured privileged academic to travel, metaphorically or literally. If you're appointed from term to term, school to school, there are no sabbaticals, travel funds, time off to play with ideas.

CONCLUSION

The marginalized academic is not so romantic, does not see her/himself cut off from the real world, but has no access to these official forms of speech that are the fabric from which official history and the issues of an age are constructed. John and Jean Comaroff (1987), drawing on the work of W.J.T. Mitchell (1986) and Paul Friedrich (1979), make a distinction between the realist text—the discourse of objectivity that forms official history and is imbedded within a hidden set of power relations that makes its legitimacy seamless (Rosaldo 1989, 202)— and a poetic discourse—a rhetoric that draws upon the metaphorical properties of language and becomes the vehicle through which group consciousness is expressed in a cultural form. From the outside, it is kind of a crypt, but for the members of an oppressed group, the tropes have meaning and significance and speak a truth about lived social relationships and the power imbedded in them that remains denied by and even masked to those in power. So we conclude where we began, with the stories and jokes told by a disenfranchised group of intellectuals that speak to the deep crisis not only within the daily ironies of intellectual life but the crisis of global production and consumption.

REFERENCES

Benjamin, W. 1968. *Illuminations.* New York: Schocken Books.
Block, F. 1996. *The vampire state: And other myths and fallacies about the U.S economy.* New York: New Press.
Bourdieu, P. 1977. *Outline of a theory of practice.* Cambridge: Cambridge University Press.
———. 1984. *Distinction: A social critique of the judgment of taste.* Cambridge, MA: Harvard University Press.
———. 1985. The social space and the genesis of groups. *Theory and Society* 14: 723–744.

———. 1988. *Homo academicus.* Stanford, CA: Stanford University Press.

———. 1990a. *The logic of practice.* Stanford, CA: Stanford University Press.

———. 1990b. The scholastic point of view. *Cultural Anthropology* 5:380–391.

Comaroff, J., and J. L. Comaroff. 1987. The madman and the migrant: Work and labor in the historical consciousness of a South African people. *American Ethnologist* 14: 191–209.

Fabian, J. 1990. Presence and representation: The other and anthropological writing. *Critical Inquiry* 16: 753–772.

Friedrich, P 1979. *Language, context and the imagination.* Stanford, CA: Stanford University Press.

Giroux, H.A. 1992. *Border crossings: Cultural workers and the politics of education.* New York: Routledge.

Goffman, E. 1963. *Stigma: Notes on the management of spoiled identity.* New York: Touchstone.

Gouldner, A W. 1979. *The future of intellectuals and the rise of the new class: A frame of reference, theses, conjectures, arguments, and an historical perspective on the role of intellectuals and intelligentsia in the international class contest of the modern era.* New York: Seabury Press.

Ivy, M. 1995. *Discourse of the vanishing: Modernity, phantasm, Japan.* Chicago: University of Chicago Press.

Jacoby, R. 1987. *The last intellectuals.* New York: Basic Books.

———. 1994. *Dogmatic wisdom: How the culture wars divert education and distract America.* New York: Doubleday.

Magner, D.K. 1996. The end of tenure? Minnesota regents' proposals stir controversy with faculty. *The Chronicle of Higher Education,* September 20, A11.

Menand, L. 1996. The limits of academic freedom. In *The future of academic freedom,* ed. L. Menand, 3–20. Chicago: University of Chicago.

Mitchell, W.J. T. 1986. *Iconology: Image, text, ideology.* Chicago: University of Chicago Press.

Press, E., and J. Washburn. 2000. The kept university. *The Atlantic Monthly,* March, 39–54.

Rigby, P. 1985. *Persistent pastoralists: Nomadic societies in transition.* Totowa, NJ: Biblio.

Rosaldo, R. 1989. *Culture & truth: The remaking of social analysis.* Boston: Beacon Press.

Said, E.W. 1983. Opponents, audiences, constituencies and community. In *The anti-aesthetic,* ed. H. Foster, 135–159. Port Townsend, WA: Bay Press.

———. 1989. Anthropology's interlocutors. *Critical Inquiry* 15:205–225.

———. 1994. *Representations of the intellectual.* New York: Pantheon Books.

———. 1996. Identity, authority and freedom: The potentate and the traveler. In *The future of academic freedom,* ed. L. Menand. Chicago: University of Chicago.

Sartre, J. 1974. *Between existentialism and Marxism* (trans. John Mathews). New York: Pantheon Books.

Scott, J. C. 1985. *Weapons of the weak.* New Haven, CT: Yale University Press.

Shumar, W. 1997. *College for sale: A critique of the commodification of higher education.* London: Falmer Press.

Soley, L. 1995. *Leasing the ivory tower.* Boston: South End Press.

Stewart, K. 1991. On the politics of cultural theory: A case for "contaminated" cultural critique. *Social Research* 58:395–412.

Tsing, A.L. 1994. *In the realm of the diamond queen: Marginality in and out-of-the-way place.* Princeton, NJ: Princeton University Press.

Wilson, R. 1996. Professor critic, professional gadfly. *The Chronicle of Higher Education,* March 22, A16.

Chapter 2

Dueling Identities and Faculty Unions: A Canadian Case Study

Mike Burke and Joanne Naiman

University faculty in both Canada and the United States have traditionally held contradictory identities. They are, on the one hand, salaried employees who share a common set of working conditions with their colleagues. On the other hand, they are semi-autonomous entrepreneurs who retain some degree of control over the nature and pace of their work. The tensions between these identities have played out in particular ways over the last twenty years as the university sector across North America experienced major restructuring. This chapter uses the case study of the Faculty Association at Ryerson Polytechnic University in Toronto, Canada, to examine the determinants and consequences of contradictory faculty identities. It shows the close connection between faculty identities and the capacity of faculty unions to respond effectively to current changes in the university sector.

DUELING IDENTITIES

A number of social scientists have noted the contradictory elements within the stratum of workers that has evolved in modern capitalist societies (for example, Wright, 1978, 1985). These are workers, such as managers, technocrats, supervisors, or other semi-autonomous employees, who concurrently embody elements of both the traditional proletariat and the petty bourgeoisie. As in the case of Erik Olin Wright, the tendency has been to take these contradictions and externalize them as different locations in the class structure. However, another approach would be to formulate these contradictory elements as opposing identities within a single individual, identities arising from the real material conditions of a worker's employment.

On the one hand, of course, employees within this stratum collectively share at least some job-related elements with others in their workplace. They are paid a salary or wage for performing work whose conditions are in some important respects determined by their employer. It is this reality that promotes their common identity as workers. On the other hand, many work, to a greater or lesser extent, within a competitive system that pits them against fellow employees, gives them some control over their daily work activities and/or the work of others, and rewards them at least in part on the basis of their individual output. This development advances an individualistic entrepreneurial identity. The real conditions of different workplaces or occupations may promote one identity over the other.

These contradictory identities can help us gain some understanding of differing organizational outcomes within particular workplaces. If employees primarily identify themselves as entrepreneurs, they would likely show at least some interest in a *competitive model*, in which personal gains are made through individual competition, private negotiations with superiors, or some type of pay-for-performance award. In contrast, if employees more strongly identify themselves as workers, they would likely show more interest in a *collective model*, in which improvements in wages and working conditions are sought jointly with others via some kind of association or union. In the competitive model, one individual's gain is frequently another's loss in a zero-sum game, while in the collective model, employees make gains as a unit.

These models are, of course, not only the result of particular identities, but a cause of them as well. For example, a strongly competitive model in a particular workplace would likely tend to encourage an entrepreneurial identity among employees by providing structural inducements that emphasize the differences between employees and individualize their work. Incentive pay schemes that reward individual effort, such as piece-rate pay or merit pay, have this kind of effect.

From the employer's point of view, in general, a competitive model has financial and managerial advantages over a collective model, as indicated by the lengths to which some owners will go to keep unions out of their workplaces. However, given the contradictory identities of many employees, their preferences regarding organizational models are not at all self-evident.

It should be noted that these models do not usually exist in a "pure" form; they are polar extremes of what is, in effect, a continuum. Hence, many workplaces may have some elements from each of these opposing models. Nonetheless, the degree to which one or the other of these two models will be emphasized in any given workplace will be determined to a large extent by the local balance of power between the employer and employees, and by the degree to which employees identify themselves either as entrepreneurs or workers. These identities will, in turn, be determined partially by the kind of model that is dominant in the workplace.

Given the nature of academic activity, one would predict that the tendency would be for most university faculty to see themselves primarily as entrepre-

neurs and, thus, favor the competitive model. While this identity may sometimes be viewed as elitism or snobbery on the part of academics, it may more
clearly be understood as reflective of the way they labor. As one author (Tudiver
1999, 161) writes:

Almost unique among employees in advanced capitalist societies, academics control most
of their own labor process. They operate essentially as semi-autonomous craft workers,
free to set procedures and methods of work provided they teach assigned courses, conduct an acceptable amount of research, and maintain an adequate publication record.
Within the boundaries of the curriculum and the length of scheduled courses, professors
determine the content and pace of their teaching. They are free from supervision in the
classroom or when they prepare lectures, and may work at any time of day, at different
locations, without constraints of time clocks or dress codes.

Moreover, the line between employer and employee is often difficult to discern
in the university setting. Aside from the obvious fact that university faculty
work primarily in the public sphere and have no clear "owners" under whose
employ they toil, the other main complicating factor is that many administrative managers are former (or even current) colleagues. Indeed, it is not uncommon in Canada for university faculty to move from leadership positions in their
unions to top levels of administration. Moreover, senior faculty or those whose
wages would surpass the average due to market factors (such as those in professional faculties) are likely to favor elements of a competitive model, in which
their remuneration could almost certainly exceed the norm. Of course, this is
the model that has traditionally dominated employer-employee relations at most
universities in North America.

Notwithstanding these realities, however, university professors are also workers who share with fellow colleagues a common set of working conditions and
problems. While certainly a privileged stratum of workers, university professors
have frequently faced arbitrary measures from their superiors, including exces-
sive workloads, inferior wages, or even dismissal. Moreover, while faculty may
have a fairly high degree of autonomy over certain aspects of their daily work
life, they have little or no influence over larger issues such as budgets, salaries,
the size of the faculty complement, the approval or elimination of academic programs, and so on. One author (Rhoades 1998) tries to embody the contradictory
nature of academic work by describing faculty as "managed professionals."

If a large group of faculty share poor or deteriorating conditions, they might
be more likely to shift attention away from their self-perception as "professionals" to their shared identity as workers and thus increase their interest in a
collective model. One obvious example would be contingent academic labor that
historically has faced extremely poor wages and working conditions. For tenured
faculty, an erosion of existing conditions might shift their identity and lead them
to favor a more collective model.

The mere fact of unionization shifts faculty, at least formally, to a collective
model, as contracts are negotiated on behalf of the entire faculty, or at least that

portion who are deemed to be part of the bargaining unit (Aronowitz 1997, 206). However, even within collective agreements there may be clauses that promote the entrepreneurial identity, including variable wage rates, merit provisions, bonus plans, managerial control over individual working conditions, and so on. For academics, the processes of obtaining tenure and promotion, in and of themselves, encourage the competitive model, even in unionized workplaces.

It should also be noted that the exceptional conditions in which academics have historically labored—as described so astutely in the quotation from Tudiver—set the stage for the particular tensions felt by university professors with regard to their contradictory and competing identities. On the one hand, the entrepreneurial identity, linked to the semi-autonomous nature of academic work, has, at times, actually encouraged university professors to collectively struggle to maintain or advance certain controls over their work and their workplace. For example, university professors have fought—and frequently won—the contractual right to have some say in hiring, the setting of program standards, faculty assessment, and promotion and tenure, as well as the right to sit on governance bodies that set university policies. Such rights and privileges are rarely seen in other workplaces.

On the other hand, university administrations may use this same entrepreneurial identity as an instrument to erode collective protections and encourage competitiveness among faculty. Indeed, academics may occasionally find themselves essentially doing the work of management in the name of faculty autonomy and professionalism. It is clear, then, that these dueling identities, and the workplace model that ensues from the ongoing struggle between these identities, must be understood in all their complexity and specificity.

The rest of this chapter focuses on the ongoing struggle between these two identities within the Ryerson Faculty Association (RFA), representing faculty at Ryerson Polytechnic University. It analyzes how the bifurcation of that faculty into two separate modes served to accentuate those dueling identities, to the detriment of faculty as a whole; moreover, it relates the changes at Ryerson to the broader political and economic forces that transformed the postsecondary sector in Canada.

THE POLITICAL AND ECONOMIC CONTEXT

In Canada, where almost all postsecondary institutions are publicly funded, academics moved toward an identity as workers in the mid-1970s. A 1971 study concluded that unionization in the university sector was coming as a result of the deteriorating job market, declining job security, increasing government control of university affairs, deteriorating relations between faculty and their administrations, and more widespread collective bargaining on campuses in other countries (Adell and Carter 1972). Canadian faculty until this time had neither a history of unionization nor a national organizing body, and faculty moved cautiously toward unionization starting in 1974.

With time, faculty across the country began to seek certification, and faculty associations increasingly joined the Canadian Association of University Teachers (CAUT), an autonomous body created to promote the general interests of faculty. However, with only one exception, professors continued to refer to their academic unions as *faculty associations*, a clear indication of their conflicting self-perception. Even CAUT was at first hesitant to support faculty unionization. Despite early resistance, by the 1980s over half of all faculty in Canada had unionized on twenty-nine campuses, while another eleven campuses agreed to voluntary collective bargaining without formal certification (Tudiver 1999, 85).

These developments were clearly linked to the fact that, by the early 1970s, capitalist economies had entered a permanent state of economic crisis. The corporate sector tried ever harder to increase the rate of profit through a variety of means, and many employers moved to what has been termed "lean production." The shift to "lean production" includes three aspects: (1) the elimination of "waste" through just-in-time production, minimal staffing levels, and the ideology of "continuous improvement"; (2) the creation of a more differentiated workforce, in which there is a minimal permanent workforce backed up by flexible workers hired on a part-time, temporary, or contract basis; and (3) new forms of work intensification that rely on stress and self-subordination (Sears 2000, 146–147).

Postsecondary education in North America has not been immune either to the shift to "lean production" or to its reflection in social policy, which Sears (2000, 146) refers to as "the lean state." In Canada, the first major transformation, beginning in the 1970s, was massive cutbacks to government funding of universities and colleges while enrollments continued to grow. This left the administrators of postsecondary institutions in a difficult economic situation, which they attempted to solve via a shift from permanent to contract faculty, increased class sizes, increased tuition fees, greater centralization of decision making, and restraints on salaries. Put simply, university administrators, like other employers, sought ways to make workers more productive at less cost.

Given these developments, one could predict that university administrations would be interested in promoting or maintaining a more competitive model of employee-employer relations. This would serve a number of useful purposes, all linked to the move to "lean production." Aside from obvious cost-savings, the competitive model would almost certainly raise output, as more and more benefits would be based on some kind of pay-for-performance scheme, with faculty repeatedly having to prove their worth. Administrators would also increase their control over this growing output, as faculty "worthiness" would ultimately be defined in fairly narrow ways—usually with concrete measures of output (number of papers published, grants awarded, students taught, etc.). In this way, the competitive model can be seen as closely linked to what has been described as "management by stress" (Parker and Slaughter 1994), an important element of lean production. This model, of course, by encouraging the entrepreneurial identity, also pits faculty against each other, thereby discouraging a more collective model and increased union activism.

At the same time, the growing commercialization of Canadian universities encouraged and rewarded the most entrepreneurial faculty.[1] As research was increasingly tied to business interests, those whose services were of value in the marketplace—such as those in business, computer science, and some engineering departments—could negotiate higher incoming wages, instant tenure, signing bonuses, and so on. At many universities in Canada, faculty also began to have a personal financial interest in their research (Tudiver 1999, 156). For this privileged component of university faculty, then, there was increased support for the competitive model.

Thus, the natural tension embodied within the contradictory identities of academics was exacerbated by the shift of the last twenty-five years to lean production and the lean state. This tension, inevitable in all university settings, nonetheless plays out differently in each academic workplace.

THE RYERSON CASE

Ryerson Polytechnic University is located in the heart of downtown Toronto, Canada's largest city, with a population of some 2.3 million. Two other major universities, The University of Toronto and York University, are also located in the greater Toronto area. Although Ryerson achieved full university status in 1993, its unique history sets it apart from most universities in Canada. Ryerson was founded at the end of World War II as a technical training school primarily for returning veterans. In 1964, Ryerson Institute of Technology became Ryerson Polytechnical Institute, and in 1971, it began to offer undergraduate degrees in some disciplines. Both Ryerson's governance structure and its relation to its workers were largely modeled on those of Ontario high schools. Faculty had to have teaching certificates, and few had more than a master's degree. The teaching load was heavier than at universities, but no research was required. Wages were determined by a rigid grid system based on level of education and years of experience.

Ryerson faculty became unionized in 1964, at the time of conversion to Ryerson Polytechnical Institute. However, from the outset, the RFA had many of the characteristics of a company union. According to faculty who were employed during this time, it was actually the new president of Ryerson, Howard Kerr, who suggested that faculty should formally organize themselves into a union.[2]

One characteristic that the RFA shares with company unions is a weak tradition of union democracy. Organizationally, a great deal of power is held by the union executive. Contract negotiations are conducted almost entirely in secret between the two negotiating teams, with only a few members of the union executive made aware of the ongoing process. To this day, RFA members do not formally set demands prior to negotiations, nor do they see the details of either the union or management proposals at the outset of the bargaining process. During negotiations, members receive, at best, occasional reports from the negotiating chair, which are almost totally devoid of specifics. The first time faculty are fully apprised of the negotiating process is at its conclusion, when they are asked either to ratify a new contract or, should there be an inability to resolve all contractual issues, to agree to final and binding arbitration.

Despite this lack of democratic process, the close relationship between Ryerson faculty and administration has not been problematic for the majority of the RFA, and indeed, many members have seen it as an asset. This may be explained by the fact that, until the late 1980s, Ryerson faculty, when compared to other teachers with similar educational credentials, did relatively well in terms of wages and working conditions. If some instructors in professional faculties were underpaid relative to those in their field, this was generally made up for by the fact that many were able to earn additional income through activities done outside the university or via overload teaching. Since faculty were not required to do research, this left time for some to undertake such remunerative activities.

Moreover, RFA salaries were determined via a single grid with relatively few steps. When one became an employee at Ryerson, the initial step was decided on the basis of educational level and experience, with automatic yearly progression through the ranks. This meant that Ryerson faculty did particularly well in their early years, even when compared to those in the university sector, as their salaries quickly escalated and they reached the top of the pay scale in a relatively short time. However, they were more disadvantaged in their later years of employment, as wages were capped at a much lower level than full professors or even associate professors at many universities.

In addition, unlike faculty in the university sector, Ryerson faculty had fairly rigid rules determining their workload. A complex clause in the contract defined maximum class sizes, maximum student-contact hours, and so on.[3] Although faculty had no teaching assistants and did all their own grading, there was no expectation that they do research, publish, or work with graduate students, as Ryerson was not yet a university. The only contractual obligation they had to their employer was teaching and teaching-related activities. The contract also guaranteed "a period of not less than two months and not more than three months per year for study, preparation and related work, and vacation."

The downside, of course, was that those faculty who wished, or were expected by their departments, to do research or write had to squeeze these activities into what time was left after attending to all their teaching and administrative duties, or during the summer break. Moreover, although relatively small class sizes enhanced teaching, the high number of stand-up hours (as many as eighteen in some cases), and number of students (as many as two hundred or so) could sometimes make for an onerous workload. In some departments, the combining of sections brought down the number of stand-up hours, if not the number of students. In those departments where much of the teaching was done in nontraditional modes (such as theater arts, dance, or nursing) the workload could be substantial indeed.

Given the relatively good wages and working conditions, the close relation between faculty and the administration, the lack of any struggle to win a union, and the fact that some faculty regularly engaged in private contract activities, the worker identity among faculty remained relatively weak in spite of having a union. For example, in its first contract, the faculty association agreed to submit any unresolved contractual issues to final and binding arbitration in the event that a new collective agreement could not be achieved. This form of dispute resolution, which essentially eliminates the possibility of strikes, has reappeared in each subsequent contract. It should also be noted that RFA presidents for many years met "informally" on a regular basis with the Ryerson president. Indeed, some faculty actually thought that the RFA was simply an arm of the Ryerson administration.

The Creation of a Two-Tiered Contract

By the mid 1980s, the Ryerson administration faced an increasingly difficult situation. The squeeze on government funding to postsecondary institutions was affecting them in the same way as other universities. However, there was little space to move in terms of the push to "lean production," since faculty had workload limits and a clear grid structure for wages, and the majority had the protection of tenure. Moreover, because Ryerson had agreed to compulsory arbitration to settle disputes, both sides knew that labor boards rarely tackled complex issues such as workloads; rather, they dealt almost exclusively with wage disputes. Thus, the Ryerson administration had fewer options than those at most other universities in terms of moving to "lean production." In order to get greater productivity at less cost, they had to get faculty to give up some of their existing benefits.

One traditional solution for employers in such situations has been the creation of two-tiered contracts that maintain or improve the wages and terms of work for current employees on the first tier, while they establish lower wage structures and inferior working conditions for all new employees on the second, or lower, tier. Such practices can be difficult for unions to resist. Employers can cleverly utilize carrot-and-stick tactics to get negotiating teams to accept such contracts. The carrot usually comes in the form of some major financial gain or benefit for the existing workers. The stick—which could include threats of layoffs or plant closures, or demands for major concessions from employees—can play on the vulnerability of particular workers to achieve the employer's aim. In such instances, it can be hard for employees to deal with, or struggle against, an abstract deterioration of their work in the future, while actual conditions remain reasonably satisfactory. Moreover, at the time such contracts are agreed to, there are no real coworkers on the second tier who will suffer the negative effects of the new agreement.

Ryerson was set to become a full degree-granting university in 1993. The impending shift to university status gave the administration what it needed to sell a radical new contract to the faculty. Full university status would give Ryerson access to millions of dollars of new funding. Many RFA members were pleased to see this development. The hope was that becoming an "official" university would lead to three key outcomes: (1) it would raise the status of both Ryerson and its faculty in the broader community; (2) it would give writing and research more formal recognition in workload allocation; and (3) it would allow the cap at the top of the salary scale to be raised in order to make wages for senior faculty more compatible with those at other universities in the province. Given that increasing numbers of faculty now had doctorates, all these concerns set the stage for acceptance of a radical new contract in early 1992.

At the same time, some faculty were opposed to, or ambivalent about, the change to university status. A fair proportion of the faculty had made teaching their career focus and were neither interested in nor trained to make the shift to a research mode. Many faculty still lacked doctorates or other appropriate graduate degrees. A good number of these would have been older faculty, not yet at retirement age, but not easily able to change careers or place of employment. It is easy to appreciate, therefore, that many faculty were looking for protections for their wages, working conditions, and status in any new contract that shifted to a university model.

Preying on these feelings, the administration, after prolonged negotiations, presented a contract to the RFA that offered a number of benefits to faculty in exchange for major alterations to wages and working conditions. However, these major changes to the collective agreement would apply only to those faculty who would be hired in future. The 1991–94 contract for the first time divided faculty into two modes. Mode I constituted all those faculty appointed before January 1, 1992. All new faculty were to be hired as Mode IIs. Because this new agreement emerged from Ryerson's move to full university status, all the newly hired Mode II faculty were contractually obliged to conduct research, like their colleagues in the rest of the university sector. Mode I members, on the other hand, continued to be defined primarily by their teaching duties and were not required to conduct research. In addition, however, the two modes also had substantially different wages and working conditions. In effect, two modes meant two tiers.

The carrot used to sell these changes came in a number of forms. Current (Mode I) faculty members received a substantial increase in wages, were all promoted to the rank of full professor, and retained all their traditional workload protections. They were also granted special veto powers in union ratification votes, in that certain key provisions in the collective agreement relating to Mode I members (workload, staffing, and so on) could be changed only by ratification by at least two-thirds of Mode I faculty.

In exchange, the employer received substantial benefits from the inferior wages and working conditions that the two-tiered contract imposed on new

(Mode II) members. There were, for example, numerous provisions in the 1991–94 agreement that applied only to Mode II members. The new salary structure cut starting salaries substantially. It also removed the salary increment system that had automatically and quickly moved faculty to the top of the salary scale and replaced it with a merit scheme that made annual salary increments contingent on the demonstration of meritorious service. The new workload language eliminated the limits on class size, student contact hours, and length of the working week. That language also increased managerial control over workload allocation for course preparation, student supervision, curriculum development, and committee work. In addition, the new staffing arrangements placed a cap of 20 percent on the number of members who could attain the rank of professor. Since only those who became professors were eligible to receive the range of substantial salary increases associated with that position, the cap on rank was also a cap on salary.

Both the RFA executive and membership had mixed views about the creation of two modes within their union. If one draws solely on the written record, there is little in any RFA documents of the time to indicate there was strong opposition to this move. Many faculty did, though, in informal discussions with us, recall the intense pressures to support the negotiating team's proposals for a two-tiered contract. Some mentioned that the argument being stressed at the time was that Ryerson would not obtain full university status unless faculty accepted the new collective agreement. Some faculty felt that, while Mode IIs would be disadvantaged, these were temporary problems that could be cleared up in later negotiations.

When the time came to vote on the new contract, the "mixed views" were transformed into strong support. The negotiating team's recommendation to ratify the new contract was endorsed by the RFA executive with only one member opposed and one abstaining. In January 1992, the tentative agreement was ratified by 82 percent of faculty, all of whom would become Mode I members according to the terms of that agreement.[4] The following year the chair of negotiations received an RFA special award for service to the Association. It appears that Ryerson faculty at that time felt the new contract gave them what they were looking for in a new university climate: improved wages and more steps at the top of the salary scale, higher status, and continued workload protection.

The lack of meaningful debate about, and muted criticism of, the move to a two-tiered contract is related to the RFA's long history of undemocratic practice. During negotiations, various administrations over many years pressured faculty bargaining teams to remain silent as a supposed requirement of the principle of "confidentiality of negotiations." As already noted, there was neither a democratic climate nor structure in the RFA that allowed for any informed discussion of negotiating positions. In this case, the concept of a two-tiered contract was presented to faculty members toward the end of the negotiating process, when there was intense pressure from both the union and the employer to ratify the tentative agreement. The quality of the debate within the RFA and perhaps even the outcome of negotiations might have been different if the RFA membership had had the opportunity to engage in meaningful discussion of the proposal for a two-tiered contract at an earlier stage of the bargaining process.

Consequences

The creation of a two-tiered contract placed increasing emphasis on the competitive model, gradually replacing the collective model. From the 1991–94 agreement onward, Ryerson has moved from an institution where most improvements in wages or working conditions had to be won by the faculty *as a whole* via negotiations (the collective model) to an institution where, increasingly, the way to improve wages and working conditions is via individual action (the competitive model).

Of course, Ryerson's mandate as a "polytechnic" made its faculty particularly vulnerable to the entrepreneurial identity.[5] Almost half the faculty teach in one of the business or engineering programs. (The remaining faculty teach in the faculties of arts, communication and design, community services, or continuing education.) Moreover, as already noted, many faculty at Ryerson engage in private consulting or other entrepreneurial activities outside of the university.

The financial implications of the two-tier structure at Ryerson become clear when comparing the salary grid of the 1989–91 collective agreement that was in place immediately before Modes I and II were created to the salary grid of the 1991–94 agreement that established the two modes. For example, the maximum salary for someone holding a PhD or master's degree rose from $69,852 to $83,646, an increase of almost $14,000.[6] Mode I members benefited disproportionately from this increase because they, unlike those in Mode II, were uniformly eligible to be paid at the rank of professor under the new contract. At the same time, the minimum salary for someone holding a PhD decreased from $44,410 to $32,800, a drop of almost $12,000. This decrease affected only Mode II members. The shift in salary structures between the two grids meant that the expansion of Mode I wages at the top of the salary scale was, in effect, paid for by the suppression of Mode II wages at the bottom.[7]

Another change worth noting was the acute elongation of the salary grid. Prior to the major restructuring of the 1991–94 agreement, there were twelve steps on the salary grid separating the minimum from the maximum salary for someone holding a PhD. After that restructuring, there were thirty-five discrete steps. This threefold increase in the number of salary steps, coupled with the 20 percent cap on the rank of professor, severely limited the salary and promotion opportunities for Mode II members.

Implications

Two-tiered contracts are, by their very nature, anathema to a collective model of behavior. The 1991–94 agreement that established two modes of faculty at

Ryerson represented the diminution of the collective model and the formalization of an entrepreneurial alternative. The creation of two modes, in the classic tradition of divide and rule, pitted the two groups against each other, with some faculty in each mode feeling that they were the aggrieved party. Some Mode I members felt that they were being marginalized by the university's new emphasis on research and researchers, while many Mode II members were increasingly alarmed by the gaping inequalities in salaries and working conditions. This division among the faculty and the accompanying inequalities were left virtually intact in the 1994–96 and 1996–98 collective agreements.[8] The structural differences in the employment conditions of the two modes, as well as the highly visible nature of the division within the faculty, frustrated the development of a common identity. This lack of commonality limited the number of issues on which faculty could present a united, collective position to the employer during negotiations.

The recently concluded 1998–2001 collective agreement brought about the most significant restructuring of salaries at Ryerson since the establishment of Mode I and Mode II in 1992. However, the nature of that restructuring was strongly and negatively affected by the weakening of the collective model that had occurred in the earlier agreement. The 1998–2001 agreement was ratified overwhelmingly by faculty members at Ryerson, including almost all Mode IIs. It gave all members a large salary increase, the first such increase in seven years for some, and it raised starting salaries and maximum salaries for each professorial rank. It also eliminated some of the most egregious differences between modes by lifting the 20 percent cap on the number of Mode IIs who could become full professors and by extending to Mode IIs, for the first time, provisions allowing for automatic annual salary increments.[9]

However popular were the terms of the 1998–2001 collective agreement among faculty, they represented a general defeat for all union members and a particular defeat for those in Mode II. The new agreement disadvantaged Mode II members in two key ways. First, it did not aggressively address the gaping salary inequalities between modes. The various forms of salary increases specified in the new agreement were not progressive. In general, Mode I members at the top of the salary scale received as much money as did Mode II members at the bottom of the salary scale.[10] The agreement also completely eliminated the salary grid, making wage inequality much harder to see and more difficult to address. It becomes increasingly difficult to see salaries as a collective problem if one knows only one's own salary, but not that of colleagues.[11] It also makes it very difficult to assess salary inequities within the university.

The second way the new agreement disadvantaged Mode II members was in terms of workload. These members, unlike those in Mode I, continued to have no workload protection limiting class sizes, student contact hours, or the length of the working week. Moreover, management continued to have relatively unfettered control over Mode II members on such central workload issues as preparation hours, curriculum development, committee work, course coordination, and student supervision. These inequalities in salaries and workloads were left largely untouched by the new agreement precisely because the incentives for collective action by faculty were fundamentally weakened by previous agreements that created and maintained division.

The 1998–2001 agreement was also a defeat for all faculty at Ryerson, not just for those in Mode II. This general defeat, like the particular one that applied to Mode II members, had its roots in the weaknesses of the 1991–94 collective agreement. We have already proposed that the 1991–94 agreement was a decisive move away from a collective model of behavior and that this move had repercussions that limited the extent of progressive change that was possible for Mode II members in the 1998–2001 agreement. Moreover, it is clear in retrospect that the 1991–94 agreement embedded aspects of the entrepreneurial model that were later generalized to the detriment of all faculty members at Ryerson.

The introduction and expansion of merit clauses in university collective agreements are archetypal expressions of the dominance of the entrepreneurial model over the collective model of behavior. At Ryerson, the principle of merit pay was first established in the 1991–94 agreement, but its application was, as noted earlier, mainly limited to Mode II members.[12] The 1998–2001 collective agreement expanded the merit system by making it apply to everyone in both modes.

Merit schemes are a form of performance-based pay that institutionalizes the individual and entrepreneurial aspects of faculty identity: Merit increments are paid to individuals on the basis of their individual achievements as determined by an assessment of individual applications. Such schemes are becoming increasingly controversial—even from the employer's perspective—in part because they may lead to the individualization, fragmentation, and commodification of work, with deleterious effects on the level of productivity (Pfeffer 1998). In the university sector, merit provisions give faculty members an incentive to withdraw from collective pursuits in their department or university as a whole and instead encourage them to focus their efforts on activities that maximize the probability of short-term individual recognition and reward.

This transformation in the structure of incentives that is typical of merit pay may also lead to the deterioration of faculty morale. The introduction of merit can fundamentally change, in deeply debilitating ways, the reasons for faculty doing what they do. Many members of the RFA give generously of their time and effort because they are committed to their students and colleagues, their teaching and research, their departmental initiatives, and their community or professional projects. Merit entangles this generosity and commitment in a competitive system of ranked valuation, a "rank-order tournament," in which one's individual worth is quantified, adjudged, and either recognized in the form of a merit award or not.[13] It is not surprising that faculty may begin to reconsider the nature and extent of their workplace contribution in the light of decisions on merit.

Merit provisions are antithetical to trade union interests in promoting worker identity and collective solidarity, although there is no mechanical connection between faculty unionization and the existence of merit provisions. At Canadian universities, the likelihood of merit provisions in collective agreements declines with the presence of a unionized faculty (Grant 1998, 663); however, in the United States, at least in those union contracts studied by Rhoades, merit structures were embedded in the salary structures of most collective bargaining agreements (1998, 44). Nonetheless, there is a manifest tension between unionization and merit: Negotiating with the employer as members of a union, faculty stand with their colleagues, trying to achieve better salaries and working conditions for everyone; applying for a salary increment in the zero-sum game of merit, faculty stand against their colleagues, trying to achieve a better pay package for themselves. The first process promotes shared identities and collective capacities, the second undermines them.

CONCLUSIONS

While a number of universities in Canada have recently had prolonged and bitter strikes that have, to some extent, radicalized faculty and increased support for their collective identity, Ryerson has been moving in the opposite direction. For example, at several union meetings during negotiations for the 1998–2001 contract, the union's negotiating committee denounced the administration's desire to remove the section of the contract that requires both parties to go to final and binding arbitration to resolve an impasse in contract negotiations. The committee's rationale was that giving faculty the right to strike would be detrimental to both students and the university.[14] The negotiating committee also openly supported merit pay provisions in that contract. In the current round of negotiations, the negotiating team has been publicly promoting the removal of the last vestiges of contractual workload protections, suggesting that, instead, faculty might negotiate workloads individually within departments. In other words, although a union, the RFA has been increasingly promoting both a competitive model and the entrepreneurial identity.

The Ryerson case demonstrates the complexity of competing identities among faculty. The competitive model and entrepreneurial identity exist side by side and in tension with other tendencies. It should be noted that on broad, noncontractual issues, the RFA executive and Ryerson faculty regularly support progressive union positions. For example, although Ryerson faculty themselves have no right to strike, they have regularly shown solidarity by providing financial and moral support to striking faculty at other institutions across Canada (including contract faculty in Ontario). They have supported students in their quest to maintain accessibility via tuition freezes, and they have opposed increasing government intervention in university governance, including the imposition of performance indicators.

The Ryerson case also demonstrates that having a union does not guarantee, in and of itself, protection of faculty members' wages and working conditions in the long term. As already noted, it is easier for adjunct faculty to see themselves as workers, where the extremely poor wages and working conditions provide a clear material basis for such an identity. However, among tenured faculty, developing or sustaining such an identity is intrinsically much more difficult. As the Ryerson case indicates, in these times of lean production, university administrations may prey on the ambitions or insecurities of faculty as a way of promoting a competitive model and an entrepreneurial identity. Unfortunately, even faculty unions with the best of intentions may end up endorsing or even promoting such developments, to the ultimate detriment of their members. Such tendencies may be exacerbated by undemocratic processes within the union that allow a few faculty in union leadership positions to shift the entire union in the direction of a more competitive model.

The current advance of the corporate agenda at university campuses could not have occurred without the complicity, even if generally unintended, of faculty. As one author (Newson 2000, 189) writes, "I want to underscore the extent to which securing faculty participation and compliance was recognised from the beginning as the key to achieving this shift [to a corporate-oriented university] so much so that many of the strategies that have been employed have been designed specifically to overcome anticipated 'faculty resistance.'" One such strategy was clearly the promotion of the entrepreneurial identity among faculty and the advancement of the competitive model.

Nonetheless, Newson (2000, 190) argues that the need for such compliance reflects the important place of faculty in the university structure, and thus, ironically, the extent to which faculty have the leverage to oppose these transformations. However, leverage for change requires both awareness and some collective response. It is therefore essential that all faculty become sensitive to the increasing push toward a more competitive model by university administrators and construct appropriate collective strategies to resist it. It is also essential that faculty constrain some of the competitive and entrepreneurial tendencies within their own unions and simultaneously promote democratic decision-making structures that will allow them to resist more effectively the shift to lean production on their campuses.

NOTES

We thank our many colleagues and friends who have contributed to the writing of this chapter, with special thanks to those Mode II colleagues who, in the course of struggling for a more equitable collective agreement, helped compile the original list of differences between the two modes. We also thank the Ryerson Faculty Association for allowing access to their documents and Diane Meaghan for providing helpful commentary on the information included in this chapter. Special thanks are owed to Deborah Herman and Julie Schmid, the editors of this volume, for their insightful suggestions.

1. It is not possible in this chapter to provide a full explication of this process, which is also referred to as the corporatization of the university. For more details, see Kenney 1986; Meaghan 1996; Newson and Buchbinder 1988; Tudiver 1999; Turk 2000.

2. Today the RFA represents not only tenure-stream faculty, but also two- or three-year contractually limited appointments, librarians, and counselors. However, for the purposes of this chapter, only tenure-stream faculty will be discussed. The majority of adjunct faculty at Ryerson are represented by the Canadian Union of Public Employees, a national body representing a wide variety of public sector workers. In the late 1970s, these part-time and sessional faculty first sought to join the RFA. However, this overture was rejected by RFA members, who felt the interests of the two groups were too divergent.

3. At this time, this was very unusual for a postsecondary institution in Ontario. In the late 1980s, community college teachers (all of whom are part of the Ontario Public Service Employees' Union and who bargain provincewide) succeeded in winning similar clauses in their joint collective agreement, drawing originally on the Ryerson contract as a model.

4. It should be noted that Mode I faculty were allowed to transfer voluntarily to Mode II, which would appeal to those who wanted fewer teaching hours in order to do major research or writing. These transferees kept their Mode I wages and thus were not affected by the drastic cut in starting salaries. The strain between the incoming Mode IIs and the transferees has increased in recent years.

5. Ryerson's mission statement reads as follows: "The special mission of Ryerson Polytechnic University is the advancement of applied knowledge and research to address societal need, and the provision of programs of study that provide a balance between theory and application and that prepare students for careers in professional and quasi-professional fields."

6. All amounts are in Canadian dollars. These comparisons apply only to those holding a PhD or master's degree because the 1989–91 collective agreement had different salary schedules for different levels of university education.

7. It is necessary to point out that most Mode II members were not actually appointed at the minimum salary. Nonetheless, in effect, the starting salary *floor* prior to 1992 became the starting salary *ceiling* after 1992, with the consequence of severe wage suppression for Mode II members. In both agreements, the usual starting salary of new employees fell somewhere between zero and eight increments on the grid. In the 1989–91 contract, however, the usual starting salary for someone holding a doctoral degree ranged from $44,410 to $62,093. In the 1991–94 contract, the corresponding starting salary range was from $32,800 to $48,427. That is, the usual *maximum* Mode II starting salary of $48,427 in the more recent contract is only $4,000 above the *minimum* starting salary for faculty members with PhDs in the earlier contract.

8. In the 1994–96 collective agreement, the maximum salary of limited-term faculty, instructors and assistant professors was increased by two salary increments, to $57,399; the maximum salary of associate professors was increased by one increment, to $71,577.

9. Such provisions are usually referred to as progress through the ranks (PTR) or career development increments (CDI), the term used in the 1998–2001 agreement.

10. These payments came in the form of automatic increments, across-the-board increases, and sector adjustments. The sector adjustments were made to bring Ryerson's salaries closer to the norm in the university sector in Ontario.

11. In Ontario, only the salaries of public servants, including university faculty, that exceed $100,000 are made public. Although faculty associations receive salary information on all their members, these figures cannot be made public for reasons of confidentiality.

12. Merit applied to all Mode IIs as a class of employees. The agreement also provided that Mode Is at the very top of the pay scale could choose to apply for a merit increment.

Mode IIs were never able to use the merit provisions of the 1991–94 agreement because they became a matter of dispute between the administration and the RFA that was only resolved with the implementation of the new merit system in the 1998–2001 agreement.

13. The term "rank-order tournaments" is taken from E.P. Lazear and S. Rosen, Rank-order tournaments as optimum labour contracts, *Journal of Political Economy* 89 (1981): 841–864, as cited in Grant (1998, 649).

14. The union's position on this issue was never tested, as the administration dropped its demand. Because negotiations are conducted in secret, there is no way of knowing more details on how this issue played out at the bargaining table.

REFERENCES

Adell, B.L., and D.D. Carter. 1972. *Collective bargaining for university faculty in Canada: A study commissioned by the Association of Universities and Colleges of Canada.* Kingston, Canada: Industrial Relations Centre, Queen's University.

Aronowitz, S. 1997. Academic unionism and the future of higher education. In *Will teach for food: Academic labor in crisis,* ed. Cary Nelson, 181–215. Minneapolis: University of Minnesota Press.

Grant, H. 1998. Academic contests? Merit pay in Canadian universities. *Relations Industrielles/Industrial Relations* 53:647–665.

Kenney, M. 1986. *Biotechnology: The university/industrial complex.* New Haven, CT: Yale University Press.

Meaghan, D. 1996. Academic labour and the corporate agenda. *Socialist Studies Bulletin* 45 (July-August-September):23–42.

Newson, J. 2000. To not intend, or to intend not ... that is the question. In *The corporate campus: Commercialization and the dangers to Canada's colleges and universities,* ed. J. Turk, 183–193. Toronto, Canada: Lorimer & Company.

Newson, J., and H. Buchbinder. 1988. *The university means business: Universities, corporations and academic work.* Toronto, Canada: Garamond Press.

Parker, M., and J. Slaughter. 1994. *Working smart.* Detroit, MI: Labor Notes.

Pfeffer, J. 1998. Six dangerous myths about pay. *Harvard Business Review* 76(3):109–119.

Rhoades, G. 1998. *Managed professionals: Unionized faculty and restructuring academic labor.* Albany, NY: State University of New York Press.

Sears, A. 2000. Education for a lean world. In *Restructuring and resistance: Canadian public policy in an age of global capitalism,* ed. M. Burke, C. Mooers, and J. Shields, 146–158. Halifax, Canada: Fernwood Publishing.

Tudiver, N. 1999. *Universities for sale: Resisting corporate control over Canadian higher education.* Toronto, Canada: Lorimer & Company.

Turk, J., ed. 2000. *The corporate campus: Commercialization and the dangers to Canada's colleges and universities.* Toronto, Canada: Lorimer & Company.

Wright, E.O. 1978. *Class, crisis and the state.* London: New Left Press.

———. 1985. *Classes.* London: Verso Press.

Chapter 3

In a Leftover Office in Chicago

Joe Berry

"WELCOME NEIGHBOR"

In December 1999, when I became a part-time, temporary, contingent, adjunct lecturer at Harold Washington College, one of the Chicago City Colleges, the polite and soft-spoken department head apologized for the pay ($1,350 for a three credit course, no benefits) and had trouble meeting my eyes. He seemed embarrassed to be hiring me at all. I did ask him if we had offices, and he said, "yes." I was pleasantly surprised, and I mentioned to him that I had worked some places with no offices for part-timers. His reply was that they used to have thirty-three full-timers in Social Science and space was very short, but now they were down to eleven, with sixteen part-timers so there was plenty of space.

I was even more surprised when I found, in the office, a wonderful welcoming note from my officemate. "Welcome Neighbor," it began. In sixteen years of part-time teaching in three states I had never before gotten a welcome like that. Soon we were exchanging notes. I found that she was, like me, part time and that she also taught at Roosevelt University, where an adjunct union organizing drive was just then in progress.

As I settled into the semester and the office where I spent the hour before and after my twice-a-week evening class, I began to look around. The office was small; the walls were dirty and looked as if they hadn't been painted for years; the furniture was battered. The desk held the detritus of many years and seemingly many occupants. A small plastic fan sat on a table—a silent indication of the airlessness of the space. A well-used cheap plastic office phone sat on the desk with two names on the option buttons, neither of them mine. The office had two full-size vertical file cabinets and two horizontal ones with shelves on top. There was one main desk and a small table next to it. Three chairs: one a desk chair, one a small secretary's chair, and one a side chair for a student, all upholstered in the bright orange popular in the late 1970s and early 1980s. All were stained and dirty. The table and file cabinets, institutional buff, still had moving stickers on them reading, "Ship to RH, Social Science Dept., 4th Floor, Harold Washington College, 30 E. Lake St." I remembered that the college building had been built in the 1980s and later named for Harold Washington, the first black mayor in "the most segregated city in America." He had died of a heart attack in office, some say hounded and pressured to death by white machine politicians in the then-famous "Council Wars." Formerly, the college had been called Loop College. These pieces of furniture had obviously made the trip when the building was opened. Then I noticed the name on all the labels, RH. He was someone who had retired and had never been replaced by another full-time tenured teacher.

Soon, I was getting curious. My officemate had suggested, via her welcome note, which drawers and shelves I could use, but now I wondered about the others. I tried the upright files first. Locked. A mystery. Papers, tests, old lunches or even body parts hermetically sealed and locked in Steelcase? Later in the semester, the department secretary came in with a large handful of keys to try to open the locked cabinets, at my officemate's request she told me. She was unsuccessful and the mystery remained. The other unlocked file cabinets held some of RH's work for programs long past, dating in some cases back to the 1960s. Open shelves held books up to thirty years old.

A MUSEUM OF COLLEGE TEACHING, AN ARCHAEOLOGICAL SITE

I was beginning to feel, especially as a labor history teacher, that I had wandered into a museum of what college teaching used to be—a stable, professional occupation where someone got hired and spent a career building their resources in an office like this one. All that was left, materially, of that long ago career and the system that allowed it to exist was contained in this musty little room. I began to look at all these artifacts with different eyes. The secretary's chair and small table probably meant that, occasionally at least, RH had some clerical support in this office, even if only a work-study student. The single desk meant that this had not been a shared office, but rather the personal home base for a full-time faculty member. The large number of files and shelves meant that he (and he was a "he") had the time and resources to develop programs and courses in some quantity over the years and to use and revise the product of that labor repeatedly. This college had once spent money on new furniture, since all, except for some of the file cabinets, were of the same vintage. He must have been an organized fellow, since there was an old set of plastic desk accessories and organizing containers sitting on the desk, in the gray translucent plastic favored in the 1980s.

I now realized it was more than a museum, it was an archaeological site.[1] This was the physical remnant of what college teaching, even in the lowest level of higher education—an urban, working-class community college—used to be before contingent, part-time labor replaced tenured, full-time faculty.

AV TECHNICIANS AND VENDING MACHINES

As I found my way around the single multistory building that made up the college, I found more archaeology. In the AV department was a complete set of old video production equipment that now sat unused, since this once-thriving operation was now staffed only by part-time students and technicians and one trained professional, a librarian who had to work the library desk part of every day as well. The library had only part-time librarians on the reference desk in the evenings, making many questions only answerable with a phone call to the full-timer during the day. Library class tours, once virtually universal for survey history classes like those I was teaching, were no longer possible due to staffing cuts. The duplicating office had more machines than the reduced staff of one full-timer could use. As I wandered further, I soon discovered that this pattern was repeated throughout the college. The building, built in the early 1980s as budget cutting was gaining steam, had been planned to be four stories higher. These floors were just shaved off the plans and never built. Perhaps it was the result of insufficient clout on the part of the local administration. (This is Chicago, after all.) As a result, there was no food service except a few truly disgusting vending machines, no faculty lounge, none of the basic amenities for students or faculty that had been routine in all colleges in the 1960s, when I was an undergraduate. This archaeology revealed that not just teachers had been affected, but students as well.

THE UNION

Into the site of this dig, some weeks later, floated a mimeographed sheet, which turned out to be the latest newsletter (May 5, 2000) of this college's chapter of the countywide American Federation of Teachers union local. Local 1600 represented the full-time faculty and some other staff. It did not represent the part-timers, who are called lecturers here. This chapter newsletter revealed that the administration of the Chicago City Colleges was asking for a new set of concessions in the current contract negotiations, including a second round of increases in class load for any new full-time faculty hired after the contract was ratified. The union was resisting, so far, but had already made this particular concession (from eight to nine sections a year) once and so, perhaps, would also concede the current demand to go from nine to ten. After all, no one voting on *this* contract provision would be directly affected by it. Another section of this union chapter newsletter detailed a recent set of increases in pay and benefits given to top administrators, vice presidents and above, which included $500/month car allowances, fully paid family health insurance until death, and other expensive perks. Looking around at my little office, I decided that never had archaeology seemed so intriguing to me, or so directly linked to the present.

WORKPLACES THAT HAVE VANISHED

At this point in the semester, while teaching the evolution of work and early industrialization, I realized that this dig I inhabited had a broader symbolism than I had realized. In fact, many other occupations had been casualized and otherwise transformed over history, but most had not left the rich set of artifacts that a college teacher's office held. Most of these jobs had not ever supplied their practitioners with a private space of this sort. In other cases, the site of the work itself had shifted from artisan shop to factory, so the archaeological record of the transition would be scanty indeed. I thought of how independent master cobblers, with their journeymen and apprentices, producing and selling to a local market, had become, first, subcontractors to the large shoe merchants. Later, most of them had become factory hands, hired by the day or the piece, doing small, routinized tasks that neither demanded nor valued their wide-ranging craft skills. Their workmates in these new factories were women and children, many of them immigrants, who could learn the necessary skill in short order and were forced to work for a fraction of the wages the old cordwainers had commanded. A few of the old master craftsmen had adapted successfully, becoming large contractors or even factory owners, but they stood out from the norm like white bird droppings on a black sand beach.

I remembered hearing how clerical work had once been the ladder to success and commercial management for somewhat-educated, white, middle-class boys in the mid-nineteenth century. By the middle of the twentieth century, most office work had long since become very routine and a professional dead end. Most recently, office work has also become physically dangerous for its mostly female and minority workers: The intensity of computer data entry and word processing has caused epidemic rates of repetitive stress disorders.

But all of this change had left little for later historians or archaeologists to look at—a few old tools, perhaps some photographs, but the old sites were largely gone as production had moved to the centralized factories and, later, to other regions and even to other nations. The continuity of place had been lost. I realized what an unusual and valuable example my own little archaeological dig was.

But how did this history apply to me? Was this process of casualization inevitable and I simply had the bad luck to have come into this workforce in the 1980s just as the Golden Age of the academic craft was passing? Was this really an example of "historical inevitability" that could have been lifted whole from the pages of Marx's *Das Kapital?*

THE BRASS RING—THE SAN FRANCISCO GENERAL STRIKE

I went back to work, trying to think of something else besides the brass ring that seemed to have been taken off the carousel just as I bought my ticket. I forced myself to outline my syllabus for next semester, when I would be teaching a recent United States history survey. And then it hit me. It was right there in front of me, even illustrated in the text: the 1934 San Francisco General Strike. Here was a battle waged, initially by the longshoremen and seamen, to reverse just the conditions of casualization (they called it the shape-up) that I was immersed in. *And they had won!*

It had taken years of preparatory struggle and organizing, many lost jobs, and two shooting deaths, but they had won! They had inspired the entire working class of San Francisco, and the whole West Coast, with their fight, not just for a few more cents per hour (though they desperately needed that too), but by their willingness to sacrifice for the goal of self-respect on the job. In their case, this translated into the end of the mass hiring crowds each day where the bosses would pick out their favorites for the privilege of a day's, or even a few hours', work. In those times, longshoremen and sailors were the lowliest of day laborers. These were the jobs men did when there was no alternative. Waiters had a better life. To get even these pathetic few hours of backbreaking, dangerous, and unhealthy labor, workers frequently had to pay off the hiring boss in the form of sleeping in his sister's boarding house, patronizing his uncle's bordellos, buying him "presents," and, certainly, doing whatever the worker was told with smiling alacrity.

"My God," I thought, "they must have felt very much like we 'adjuncts' feel right now; doing honest labor, but giving up a little of their humanity every time they tried to get a day's work (or, in our case, another class)." Then the International Longshoremen's and Warehousemen's Union (ILWU) won a centralized, union-controlled hiring hall with a worker-elected dispatcher, and the world was turned upside down. Within a generation, the lowest of the low became the "kings of the waterfront" with the highest wages and most job security (and the strongest union) of any noncraft manual work. I remembered the pride in their faces when they marched in parades in San Francisco with their white hats and their cargo hooks. The ILWU (since 2001, without "men" in their official name) had appealed to the formerly excluded African-American workers to respect their strike lines and not scab in exchange for a promise for fair hiring and an end to gross discrimination after the battle for a union hiring hall was won. They had kept that promise and, by the time I lived in San Francisco in the 1970s, the Longshore local there was mostly African American. The ILWU continues to be the most progressive, solidaristic wing of the West Coast labor movement, bringing democratic, militant unionism to workers as diverse as booksellers and bicycle messengers.

WHAT WINNING CAN LOOK LIKE

It had not all been sweetness and light after 1934. Automation, in the form of containerization, eventually cut new hiring to a trickle, and the union had only protected the current workers, not the next generation, with the result that there were many fewer American longshore workers (and sailors) than two generations before. There had been limits to even founder Harry Bridges's and the ILWU's left-wing sense of working-class solidarity and their stomach for seemingly hopeless fights in the 1950s. Nevertheless, the memory of what they did achieve brought tears to my eyes and a more rapid beat to my heart.

After this eureka moment, more examples came to mind. The farm workers, after three generations of struggle, had finally, however briefly in the 1970s, regularized work in the California fields. They destroyed the hated labor contractor system, replaced it with union hiring halls and brought health care and other social services to this workforce. The farm workers' plight, then and now, makes contingent teachers look like nobility. "But," I thought, "health insurance would be really nice, since I'll never see fifty again and may not ever live to see socialized health care instituted in America."[2]

The United Farm Workers (UFW), like the ILWU, had done this not only by organizing on the job, but by building a movement that reached out to entire communities for allies and fought for a broader vision of social justice than just wages and hours. It was even broader than job security and dignified, fair hiring procedures for themselves. The UFW was the godparent of the whole Chicano movement in the 1960s and was based upon a strategic alliance with Filipino farm workers as well. They appealed to the students of the 1960s, especially the Latinos, to rally around *La Causa* and built a national grape boycott that mobilized progressive America. Here, too, all was not perfectly fair, democratic, or uniformly principled. Who in the movement can forget the terrible lapse when Caesar Chávez allowed cooperation with the Immigration and Naturalization Service (the hated "Migra") at the border? Or the tremendous embarrassment felt by many when he visited Philippine dictator Ferdinand Marcos in Manila? Nevertheless, much was won, and not just by farm workers, but by the whole movement they sparked in Chicano/Latino communities across the nation. The hundreds of committed young organizers they trained now help lead many of the most progressive unions and community organizations nationwide.

Then I really let my mind go and realized that the most improbable example of successful resistance to casualization, and perhaps the biggest single group of contingent workers in the economy, was the building trades. Here were workers who had not only succeeded in overcoming their status as day laborers (still true in many parts of the world), hired mainly for their strong backs, but had become the aristocracy of the labor movement. They had gained control about one hundred years ago of the hiring of their labor through union hiring halls and had fought bitterly to force contractors to come to terms. They had made construction a job a worker could reasonably hope to afford to retire from and still walk away able-bodied. The United Brotherhood of Carpenters and Joiners (Carpenters) also led the struggle for the eight-hour day and helped to found the workers' holidays of May Day and Labor Day in the process.

Construction craft unions' history was also marred by unconscionable racism, sexism, and a general strategy of exclusion. Most of these unions were so successful in their exclusiveness that they fought all attempts by African Americans, Latinos, Asians, and women to enter the trades, and antidiscrimination court orders ("consent decrees") dating from the 1960s and 1970s are still in effect for some of these unions. Their influence since the 1880s in the American Federation of Labor (AFL) was frequently extremely backward, such as when Carpenters' President Bill Hutchinson led the opposition in the 1920s and 1930s to organizing workers in the mass production industries, arguing that "unskilled" factory workers, many of them immigrants and their children, could never be good trade unionists. This obduracy essentially forced the Congress of Industrial Organizations (CIO), led by United Mine Workers of America president John L. Lewis, to leave the AFL in the 1930s in order to organize the workers in the factories in the only possible form, single organization industrial unionism.

In recent years, however, the force of employers' renewed, and nearly successful, drive to destroy the unions in the interest of higher profit has brought many building trades workers and unions back around to a vision of broader social unionism, movement building, and bottom-up organizing that would be familiar to Carpenters founder, socialist Peter J. McGuire. This vision would likely be unrecognizable, and surely amazing, to old standpatters like the late New York plumber and AFL-CIO president from the 1950s to the 1970s, George Meany, who bragged he had never been in a strike and saw no need to organize new workers. This was the man who, along with the CIO's Walter Reuther of the United Auto Workers, engineered the merger of the AFL and the CIO in 1955, largely on conservative AFL terms, and then presided over the first years of labor's decline in numbers and influence.

Recently, we saw one of the historic building trades unions, the International Brotherhood of Electrical Workers, developing the very prototype of internal support for new organizing with their Construction Organizing Member Education and Training program, which has been adopted by the entire AFL-CIO in the form of Member Education and Mobilization for Organizing. In many parts of the country, and for the first time in many years, one now can see building trades banners in solidarity demonstrations for other unions in struggle.

Heady with all this inspiration, I decided to take a break and call up a couple of students who had been missing class lately to see what was up. As I looked through the student information questionnaires I give out at the start of every semester, I noticed the question on current work. Nearly all community college students now work, most full-time, and my eyes fell on one student's form. There it was, big as life, and I had not even thought of it when I was feeling so sorry for myself. *UPS*. Just saying the initials made me feel better. Of course!

The 1997 United Parcel Service (UPS) strike, a rare national strike victory in a decade of losses, had been fought largely by, and about, people just like my student here. The recent growth of part-time, poorly paid and insecure labor at UPS had been a major scandal and a key reason for the rise to power of the re-form movement in the Teamsters in the early 1990s. When the contract came up, the new leadership had pledged a real fight to reverse this trend and win back some full-time jobs, with preference going to the present part-timers. A massive national strike, the first largely publicized and organized via the Internet's World Wide Web, had brought out nearly 100 percent of the workers, and had won the support of the entire working class, who were then inspired by the un-expected victory over one of the largest corporations in the world. The strike had hit a massive chord of sympathy among the downsized, casualized, part-timed, re-engineered, teamed up, contracted out, outsourced, broken down, generally fearful, but deeply resentful workers in all employment sectors. This was true in Europe as well, where planned solidarity job actions were a significant factor in forcing the eventual settlement at UPS. They had won a fight for dignity and fairness under the slogan "A Part-Time America Won't Work" that reached far beyond their own membership.

COLUMBIA COLLEGE PART-TIMERS: WHY NOT US?

The next week brought my final hopeful reminder, just in case I had missed the point. I was pleased when a friendly Illinois Education Association (IEA) union organizer told me that a small, new local union of part-time faculty had been formed at a downtown private college, Columbia College: the Part-Time Faculty Association at Columbia (Pfac/IEA/NEA). They had achieved a first contract but had been forced to agree to a bargaining unit that excluded over 350 junior part-timers, under the threat by the administration of delaying the election for months in National Labor Relations Board hearings. Now the local was trying to go back and add the "left outs" to the unit and to the union, and they were looking for an organizer (part-time temporary, of course) to make the calls. Like most contingent faculty, I was always on the lookout for another part-time job, even one as endless as organizing.

I took the job, and in that first conversation with the local president, who was a computer instructor new to unionism himself, I asked him how he first got in-volved and how the union began. He told me that part-time college teachers' gripe sessions had been transformed into organizing discussions by the example of the Teamsters' UPS strike. He said that they thought if part-time pack-age loaders, some of whom were their students, could do it, "why can't we?"

As I finish this piece, I just found out that, with five days to go, we won our little add-on unit modification effort, with a few cards to spare and more in the mail. This victory demonstrates two lessons. The first is that even relatively new part-timers will respond to a union message in overwhelming numbers if we can actually talk with them. The second is that the college administration, now sufficiently reconciled to the union to agree to voluntary recognition for this group if we got a majority to sign union authorization cards, may have surmised that we would never make it, since they only give us a correct list three weeks before our end-of-semester deadline. If they thought so, they were merely the most recent employer to underestimate their own workers—a frequent strate-gic mistake that all unionists must learn to take advantage of. This will be the third bargaining group of part-timers certified in a private Chicago college in two years. It is not yet a movement, but I can hear the clock ticking.

JANUARY 2001

In revising this chapter for publication months later, I am struck by how little changes with the updating. Pfac successfully renegotiated their contract, bring-ing in those hundreds of new members. Their newer sister local at Roosevelt University, the Roosevelt Adjunct Faculty Organization (RAFO/IEA/NEA) is deep in bargaining for their first contract with an administration whose ideas of job security and academic freedom for adjunct faculty could be summed up as "You teach and say what we want, when and where we want you to, and go away when you are finished."

Meanwhile, the national meeting of the American Council on Education (higher education's top administrators' trade association) was held in Chicago. I attended and discovered that their focus was on competing with the corporate for-profit schools (University of Phoenix, DeVry, etc.) on their own terms. I found that these terms included "unbundling" the tasks that make up faculty jobs (curriculum de-velopment, presentation, tutoring, advising, correcting student work, and grading and evaluation) and doling most of them out to a variegated, less skilled, and lower compensated contingent workforce. Now that most faculty work has been casu-alized, and with the majority of postsecondary teachers nationwide now hired without job security (much less tenure), the second part of the transformation of faculty work is now in the offing: deskilling through division of labor.

This entire process would be desperately familiar to our old nineteenth-century artisan cobbler if he could be brought back to life. He might also have more than a few words for us about the motives of our employers and how we might fight for a different future. In the absence of our working-class ancestor, let me suggest a few tentative considerations for the future.

WHAT THE OLD COBBLER MIGHT SAY

First, the old days of the professorial guild are gone forever, along with the perks and individual prerogatives that went with membership in it. What will ultimately replace that pattern of faculty life and work is the most important question for all of us in, or interested in, higher education today.

We have a new-majority faculty: contingent and highly varied, including graduate employees, adjuncts, part-timers, nontenure track full-timers, and a hundred other labels at all levels of higher education, from noncredit adult educators to even faculty in some graduate programs. Only this new-majority faculty has both the potential collective power and the collective enlightened self-interest to lead a fight for a different future for higher education than that which befell shoe manufacturing and the artisan cordwainers.

The lessons of the victories, however partial and transitory, of fellow workers like those on the docks, fields, and construction sites, teach us that we cannot wage this fight alone, though we do have a responsibility to lead it. We will need to open ourselves to alliances with our students, their parents, other campus workers and their unions, and the labor movement and working class generally. It is their social interest in a better, fairer, more inclusive and equitable system of higher education that will both transform our struggle for equity as faculty into something broader and also will give us the additional social force to win. Within this struggle, no tactic should be rejected out of hand, but none should be embraced that does not create a broader stronger movement.

With the lessons of the democratic social movements of the past to guide us, we can help create a future where higher education serves the real interests of the working-class majority, not just the elite or the employers of labor. When that occurs, higher education will both be staffed and controlled by its fairly treated workforce and will be a force for a more equal, less stratified, and less exploitative society in general. Higher education will then be even more fun to teach in.

NOTES

1. After completing this essay, I discovered a similar anecdote. See C. Nelson and S. Watt, *Academic key words: A devil's dictionary for higher education* (New York: Routledge, 1999), p. 210. Nelson's story is of a new full-timer who discovers that he has been assigned to a former part-timers' gang office and he chooses to keep the stenciled notice "Part-Time Faculty Office" on the wall, "wanting some residue of the school's labor history to remain."

2. For a discussion of the application of the hiring hall model to K-12 teachers, see Charles Taylor Kerchner, Julia E. Koppich, and Joseph G. Weeres, *United mind workers: Unions and teaching in the knowledge society* (San Francisco: Jossey-Bass Publishers, 1997). For recent efforts at organizing casualized college teachers in other regions of the United States, see, for example, the webpages of the Boston Coalition of Contingent Academic Labor <http://omega.cc.umb.edu/~cocal/>, the California Part-Time Faculty Association <http://www.cpfa.org/>, the Chicago Coalition of Contingent Academic Labor <http://www.chicagococal.org>, and Campus Equity Week <http://www.CEWaction.org>.

Part II

The Next Generation: Charting New Waters

Chapter 4

More than Academic: Labor Consciousness and the Rise of UE Local 896-COGS

Susan Roth Breitzer

The history of the graduate employee unionization movement has in the last few years become increasingly recognized as a legitimate topic of historical study. Much of what has been written about for public consumption, however, has focused on struggles and setbacks. By contrast, the story of the Campaign to Organize Graduate Students (COGS) has received comparatively little general publicity. Similarly, the seeming incongruity of COGS's affiliation as Local 896 of the traditionally (and still predominantly) blue-collar United Electrical, Radio, and Machine Workers of America (UE) has been a subject of much discussion but no formal study.

Although in the University of Iowa the legal status of graduate assistants as employees was apparently never an issue,[1] more than legal recognition was necessary for COGS to succeed. Throughout the long and difficult history of graduate employee unionization at Iowa, there is evidence of the development of a labor consciousness that has gone well beyond the simple recognition of graduate assistants as employees to genuine efforts to connect this union's concerns with those of other workers at the University of Iowa, in Iowa City, and throughout Iowa, as well as with the rest of the UE.

This chapter examines the history of this development of a labor consciousness and how that in turn facilitated the development of a successful unionization movement. Although I look primarily at the two most recent union campaigns and the negotiation of the first contract, I also compare the recent campaigns with the earlier unionization campaigns that took place in 1968 and 1984. I examine the reasons for the failure of past campaigns, what some of them accomplished in terms of changing working conditions, and, most importantly, how each of them advanced the idea of graduate students as graduate employees to the point that unionization was not only desirable but possible. Beyond the successful 1995 election, I examine how COGS has continually worked to grow as a labor—as opposed to a student—organization and to establish its unique identity as (so far) the only graduate employee local of the United Electrical, Radio, and Machine Workers of America. To examine these issues of changing identity within the narrative framework, I have made significant use of oral histories, in addition to archival material and union and general publication accounts.

THE EARLY UNION MOVEMENT AT IOWA

The graduate employee unionization movement at the University of Iowa has a longer history than is generally acknowledged. Although the first campaign under the acronym COGS goes back to 1993, at least two unionization drives among graduate teaching and research assistants took place well before then. The first organization attempt took place in the late 1960s, around the same time that the first graduate employee union was organized at the University of Wisconsin, Madison. During this first Iowa campaign, the principle issue was salaries, which at $2,400–2,600 per year were abysmally low (even in 1968 dollars) and continued to devalue as the fighting of the Vietnam War spurred new inflation. However, there were also other issues, including free tuition for all graduate students (a goal that still has yet to be achieved), just suspension and dismissal procedures, and more control for teaching assistants over their course-work.[2]

This first union campaign (which involved only teaching assistants) arose in 1968 and died down by April 1969. The following year, according to early graduate employee union activist John Schacht, a remnant of the organization existed, but it was not nearly as strong as in the previous year. When it came to affiliation, the early union activists sought and received adjunct membership with the American Federation of Teachers (AFT), something usually reserved for student teachers, which according to Schacht, had most of its significance in that it really made the University of Iowa administration sit up and listen. The early union's name was the University of Iowa Student Federation of Teachers.[3]

The first union campaign at the University of Iowa was, in some ways, a victim of its own success. In response to the union's efforts, the administrators raised salaries to $3,400–$3,500 per year, a dramatic rise that undoubtedly brought relief to many teaching assistants, but also took away the union's principle reason for being. Yet the raise was not the only reason for the demise of the early unionization effort. According to Schacht, it also died out because the organizers "just didn't have the organizational apparatus or a commitment on the part of people to have continuity," because, he explains "we were graduate students" who had to finally go back to academic work and were unable to pass on the movement to another core group of activists. Finally, Schacht theorizes that the most insurmountable problem was the idea of a graduate assistant union at a time when there was little labor consciousness among graduate students.[4]

While there were possibly other organizing efforts in the intervening decades, the second known organization attempt took place in early 1984, as part of a large wave of graduate student protest over cuts in teaching assistant appointments. Other graduate employee concerns at that time included lack of benefits, such as health insurance.[5] According to then undergraduate eyewitness (later COGS activist) Robert Hearst, all of the students involved were part of a "radical student coalition" who "went pretty much around to all the activists they knew." Hearst also remembers that "they didn't do a lot of things really effectively, but they did ... have a lot of really big rallies."[6] In this instance, there was no evidence of efforts to affiliate with any established union. While a great deal of effort was expended and some tangible benefits were obtained, in the end no permanent graduate employee voice was established.[7]

THE FIRST COGS CAMPAIGN—HEARTBREAKING LOSS

The third known unionization campaign, which was also the first COGS campaign, began in spring 1993. By this time, Iowa graduate employees were becoming increasingly dissatisfied with low pay, lack of tuition waivers and health benefits, and lack of respect. Even as the founders of COGS were aware that finishing one's degree expediently should be every graduate student's goal, they were also aware that graduate employees were doing an increasing amount of the teaching, research, and other work that kept a major research university going and therefore deserved adequate compensation.[8] They had seen, through examples of universities with long-established graduate employee unions, how a union could make a positive difference when it came to working conditions and benefits. Furthermore, COGS founders learned that unionized, part-time clerical staff at their own university had superior health care plans.[9]

During this period, Iowa graduate students, like their colleagues elsewhere, were also aware of the changing profile of the average graduate student, who was increasingly likely to be self-supporting or even (somehow) supporting a family of his or her own. For example, a campus newspaper article described the pro-union testimony of Mark Stemen, then a graduate student and new father, working three jobs to stay barely above the poverty line.[10] Additionally, they were keenly aware of the growing corporatization of the American university, a phenomenon from which the University of Iowa was hardly exempt, and its attendant concern for the bottom line. Across the country, tenured professors were being replaced by part-time adjuncts, with substandard pay and benefits; and graduate assistants, at Iowa and elsewhere, had become an unacknowledged source of cheap labor.[11]

As a result, a group of about thirty to forty grads gathered to discuss their working conditions and the possibility of unionization, which initially was not a given except among the very core activists. Recalls Hearst, "Early on it was more of an approach of how do we get things like better health care, or ... higher pay, or things like that," adding that "there were a lot of different sort of ideas floating around" including the argument that "all we needed to do was take over the Graduate Student Senate." Even when it was generally agreed that a union was the best solution, there was the question of affiliation, whether to be "an independent association of Iowa graduate students" or affiliate with an existing national labor union. Due to the developing labor consciousness among COGS activists, the decision to affiliate with a national union carried the day. Explains Hearst, "One of the things about unions, even among people who didn't like unions is, unions actually have the power to do things. And so we convinced people that if we have a union, we might actually be able to get all these things we know we deserve." Also, on the basis of practical considerations such as financial resources and organizing assistance "we needed to be affiliated with ... an international [union] to get those things."[12]

The first COGS campaign commenced, however, even before affiliation. That summer of 1993, COGS activists mounted an unofficial campaign, called a canvass. In this canvass, as Hearst recalls, "we were basically going out to graduate students and asking them to join COGS" by signing interest cards; new canvassers were simultaneously recruited. By the end of that summer, the COGS Affiliations Committee had conducted extensive research into a large number of unions, including the AFT, the Service Employees International Union (SEIU), the American Federation of State, County, and Municipal Employees (AFSCME), the Communications Workers of America (CWA), and the United Electrical, Radio, and Machine Workers of America (UE).[13] UE, with whom COGS would later affiliate, was in 1993 just beginning to re-establish a presence in Iowa, after having been driven out by McCarthyism decades earlier.[14] Aside from the fact of UE's lack of structure in Iowa at that time, other concerns included the fact that it was not part of the AFL-CIO, which gave it a comparatively marginal status; its smallness in sheer numbers; and (at the time) its lack of experience organizing in any educational setting.[15] Even so, Hearst recalls, UE was attractive to a number of COGS activists because "they had a very good reputation" adding that "a lot of us ... who knew a little bit about labor history" were excited about the possibility of organizing with UE.[16] In the end, SEIU was chosen, in large part for its reputation for political progressivism, its affiliation with the AFL-CIO, and for its past history of aggressively organizing workers in low-wage, underorganized job classes. The last of these would be especially valuable for a transient bargaining unit that would require any union to remain in constant organizing mode, long after any campaign was won. Hearst also points out that people were impressed by SEIU's willingness to organize in "a lot of sectors of the economy that hadn't been traditionally unionized," which boded well for organizing the nontraditional constituency of graduate employees. Additionally, according to COGS activist Jason Duncan, at the time SEIU appeared to be the most interested of any of the unions considered and "really committed to helping us win."[17]

Following the decision to affiliate with SEIU, the canvass was transformed into an official organizing drive in which, says Hearst, activists were then asking people to not just "join a group called COGS that wanted better conditions for graduate students," but sign authorization cards for SEIU Local 150 to be the official bargaining agent for graduate employees. The COGS-SEIU campaign began with high hopes but, by the end, had lost the momentum that might have ensured a victory. To start with, admits Hearst, while SEIU provided assistance and resources during the campaign, "they didn't provide an experienced organizer" until near the end, which he recalls as being "the fatal mistake."[18] There were also other tensions over tactics within the campaign, stemming from the observation of one activist that "SEIU never could understand COGS's desire to run its own campaign or maintain an independent identity."[19] This unresolved tension—between maintaining a separate identity as a graduate employee union and being part of a large, occupationally diverse national union—did not help matters during the first COGS campaign, in which, Duncan recalls, "we were overconfident" and not prepared for the challenge of broad-based organizing on a large, diverse campus. Nor were COGS activists prepared for the antiunion onslaught that developed near the end of the campaign. Says Duncan: "We hit our peak of momentum in the early fall of '93 and never really built on the initial momentum."[20]

As a result, COGS activists found themselves unprepared to fend off a late-campaign antiunion assault by a small group of graduate students, calling themselves STOP (Students Tired of Propaganda).[21] According to Duncan, the real problem was that the local press, in the name of "equal time," "portrayed it as ... two groups battling it out the whole way," when, in fact, STOP did not appear until the last two weeks of the campaign. Furthermore, according to Duncan, STOP had the comparatively easy task of scaring people through disinformation, whereas COGS organizers "had to come out and convince people to be for something." Typical threats included predictions that tuition would be dramatically raised and assistantships drastically cut.

STOP's legitimacy was possibly aided in the press by earlier letters from unorganized opponents who expressed similar fears and also questioned COGS's legitimacy to address employment issues. For example, Nancy Anderson Mortenson, a May 1993 graduate of the art history M.A. program, wrote to the *Daily Iowan* in September 1993 and argued that many union proponents "are either conveniently forgetting or completely clueless" about lobbying efforts mounted by the Graduate and Professional Student Senate (GPSS), and the result of "the Legislature and the governor paying increased attention to graduate education here." She also argued that Dean of the Graduate College Leslie Simms had "worked endless hours to see that the health-insurance needs of graduate students be recognized within the university system" and that "his door is always open." In her defense of earlier GPSS lobbying efforts and of Dean Simms's goodwill however, she failed to address the fact that a union could address problems such as health care in a way that lobbying by student government organizations could not—through a legally binding contract.[22] At that time, she and others continued to believe that graduate students could best solve their problem by lobbying as students rather than bargaining as workers.

The university administration also weighed in with "informational" letters, including one in which Dean Simms smoothly praised "the professional manner in which COGS/SEIU participated in negotiations to define a bargaining unit," but he insisted *I would prefer to work with graduate students in the collegial manner that is the hallmark of higher education, and not through the formal structures imposed by collective bargaining* [emphasis in original]. He then went on to warn about "the impact of collective bargaining on the mentor-graduate student relationship that is at the heart of graduate education," suggesting, for example, that the line between research and employment hours was often so blurred that it "could not easily be accommodated by collective bargaining." Finally, he cited the Plan for Revitalizing Graduate Education developed by the faculty senate to improve salaries and the Health Insurance Allowance (HIA) that had been instituted the previous fall, to promote the idea that administrative goodwill was the preferable solution.[23]

Beyond these external factors there was also by late in the campaign a palpable sense that the University of Iowa graduate employees were simply not ready to unionize, even with the recognition that the problems the union addressed were real. As former vice president for organizing Julie Schmid recalls, contrasting the SEIU campaign with the subsequent UE campaign: "I felt people were still timid, or sort of scared ... they were unhappy with their working conditions but they weren't really angry yet."[24] Union opponents such as STOP proved more than willing to play on these fears and the willingness to give the administration another chance. In the end, Duncan has pointed out, "our support was soft in a lot of places" and furthermore, when it came to the April 1994 election, "we didn't get our people to the polls, and they did." On April 13, 1994, COGS-SEIU narrowly lost the vote to unionize.[25]

COGS REGROUPS, CHOOSES UE

Although the defeat of the COGS-SEIU campaign was a significant setback, in the long run it proved helpful by providing the activists who stayed on for the COGS-UE campaign the opportunity to analyze and reconsider campaign strategies. At the time, however, the defeat was devastating. Adding to the COGS activists' distress, shortly after the electoral defeat, the SEIU organizers simply closed up shop and left town. During the year between the campaigns, a small group of activists tried to keep COGS alive through social events and writing occasional letters to the editor of the campus newspaper to remind people of COGS's continued existence. The letters, according to Duncan, were more of a smoke screen than anything else, but were effective in making at least some think that COGS would be back with another union campaign. As he recalls from attending a Graduate Student Senate meeting in May 1995: "I remember a couple of people saying 'next year when COGS comes back for an election again....' I was stunned ... what did they know that I didn't? I was really surprised to hear that." But, he adds, "we had sort of created the image, more than anything, that we were still viable."[26] Even so, according to Hearst, by the spring of 1995 "we had hit rock bottom." Yet just a few months later a group of grads gathered informally and at one point someone said, "Let's make one more try to get COGS going." That same summer a new organization drive began, and many graduate employees who had been around but uninvolved during the previous campaign became active this time.[27]

In the second COGS affiliation vote, the main contenders were the American Federation of Teachers and the United Electrical, Radio and Machine Workers of America. AFT was a strong contender, partly because of its earlier successes organizing graduate employees, and partly, COGS activists have admitted, on the basis of name recognition. Many activists reasoned that joining with the AFT would be easy for most graduate employees to understand; whereas with the UE, the initial reaction would likely have been to wonder just where graduate teaching and research assistants fit in with electrical, radio, or machine workers. In the end, what swayed the affiliation vote were the impressions garnered from the meetings with representatives from the respective unions. According to former COGS co-president David Colman, the AFT representatives simply turned people off for a number of reasons. One AFT representative was "a bit too conservative" and offended people, especially when he "started talking about members' money in a kind of flippant way and ... trying to impress us with ... the big building they owned in Washington, D.C.... and how much money their executive officers made." Far from being impressed, Colman recalled that he and other COGS members "thought it was very inappropriate and certainly wasn't the kind of union that we wanted to ... represent us." More importantly, the AFT representatives told them that it was just too difficult to organize a graduate employee union in Iowa, a "right-to-work" state,[28] referring to the fact that under Iowa law union membership may not be made a condition of employment, nor can "fair share" dues be negotiated.[29] Even those who, like Schmid, did not share Colman's harsh assessment of the AFT, were left shaking their heads. As Schmid admitted, "nobody was terribly impressed by their presentation."[30]

By contrast, the UE representatives gave COGS activists a positive impression of their union and their commitment to helping COGS. As Colman recalls about his first impressions of the UE representatives: "[They] just gave off very good energy" and were "very kind of 'up' and optimistic." When it came to learning UE's political views, he adds, "they just seemed to have a different understanding of the world and unions." Schmid remembers that she and others were impressed by the fact that UE was pointedly not a "business union," by UE's democratic principles, and by "the fact that they hadn't ... been involved with Red-baiting during the McCarthy era." As COGS members evaluated each union, Schmid also remembers that the late UE Local 893 President Dan Kelley[31] "was a real presence during our decision to affiliate."[32] For example, in a lighter moment, when someone raised the question of how UE's reputation as a "Communist union" would affect the campaign, Kelley looked at the assembled group, most of whom were comfortably to the left politically, and replied, "Well, judging from this room, you don't need the UE to get Red-baited."[33] In the end, says Hearst, UE won the second affiliation vote because "there had been so much support for them the first time, and there was still a lot of support for them for many of the same reasons."[34]

The second COGS campaign benefited from the experience of the veterans of the previous campaign. The organizational support of UE, which included the installment of a team of organizers led by field organizer Sam Smucker and international representative Carol Lambiase, was also of immense help. All of the field organizers were chosen for their relative youth (late twenties to early thirties), and, hence, ability to blend in with the graduate employees they were trying to organize. Although having a graduate-level degree was not a criteria for choosing field organizers, at least some of them had such a degree, and one organizer had even been a graduate employee union activist. While the UE staff was important to orchestrating the campaign, it was the level of organization among the rank and file that really made the campaign as successful as it was. As former UE field organizer Todd Ricker recalls, "What really made the difference was that there was key leadership and activists who were graduate employees who were basically doing the work," which included housevisiting and follow-ups, making contacts, finding issues and reporting them back to UE staff. Says Ricker: "The five of us, who ... weren't from the university, who didn't understand how the university worked, could not have pulled this off." This rank-and-file activism was also in keeping with UE's philosophy of organizing, which is that active union building by the membership must begin even before an election is won so that the election becomes a ratification of the organization already in place.[35]

Despite the national union's lack of experience working with graduate employees, the UE organizers who worked with COGS were able to quickly adapt their organizing strategies and tactics to a university setting. For example, Schmid points out that the UE representatives were well aware of the effect of the academic calendar on the momentum of the organizing campaign and, therefore, "they couldn't let it peak at the wrong time," such as just before winter break. UE representatives also proved much more prudent in timing the election, setting a goal of talking to 70 percent of the graduate employees before calling an election. All in all, compared to the SEIU campaign, says Schmid "They were just much more organized and it was much more of a campaign."[36]

All of this was not to say that UE staff and COGS volunteer organizers alike did not encounter resistance, and even hostility, from some grads, as had occurred in 1993. This was especially true among science and engineering graduate employees, many of whom regarded the unionization campaign as a threat to their academic careers and (by graduate student standards) high salaries. In addition, for science and engineering graduate research assistants, the line between work and research was often genuinely blurred. As COGS organizer Jolene Stritecky pointed out: "They don't see themselves as exploited. They don't see the work they do as essential to the university, they see it as being essential to their career. But they don't see … how the two overlap and that they should be compensated for it … they think it's a privilege to work for Professor X." Plus, she added, "a lot of them have tuition waivers, too, so they don't feel the crunch."[37]

Even beyond the sciences, union opponents scoffed at the idea of graduate employees affiliating with the United Electrical, Radio, and Machine Workers of America, knowing little if anything of UE's recent efforts to broaden its constituency beyond its traditional industrial base and not caring to find out. For example, graduate assistant and anti-union activist J. Mark Wrighton, in a letter to the editor of the university newspaper, castigated COGS activists for choosing UE over the AFT, "a union that at least has a discernable link to graduate assistants" and asked: "What possible experience can UE bring to the enhancement of the situation of graduate assistants?" Wrighton concluded, "As for me, I'll pass on the rubber boots and tool belt."[38]

Nor did the university administration's hostility to unionization abate. As in the previous campaign, they sent out "informational" letters to the graduate students.[39] The letter that achieved the most notoriety was sent by Graduate College Dean Simms shortly before the election, a multipage, single-spaced rationale advising grads to "retain the present collegial relationship between graduate assistants and the university" as the preferable alternative to collective bargaining. The letter repeated some of his earlier arguments about the Revitalization Plan, and repeated the phrase "the impact of collective bargaining on the mentor-graduate student relationship that is at the heart of graduate education."[40] This particular letter may have backfired since many graduate students by this time had become aware of just what Dean Simms and many members of the university administration meant by "collegiality." As Schmid pointed out, "we had learned to see through his rhetoric."[41] Former COGS President Deborah Herman recalled how this letter sealed her decision to vote yes for the union: "We don't have any collegiality [with upper level administrators]. They're in control and they tell us what to do and we suck it up and hope that we can get through without crossing any of them."[42]

According to Colman, there were two particular strategies that made a difference in the second COGS campaign. The first involved the authorization cards, which in the previous campaign were treated as just that—authorization for an election and were, therefore, easy to get people to sign. This time, however, "[the] UE and Carol and Sam were very forceful about the idea that, we're not [asking] people to sign cards for an election, we're getting people to sign union cards." While this strategy took more time and effort, in the end it paid off by ensuring that those who signed cards would be more likely to vote yes. The second strategy involved a more planned and coordinated response to the renewed emergence of an anti-union student group, this time called "Students Against COGS" (SAC). Like its predecessor STOP, SAC received equal time from the local press. COGS's strategy this time, however, was to not engage SAC in what Colman termed "a war of words" and an exchange of accusations; rather, COGS simply kept putting out the facts to counter the anti-union propaganda and stayed "on message."[43] Although the anti-union rhetoric from SAC was not as pervasive as had been the case in the previous campaign, throughout, asserts Duncan "we took nothing for granted. We never assumed we were going to win."[44]

Beyond these strategies, the second COGS campaign was able to capitalize on the change in the general graduate employee attitudes that had taken place between the two campaigns, with more grads visibly appearing to want unionization, having lost faith in the university administration's promises of change. Says Schmid: "A lot of people who had been laissez-faire with the first campaign became more active the second time around because they felt like they had been betrayed by the university." This betrayal came with the university's failure to fulfill promises made during the first campaign. "I think a lot of people ... really wanted to give the Graduate College and the administration the benefit of the doubt the first time around" and assumed that administrators "just didn't know how bad it was," only to see very little change in the interim.[45] In the end, the teamwork between the UE staff and the many rank-and-file volunteers, and COGS's willingness to build on the previous campaign and learn from its mistakes, brought the campaign to an electoral victory of 949 to 667 on April 16, 1996.[46]

CONTRACT NEGOTIATIONS: HARD DECISIONS

Shortly after the electoral victory, even before the completion of the local's constitution and vote for regular officers, COGS members elected a negotiating team. Months before formal collective bargaining began, the COGS negotiating team began talks with university administration, winning significant pay increases for Iowa graduate employees that went into effect immediately.[47] Formal bargaining began in early September, 1996. The main issues of the first contract negotiations included access to a more comprehensive and affordable health care plan; further pay increases; protection against overwork; timely announcements and notifications of appointments; and a formalized grievance procedure. In the end, all of these issues were addressed in the Iowa graduate employees' first contract, which was by no means easily achieved. As Stritecky, who served on the first negotiating committee, recalled: "Mary Jo [Small, the vice president for University Finances] just expected us to come in and sit down and take whatever they gave us," adding that Vice President Small quickly found out that, instead, "she had a fight on her hands."[48]

Although the main action took place in the closed negotiations, on the outside the union's rank and file backed up the committee's efforts to pressure the administration. COGS members staged informational pickets and a public "grade-in." The grade-in participants demonstrated the work that graduate employees did for the university and "flunked" the administration on how they compensated this work.[49] Even so, on certain mandatory bargaining issues, including health care, the university administration refused to budge, forcing the decision to go to binding arbitration. Then, on the night before arbitration was to begin, with no more than ten hours to go, the administration reversed itself on these issues.[50]

On one issue, however, the administration remained unmoving, and because it was only a permissive, as opposed to mandatory subject of bargaining, arbitration was not an option.[51] This was the inclusion of the University of Iowa's own no-discrimination clause in the contract.[52] The university's no-discrimination clause, also known as its human rights clause, was broad enough to include just about every conceivable category of discrimination, including sexual orientation and HIV status. If, as the university claimed, graduate employees were automatically covered by the clause, it should have posed the administration no problem to include it in the contract. However, the university refused, in part "under orders from Des Moines [Iowa's capitol]" to prevent the possibility of, for example, discrimination against gays being taken through a formalized grievance procedure that included binding arbitration at the highest level.[53]

Far from being a lost cause, however, the no-discrimination clause became a cause célèbre for COGS, as well as the source of what has been its most controversial political action to date. In January 1997, the university, as the opening event of its week-long commemoration of Martin Luther King Day, arranged a speech by civil rights historian Taylor Branch about (interestingly enough) the role of students in the civil rights movement. A number of COGS leaders decided to plan a demonstration at that event in protest of what they saw as the chutzpah of the administration celebrating the life of Martin Luther King while refusing to subscribe to his principles.

The decision to mount a protest, however, was not taken lightly. Not long after the initial plan was agreed to, one of the UE international representatives intervened to object to the planned protest as having the potential to "back the university into a corner and not let them get out gracefully." According to Stritecky, another meeting was called and the initial plan to disrupt the event was altered to a far less visible demonstration. The organizer of the initial plan, who had been informed of the change only after the fact, then addressed yet another meeting to object to the changes as shunting aside the union's growing commitment to social justice for fear of hurting bread-and-butter gains.[54] After a heated debate over how militant an action to take, the plan decided on was for a group of union members to march in just before the speech, singing "This Little Light of Mine," after which co-president Margaret Loose would make a brief speech before they marched out. The planners of the demonstration decided to inform the speaker in advance what was happening, in part out of courtesy and in part as a bid for support. The speaker's response was to accuse them of distorting the tactics of the civil rights movement while claiming that he hadn't heard the university's side of the story.[55] The activists went ahead with their demonstration and received an overall positive response from the audience, many of whom sang along. It was also reported that as the university's president Mary Sue Coleman sat in the audience, one person leaned over to ask why the administration didn't just give the graduate employees the no-discrimination clause? President Coleman's response remains unknown.[56]

Before and after the event, the organizers and their supporters defended the protest (and all its potential to offend the administration) with the argument that COGS's philosophy of a union should be inclusive, rather than exclusive, and that any material gains by the union are worthless if any member is left behind. As Herman pointed out, by simply giving in on the matter of the no discrimination clause for fear of losing material benefits, the union would lose the moral high ground by displaying that when the chips were down, discrimination (which for minority and international students was likely to be more than an academic issue) was less important than concrete bread-and-butter issues (a distinction that, it could be argued, was more rhetorical than real).[57] Beyond the moral concerns, Herman also argued that failure to speak out on the issue was shortsighted from an organizing perspective because, in a "right-to-work" state, "the future health of the union ... is dependent on constantly attracting new members." Therefore, "even for those who might not care, such abandonment [of minority rights] might signal an inability on the part of the union to stand up for any cause that could jeopardize short-term monetary gains."[58]

COGS's stance on the no-discrimination clause was noted by many inside and outside the union. John Scott, a forty-something African-American graduate assistant and long-time union activist, remarked after the event that it was the first time he had been in a union willing to put economic gains on the line for the sake of social justice.[59] Beyond the university community, the MLK action was cited by cultural historian Robin D.G. Kelley as "a sparkling example" of a university union's recognition that civil rights questions should not be subordinate to bread-and-butter issues, and as proof that "it is possible to build a dynamic labor movement without subordinating race or gender."[60]

No one would dispute, however, that the stress and anxiety inherent in the negotiation of a first contract were quite real; the weight of this responsibility was a factor in the decision of some COGS activists to oppose the MLK event. The group of graduate employees who made up the negotiating committee spent long hours—unpaid and in addition to the usual employment and academic responsibilities, as was true of all activists—meeting with the university administration's representatives and preparing new contract language from scratch, researched from various existing similar contracts. The work could be so all-engrossing that, as Stritecky recalled, "I have no idea what else I did that year."[61] While not all of the negotiators were opposed to the MLK action, for some, the fear of the ill effects of a disruptive protest was very real. As former negotiator and chief steward Mike Evces recalls, "At the time, I just wanted the contract to be successful. I thought that was paramount.... That was my measure of success—if we ratify the contract," and when it came to the MLK protest, "I feared that it would damage negotiations because that was what I was being told, and I had no reason to think otherwise." Evces recalled being advised by the UE international representatives assisting in the negotiations that mounting such a protest was "a horrible idea," a view he has since rejected.[62] Beyond the negotiating committee, other COGS members viewed the event with a certain degree of ambivalence. While few would have doubted the rightness or necessity of the no-discrimination clause, as Schmid pointed out, "the reality of it was that [the negotiating team] had a responsibility to the membership to get them better wages, and to get them health care," a responsibility the union, unlike a purely student organization, could not dismiss lightly.[63]

How did the protest affect the first (and subsequent) contract negotiations? There is no single answer. Herman recalls that she believed that the chances of getting the no-discrimination clause at the time were "slim-to-none" and that the only way the administration would budge was through "an incredible amount of public pressure," adding: "They were not going to give it to us by us being nice at the bargaining table."[64] Similarly, Loose, who was on the negotiating committee, later asserted the university was firmly opposed to it from the beginning and "no matter how many opportunities we gave them and how many crafty, artistic, linguistic acrobatics we did in the language we proposed for a no-discrimination clause, they were intransigent." If anything, she suggested that the failure to achieve the clause was the result of the university administration's "moral bankruptcy."[65] On the other hand, negotiating committee member Stritecky has raised the possibility that the administration did retaliate against the Martin Luther King protest by refusing to discuss the no-discrimination clause, though she still insists that it was nonetheless the right thing to do and that "ultimately in the long run, our activism paid off."[66]

As to the long-term effect of the MLK protest, Schmid has pointed out that it may have forced the university to take a less hard line against the no-discrimination clause in subsequent contract negotiations.[67] Although the MLK action was not repeated in subsequent years, the issue of the no-discrimination clause did not go away. By the time the second contract negotiations rolled around, the university, looking to avoid another public relations nightmare, agreed to a "Memorandum of Understanding" in the contract. This compromise language restricted complaints under the university's human rights policy to resolution by the "Human Rights procedure established by the university policy," rather than through the legally binding grievance procedure established by union contract; it did, however, guarantee that a union steward could accompany the complainant through the process. Commented Herman, a member of the negotiating committee for the second contract, "What we ended up with was very much a political compromise, which essentially pleased no one."[68]

Nonetheless, the membership approved it, in part on the basis that, says Herman, "they did put enough on the table that if we rejected it ... it would have put us in a rather difficult position" when it came to explaining an "all-or-nothing" hard line to union members and the general public. Herman adds that at least the memorandum "made it very clear that people have the right to take a union steward with them at all points in the university process," a point that had previously been in contention; nevertheless, it did not address the essential unfairness of a complaint process controlled by the very university that the complaint was being made against. Herman concluded that to win a true no-discrimination clause it might require a test case "where we'll be able to show in a public way that their system is a failure, that the compromise we agreed to, as we predicted all along, doesn't work."[69] In the meantime, the issue has still not gone away. Says UE field organizer Ryan Downing: "The fight's going to continue to get a standard nondiscrimination clause in the contract."[70]

STUDENT ACTIVISTS OR UNION MEMBERS?

While the concrete issue of the no-discrimination clause has been generally agreed upon as a bargaining priority, the larger issue of how "political" an organization COGS should be is one on which the members continue to agree to disagree. Some favor maintaining a militant edge that includes a willingness to address social issues that are connected to, but go beyond, the immediate concerns of the union and the workplace.[71] Others hold the view that organizing is at bottom the union's purpose and should remain its focus; they assert that while COGS may give support to and engage in limited cooperation with student or political organizations such as the University of Iowa Students Against Sweatshops, COGS's role as first and foremost a labor union should remain dominant.[72]

As COGS has worked in its post-campaign phase to define itself as a graduate employee union, it has also worked to define itself as a part of UE, and in the process educate its members and potential members about their role in the larger labor movement.[73] Within the local labor community, this had meant solidarity action with other unions, from going out to support picketing Rockwell-Collins electrical workers (members of the International Brotherhood of Electrical Workers Local 1634) to taking part in a rally in support of the University of Iowa Hospitals and Clinics nursing and other staff workers' union campaign in the face of the hospital administration's use of a notorious union-busting firm. COGS's solidarity efforts have been starting to pay off, as other local labor organizations come to recognize COGS as a genuine part of the labor movement. For example, COGS maintains ties with the Iowa City Federation of Labor (the local arm of the AFL-CIO), even though UE is not a member of the national organization.[74] More recently, COGS, AFSCME Local 12, and SEIU Local 199 staged a joint rally in front of a Board of Regents meeting to draw attention to common issues such as wages, benefits, and working conditions that each group of workers at the university would face as they commenced 2001–2003 contract bargaining.[75]

As for COGS's relationship with UE, despite the initial misgivings on both sides, things have worked out well. One of the most palpable measures of this mutual adjustment has been COGS's active participation in the union's district council and national convention meetings since certification. Here, as perhaps nowhere else, does the incongruity of being an academic worker in a traditionally industrial union become apparent. As a national convention delegate, Evces, who served on the resolutions committee of the 1997 UE national convention, recalls being puzzled when the committee chair, District 11 president Carl Rosen, chose him to read the resolution on health and safety before the assembled delegates.[76] Evces marveled: "So here's me, a rhetoric instructor from the University of Iowa, reading a resolution about safety in the workplace in memory of our sisters and brothers who lost their lives in dangerous workplaces and how important it is to have a union and guarantee safety procedures in a union contract.... If I had been in the audience ... I would have smelled irony."[77]

By a similar token, interacting with other UE members involved a certain measure of self-consciousness and explaining just what members of UE Local 896 did as teaching and research assistants. As Evces admitted, there were other UE members he met who were at least initially puzzled at how he and his colleagues ended up in "a blue-collar, working-class union" but who proved to be open-minded about the seeming anomaly. For example, shortly after Evces read the health and safety resolution, an older delegate, who was planning to give a shop report at a forthcoming district council, approached Evces to express admiration for his speaking style and ask for some tips on public speaking.[78] On the other hand, as Loose has pointed out, the process of face-to-face education at these events has been mutual. UE members have learned that a college education no longer guarantees a comfortable future; and COGS members have learned, for example, the realities of what it means to be an airbrush operator in today's economy, as well as receiving invaluable advice on handling grievances and organizing workplace actions.[79]

Yet from the beginning, the UE National made a public point of emphasizing similarities of issues, rather than what Ricker described as "material differences" between Local 896 COGS and the more traditional industrial locals.[80] They also made it clear that their latest and perhaps most distinct effort to expand their constituency was just another part of the recent larger effort to rebuild UE, decimated by McCarthyism in the 1950s and by plant closings in the 1980s.[81] During the 1996 UE National Convention, at which COGS made its official debut as a chartered UE local, the director of organization Robert Kingsley hailed COGS's victory, a bargaining unit of 2,600, as "the largest single UE organizing election win in at least 30 years. It was the largest organizing triumph in Iowa in more than a decade and it ranks as one of the five largest victories of any union in the United States of America in 1996."[82] Within Iowa, there has been little question of the importance of UE Local 896-COGS as a major step in re-building UE.[83]

If UE national officers and staffers emphasized any distinction, it was the challenge of successfully organizing a bargaining unit that was not only much larger than most, but whose members were occupationally diverse and widely dispersed among many small "shops" within a geographically sprawling "plant." The other structural distinction with which COGS members and UE national staff alike have had to deal is the transitory nature of the bargaining unit, requiring the union to be in continual organizing mode to survive and succeed. Beyond these distinctive structural factors, however, Downing, who has been the assigned national staff organizer at Local 896 since 1998, insists that "this is just as conventional a local" as any of the other locals he works with, whose members range from electricians to die-cast workers to public education support staff. Rather than attributing post-campaign stresses such as the difficult MLK demonstration decision to COGS being a local of student-workers who are "too hung up on ideology, theory, and abstraction," recalls Evces, the national staff instead reassured them that these were problems faced by every new local "in some form or another."[84]

In return, members of COGS have made a concerted effort to become a regular part of UE. One way has been involvement by COGS members in other UE organizing efforts, on both a volunteer and a paid basis. Stritecky, who was a project organizer for two summers, recalls that her and her colleagues' graduate student status proved no impediment to successful organizing because "it's not like they're dealing with a huge mob of eggheads.... We're able to slip back into our human roles."[85] COGS members who have assisted other organizing on a volunteer basis have reached similar conclusions.[86]

Another example is COGS's involvement in UE's cross-border solidarity movement with Mexico's progressive labor organization, *El Frente Auténtico de Trabajo* (FAT) (the Authentic Workers' Front). In November 1997, then Labor Solidarity committee chair Mary Crippen was part of a small delegation of UE women visiting Mexico in a worker-to-worker exchange program. After the visit, Crippen remarked that "hearing the stories from the workers themselves really brought their struggles home."[87] The following year, two Mexican workers visited Iowa City as part of the ongoing UE-FAT exchange and were impressed by COGS members involvement as both students and workers (something almost unheard of in Mexico).[88]

COGS has also made a concerted effort to join other UE locals in political matters. On February 4, 1998, COGS members joined their UE brothers and sisters in Local 893-IUP (Iowa United Professionals, representing human services and other state employees) at UE's annual lobby day in the state capital to protest the state legislature's threats to privatize social services and attacks on public employee collective bargaining rights.[89] More recently, in the last presidential election, COGS passed a resolution endorsing Green Party candidate Ralph Nader, paralleling the national union's endorsement.[90]

Finally, it has been the self-consciousness of COGS members of their unique place both in UE and the graduate employee unionization movement that has helped allay concerns regarding academic snobbishness (perceived or actual). Says Evces: "We've been fortunate to have officers in our local who are incredibly sensitive to issues of class identity ... they're very aware of how they deliver their shop reports ... how they interact with people socially" and how these things represent the local, adding: "I think people appreciate that."[91] Schmid has viewed the shop reports as opportunities to explain to other UE members why they, a union of graduate students employed as teachers and researchers, were part of UE; and in turn enable COGS members to connect their issues of wages, health care, and overwork to the same issues presented by other delegates in their shop reports.[92]

CONCLUSIONS

The ongoing success of UE Local 896-COGS can be attributed to three important factors. First, the decision of COGS activists from the beginning, despite the criticism from some grads, to identify themselves as a "real" labor organization. Next, COGS members have retained a commitment to social justice activism that has, so far, remained focused on work issues, while nevertheless expanding that definition beyond wages and benefits or the exclusive concerns of the local. Finally and perhaps most significantly, COGS members, despite the challenges of an annual turnover rate of 20–25 percent in the bargaining unit, have embraced and worked hard to enact UE's principles of rank-and-file democracy. These factors have not only brought Iowa graduate employees to union victory after a generation's worth of activism, but have made COGS a powerful advocate for graduate employees that is also capable of looking well beyond the confines of the campus.

NOTES

The author would like to acknowledge and thank everyone who sat for interviews, all of which were integral to the research for and production of this chapter. She would also like to acknowledge and thank UE Local 896-COGS and Robert Hearst for permission to use archival material, and Michael Innis for providing a copy of the elusive "Dean Simms letter."

1. Employed graduate students, unlike undergraduates, are permitted collective bargaining rights. Public Employee Relations Act 20.4, Iowa Code, 1995.

2. John Schacht, interview by Dennis Deslippe, COGS-SEIU Archives, State Historical Society of Iowa, Iowa City, Iowa; "Graduate assistants at Iowa to present demands," *Cedar Rapids Gazette*, April 1, 1969, p. 4A.

3. Schacht, interview.

4. Ibid.

5. "T.A.'s seek contract, want union," *Daily Iowan*, February 14, 1984, p. 3A; "T.A.s plan walkout in protest of proposed cuts," *Daily Iowan*, February 16, 1984, p. 1A, 6A; "More than a walkout," *Daily Iowan*, February 21, 1984, p. 7A; "Open letter to UI students, faculty, staff," *Daily Iowan*, February 21, 1984, p. 7A; "'Teach-ins' offered as strike alternative," *Daily Iowan*, February 22, 1984, p. 3A; "Graduate interest," *Daily Iowan*, March 12, 1984, p. 7A; "Issues not addressed," *Daily Iowan*, March 12, 1984, p. 7A; "Big Ten T.A.'s see benefits of unionizing," *Daily Iowan*, April 9, 1984, p. 1A, 8A; "A real bargain," *Daily Iowan*, April 30, 1984, p. 7A; "Help yourself," *Daily Iowan*, April 30, 1984, p. 7A.

6. Robert Hearst, interview by author, Iowa City, Iowa, April 28, 1998.

7. Shelton Stromquist, electronic mail correspondence with author, September 1998.

8. D. Colman, "A short history of COGS," union flyer, Iowa City (also, author's private collection), n.d.

9. D. Colman, "There is power in a union," *COGNITION*, union newsletter, April 19, 1996, p. 4.

10. "COGS-SEIU, GSS both serve grad students," *Daily Iowan*, October 5, 1993, p. 8A; E. Marty, "Father hopes for union and better life," *Daily Iowan*, April 11, 1994, p. 2A.

11. "Casual nation: The American system of higher education faces an unprecedented crisis: Half of all college teachers work for inadequate pay and benefits and have no institutional voice," report by the Coalition of Graduate Employee Unions, n.d.; K. Bronfbrenner and T. Juravitch, "Universities should cease hostilities with unions," *Chronicle of Higher Education*, January 19, 2001, p. B24.

12. Hearst, interview.

13. Ibid; "COGS members talk with SEIU representative of future," *Daily Iowan*, September 7, 1993, p. 4A.

14. J.J. Matles and J. Higgins, *Them and us: Struggles of a rank-and-file union* (Englewood Cliffs, NJ: Prentice-Hall, 1974; reprint, Pittsburgh, PA: United Electrical, Radio, and Machine Workers of America, 1995): 319–320.

15. Curiously, this consideration was not a deciding factor in the second affiliation vote.

16. Hearst, interview.

17. Jason Duncan, interview by author, Iowa City, Iowa. May 18, 1998.

18. Ibid; Hearst, interview.

19. D. Swinarski, "Painful lessons: The failed attempt to unionize graduate employees at the University of Iowa," paper written for distribution at the Coalition of Graduate Employee Unions, August 19–20, 1994, Robert Hearst private collection, Council Bluffs, Iowa.

20. Duncan, interview.

21. E. Marty, "STOP formed in opposition to grad union," *Daily Iowan*, April 12, 1994, p. 3A.

22. "Who we are—What we want," *COGNITION*, union newsletter, September 1993, p. 1; N. Anderson, "COGS not the first to work for change," *Daily Iowan*, September 14,1993, p. 9A; S.J. Bucklin, "Perhaps not time for UI grad students to unionize," *Daily Iowan*, September 29, 1993, p. 9A.

23. Letter, Dean Leslie B. Simms to the University of Iowa graduate students, March 7, 1994.

24. Julie Schmid, interview by author, Iowa City, Iowa, March 20, 2001.

25. "Significant events in COGS history," Robert Hearst, private collection, Council Bluffs, Iowa; M. Gehraghty "Union vote fails at U of I by 81 votes," *Des Moines Regis-*

ter, April 13, 1994, p. 6M; E. Marty, "Unionization denied: COGS may contest election after efforts fail," *Daily Iowan*, April 15, 1994, pp. 1A, 10A. The exact number of votes by which COGS lost the 1994 election has been variously reported as 80 or 81.

26. Duncan, interview.

27. Hearst, interview; David Colman, interview by author, Iowa City, Iowa, May 6, 1998.

28. Colman, interview.

29. According to the Iowa Public Employee Relations Act, public employees have the right to "refuse to join or participate in the activities of employee organizations, including the payment of dues, fees or assessments of service fees of any type." <http://www./IACODE/1999SUPPLEMENT/20/8.html>, 3/21/2001.

30. Schmid, interview.

31. Kelley died December 19, 2000. See "Dan Kelley, Local 893 founder and president, dies," *UE News*, January 2001, p. 12.

32. Schmid, interview.

33. Colman, interview.

34. Hearst, interview.

35. Todd Ricker, interview by author, Iowa City, Iowa, December 17, 1997.

36. Schmid, interview.

37. Jolene Stritecky, interview by author, Iowa City, Iowa, January 13, 1998.

38. J.M. Wrighton, "COGS is a secret elite," *Daily Iowan*, November 17, 1995, p. 7A.

39. Deborah M. Herman, interview by author, Iowa City, Iowa, April 22, 1998.

40. Leslie B. Simms, letter to the University of Iowa graduate students, April 2, 1996.

41. Schmid, interview.

42. Herman, interview.

43. Colman, interview.

44. Michael E. Evces, interview by author, Iowa City, Iowa, January 23, 2001; Duncan, interview.

45. Schmid, interview.

46. Colman, "A short history of COGS."

47. Ibid.

48. Stritecky, interview.

49. B. Brown, "Educational quality and the UI: COGS protest allocation of funds,"*Daily Iowan*, February 20, 1997, pp. 1A, 8A; C. Eby, "COGS-UE stage 'grade-in,' to support negotiations," *Daily Iowan*, December 19, 1996, p. 3A.

50. "Vote on your contract!," *COGNITION*, union newsletter, February 1997, p. 1; "Happy birthday to COGS," *COGNITION*, union newsletter, April 1997, p. 1.

51. Under the Iowa Public Employee Relations Act, certain topics are designated "mandatory," that is, the employer must negotiate them with the union. Other topics are "permissive," that is, the employer is permitted to negotiate them, but is not required to do so. If the contract is submitted to binding arbitration, the employer has the right to (and generally does) abandon all previously negotiated permissive topics.

52. "Administration fails to accept non-discrimination," *COGNITION*, union newsletter, November 1996, p. 2.

53. Herman, interview.

54. Jolene Stritecky, telephone interview by author, Madison, Wisconsin/Seattle, Washington, March 13, 2001.

55. Ibid.

56. Ibid.

57. Herman, interview.

58. Deborah M. Herman, electronic mail correspondence with author, March 21, 2001.

59. Margaret Loose, interview by author, Iowa City, Iowa, March 20, 1998.

60. R.D.G. Kelley, *Yo mama's disfunktional!: Fighting the culture wars in urban America* (Boston: Beacon Press, 1997): 143–144.

61. Stritecky, interview, January 13, 1998.

62. Evces, interview.

63. Schmid, interview.

64. Herman, interview.

65. Loose, interview.

66. Stritecky, interview, March 13, 2001.

67. Schmid, interview.

68. Deborah M. Herman, interview by author, Iowa City, Iowa, June 11, 2000.

69. Ibid.

70. Ryan Downing, interview by author, Iowa City, Iowa, January 24, 2001.

71. David Colman, interview by author, Iowa City, Iowa, June 23, 1998; Loose, interview.

72. Evces, interview; Herman, interview, June 11, 2000.

73. Stritecky, interview, January 13, 1998.

74. A. Coutee, "Walking the line with strikers," *Daily Iowan*, June 10, 1998, pp. 1A, 7A; Herman, interview by author, Iowa City, Iowa, July 16, 1998.

75. "AFSCME, COGS, SEIU show solidarity at Regents' meeting," *Daily Iowan*, September 14, 2000, p. 2A.

76. Michael E. Evces, electronic correspondence with author, June 7, 2001.

77. Evces, interview.

78. Ibid.

79. Loose, interview.

80. Ricker, interview.

81. *Solidarity and democracy: A leadership guide to UE history*, 2d ed. (Pittsburgh, PA: United Electrical, Radio, and Machine Workers of America, 1996): 81–83.

82. *Proceedings of the UE 61st National Convention* (Pittsburgh, PA: United Electrical, Radio, and Machine Workers of America, 1996): 147.

83. Downing, interview.

84. Evces, interview.

85. Stritecky, interview, January 13, 1998.

86. Evces, interview.

87. "UE activists discover union sisterhood is powerful, despite borders," *UE News*, February 20, 1998, p. 7.

88. M. Crippen, "UE FAT representatives visit UE locals across the midwest," *COGNITION*, union newsletter, November 1998, p. 5.

89. "Biggest-ever Iowa political action day," *UE News*, February 20, 1998, p. 4.

90. "COGS issues political endorsements," *COGNITION*, union newsletter, November 2000, p. 3; J. Sherer, "Delegates report on national convention: UE sets union priorities, endorses Ralph Nader," *COGNITION*, union newsletter, September 2000, p. 2.

91. Evces, interview.

92. Schmid, interview.

Chapter 5

Pyrrhic Victory at UC Santa Barbara: The Struggle for Labor's New Identity

Richard Sullivan

A spirited dialogue is occurring concerning issues of union transformation, organizing the unorganized, promoting union democracy, and developing new strategies to re-establish unions as a powerful voice for workers (Mantsios 1998; Nissen 1999; Tillman and Cummings 1999). Several developments provide reasons for optimism: the rise of reform-minded John Sweeney as president of the AFL-CIO, a new commitment by some unions to dedicate resources for organizing, and several highly visible union victories.

The organizing efforts of graduate employees are indicative of this renewed enthusiasm—both embodying the promise of a new labor movement and serving as laboratories where much needed experimentation is taking place. Among the more notable recent examples was the United Automobile Workers' (UAW) campaign to organize graduate employees at the University of California (UC). Having gained union recognition and a contract covering over nine thousand graduate workers on eight of the system's nine campuses, the campaign represents one of largest recent victories for labor—in or outside of the academy. UAW vice president Elizabeth Bunn has called it "an inspiration to the labor movement." Labor scholar David Montgomery agrees "that the victory of the UAW in California gave a great shot in the arm to graduate employees trying to win recognition elsewhere."[1]

Our eagerness to find evidence of labor's rebirth and to identify movement victories is understandable. But it is the job of labor scholars to critically examine the quality of these victories. What do the worker-activists have to say about the UAW's victory? On the UC Santa Barbara (UCSB) campus, where I was a participant observer, I found that the graduate employees and campus activists there, who stood to benefit the most from the successful campaign, are not celebrating. Therefore, in this chapter, I attempt to explain from their perspective why this is the case. What follows are two accounts of the union drive at UCSB that occurred two years apart that will demonstrate why a more critical examination of this union success is needed.

In spring 1998, the graduate employee union at the Santa Barbara campus of the University of California seemed to fit the description of what is being called the "new labor movement." Graduate employees had built a union based on the principles of rank-and-file democracy and collective empowerment. In May of that year, they organized a strike vote to force the UC administration to recognize their union. At the time, their membership numbered more than one thousand, and a dedicated group of fifty volunteer activists were busy organizing, holding department meetings and talking to fellow graduate employees about the union. After months of organizing, six hundred members turned out for the vote—five hundred of whom voted to strike. Activists were inspired by this success, which seemed to validate their belief that democracy and grassroots activism are essential elements of union strength. Confidence was growing among graduate employees, there was a palpable sense that they were making history, and there was no doubt that they were a union.

But two years later, the situation was much different. Although graduate employees had gained recognition and secured a contract, the mood within the local union was somber. Missing were the energy and commitment that had characterized the union. Nearly all of the activists who had worked so hard to build the union over the preceding six years had disengaged entirely. Among the rank and file, enthusiasm for the union was at an all-time low. Support had eroded so much that the UAW had to resort to sending paid staff to Santa Barbara whenever a public presence was required at UCSB. When the UAW called a one-day strike during contract negotiations, only two members walked out. And when the contract was presented for ratification, fewer than 150 members voted to approve it. Six months later, union membership at UCSB had dwindled to just fifty-three. In the span of two years, despite gaining union recognition and a contract, the dynamic pro-union culture was gone.

In this chapter, I examine the events leading to this dramatic change at UCSB. In light of the labor movement's current effort to transform itself, this story raises doubts about whether it can—or should—count such outcomes among its victories. Many unions and their leaders continue to resist change despite growing recognition within labor's ranks for the need to expand the mission of the movement, promote greater democracy within it, and increase rank-and-file participation. Those seeking reform and those resisting it are essentially engaged in a struggle over the identity of the labor movement. The UCSB case illustrates what this struggle looks like on the ground and identifies some of the challenges workers face when trying to incorporate new visions for the movement into existing union frameworks.

My primary goal is to examine the UCSB organizing drive from the point of view of graduate employee activists who played leading roles in the campaign.

Collectively, these activists' stories highlight the critical need for labor to welcome innovation. Their experiences demonstrate how organized labor's resistance to change undercuts the efforts and undermines the commitment of those who answer the call to help rebuild the movement. From a distance, the UAW's campaign at UCSB might appear to have been a victory, but closer scrutiny reveals that a promising pro-union culture was destroyed in achieving it.

METHODS

This chapter focuses on events occurring at UC Santa Barbara during 1998–2000. The data on which it is based come from semistructured interviews with graduate employees active in the campaign during this two-year period. I interviewed fifteen (former) activists from nine different academic departments between April 2000 and March 2001. The tape-recorded interviews ranged in length from forty-five to ninety minutes. I identified interview subjects based on my personal knowledge of who was most involved during the period being examined. Each of the interviewees agreed to allow me to use their names. I drew additional data from union newsletters, web sites, campaign literature, e-mail correspondence, and newspaper stories related to the events.

In order to situate the Santa Barbara case and to corroborate certain statements made by UCSB informants, I interviewed five current and former graduate employees who had been activists or UAW staff members on other campuses. Because some subjects in this group continue to work for organized labor, they will remain anonymous. Despite occasional references to the UC-systemwide campaign or the drives at individual campuses, it is beyond the scope of this chapter to draw conclusions about the campaigns at other campuses, and I make no claims to do so. I am also unable to speak to the motivations and perspectives of UAW employees. The aim of this study is to give voice to the perspectives and experiences of the USCB graduate employee activists.

Finally, I witnessed and actively participated in many of the events described. I joined the union when I came to UCSB in the fall of 1997 and was an active member of the organizing committee until spring 2000. I held elected positions on the strike committee in 1998 and the bargaining team in 1999. As such, I draw extensively from personal notes and my own recollection of this period.[2] Although I was personally involved during many of the events, for the sake of clarity I will retain the third-person voice throughout except in instances that warrant otherwise.

GRADUATE EMPLOYEE ORGANIZING
AT THE UNIVERSITY OF CALIFORNIA

The University of California system comprises eight campuses providing education to over 137,000 undergraduate students.[3] It is one of the largest public research universities in the country, producing 10 percent of the nation's PhDs annually.[4] The largest and more widely known campuses, Berkeley and UCLA, each have enrollments of over thirty thousand while the smallest schools in the system, Riverside and Santa Cruz, have total enrollments of just over eleven thousand. Santa Barbara, located on the state's central coast approximately ninety miles north of Los Angeles, ranks as one of the midsized UCs, with twenty thousand undergraduate and graduate students.[5]

Although the campaign to organize UCSB's seventeen hundred graduate student employees began in 1992, it was part of the effort to organize more than nine thousand graduate employees throughout the UC system that began at Berkeley in 1983. That year, the recently formed Berkeley union filed an unfair labor practice with the state's Public Employee Relations Board (PERB) after the administration refused to negotiate with graduate employees. This marked the beginning of a seventeen-year struggle for union recognition—eventually involving eight UC campuses—that would not be resolved until 1999 when PERB ruled decisively in favor of the union and ordered certification elections to be held at each campus.

But for nearly two decades, the UC administration used the courts in an effort to block the unionization of graduate student workers by arguing that they were not actually employees. UC administrators maintained that the work done by teaching assistants, readers, and tutors was a central part of their academic training and as such made them student apprentices, not employees. This distinction was crucial since under California's Higher Education Employee Relations Act (HEERA), student workers do not have collective bargaining rights. The administration spent millions of dollars litigating the effort to thwart unionization.[6] Even in the current era of employer resistance to unions, the opposition of the UC was remarkable. That a prestigious public institution of higher learning engaged in such rigorous resistance indicated the extent of antiunion sentiment shared by the UC president and Board of Regents.

In 1987, the Berkeley union affiliated with District 65/UAW, partially motivated by the need to meet the UC's court challenge. District 65 was an independent union based in New York that organized workers in a wide range of occupations, including large numbers of "knowledge" workers. It had a reputation as one of the more socially progressive and democratic unions in the United States. In 1979, financial troubles prompted District 65 to form an alliance with the UAW (Hoerr 1997). The arrangement between the two unions allowed District 65 to retain much of its autonomy while benefiting from the UAW's superior resources. For the new graduate employee unionists searching for a national affiliate, it seemed to be a good combination—the financial strength of the UAW with the more democratic tradition of District 65. In 1994, after District 65's financial condition failed to improve, it was fully absorbed into the UAW. In the process, all of 65's locals became part of the UAW's Technical and Office Professionals (TOP) division, including the UC's graduate employee unions.

While the court cases dragged on, graduate employees at each of the other campuses began their own organizing drives. One of the first things campus activists did was conduct membership card drives. Not only was this a way to build early momentum for the union, but it also increased pressure on the UC in an arena outside of the courtroom. Once membership surpassed 50 percent of a bargaining unit, the union could file the cards with PERB. PERB would then certify that a majority of graduate employees wanted collective bargaining and inform the employer they could voluntarily begin negotiating with the union. Berkeley gained this state-certified majority status in 1988, followed by Santa Cruz in 1990, San Diego in 1991, Davis in 1993, Los Angeles and Santa Barbara in 1994, Riverside in 1996, and finally Irvine in 1997.[7] Initially, each campus's activist group conducted its own campaign independently from one another and, for the most part, from the UAW as well. The UAW supported the individual drives primarily by directing the legal battle, but also by allocating funds to hire graduate employee organizers at each campus to coordinate the local campaigns. Nevertheless, the campaigns were conducted almost entirely by local graduate employee activists.

The eight campus locals were loosely affiliated with each other through an informal coalition called The California Alliance of Unionized Student Employees (CAUSE). "The Coalition," as it was more commonly called, was an ad hoc collection of activists from each campus who met roughly every six weeks to discuss strategy and coordinate actions. The Coalition had no formal guidelines regarding its operations nor did it have authority to set policy for the campus locals. The decisions it reached were regarded as recommendations to be taken back to local campuses for consideration.[8] Having been left to their own devices for many years, most campuses operated on the assumption that they were independent locals with the autonomy to make decisions and implement strategies. This assumption would ultimately cause problems for graduate employees at UCSB.

THE UCSB CAMPAIGN: A VISION DENIED

In 1992, a group of graduate employees at UCSB began organizing the seventeen hundred graduate employee workers at their campus. They founded the Associated Student Employees (ASE/UAW). The activist group, called the ad hoc organizing committee (AHOC), became the nucleus of the new union. Starting with a handful of volunteers, by the time the local achieved its state-certified majority in 1994, the membership had grown to twelve hundred.[9]

The issues motivating UCSB graduate employees to unionize were similar to those that concern other academic workers—desire for a voice in the decisions that affected them, respect for the contribution they made to the university, decreased workloads, better pay and benefits, and a belief that achieving these goals would improve the quality of education at the university. Winning recognition was the necessary first step. These goals may not have been unique, but the methods used to achieve them were noteworthy.

Perhaps the defining characteristic of the ASE was its uncompromising commitment to democracy. For the organizing committee, democracy was more than an abstract ideal. It represented the source of union strength; it shaped the way they structured their organization and conducted its affairs; it was a value around which union identities could be formed; and ultimately it was the process used to achieve their goals. In the words of Glyn Hughes, a veteran activist from sociology at UCSB, "there was a ... realization that whatever outcome we wanted was going to have to come from a process that we believed in as well. And that was going to have to be collective."[10]

The commitment to democracy had a strategic as well as moral logic. The organizers felt that union strength and success was predicated on having a broad base of rank-and-file participation. This perspective was consistent with their goal for the university to become an institution in which the people who did the work had a say in the way it operated. The activists at UCSB possessed a critical understanding that without high levels of member participation, the union's actions would be prone to fail. Relying on a handful of militant leaders would not produce a vibrant union and would appear weak to the UC.[11] However, understanding this in theory was one thing; achieving it was another.

Activists sought to increase participation by developing a union culture on campus and cultivating union identities among graduate employees that could sustain the struggle and eventually form the foundation of a more equitable relationship with UC administrators. As one of ASE's founders remembered: "We were committed to a more educational approach ... to develop union identities among graduate employees who typically identify with their research or their mentors. We felt we needed to develop this identity with the union."[12] If graduate employees identified with the union and felt a sense of ownership of the campaign, there was a better chance they would be willing to actively participate.

One of the more challenging tasks activists faced was figuring out how to get graduate employees to identify with the union. Campus organizers had to confront existing attitudes of many graduate employees who did not view unions as relevant to their work lives. Most identified as professionals and saw themselves as soon-to-be professors with no need for organized labor. For others, it seemed incongruent for academics to be joining a union (the UAW) that traditionally represented auto workers. They also held many of the typical conceptions of unions as outsiders interested solely in dues and as bureaucratic, corrupt, and potentially detrimental to collegiality among graduate employees and faculty.

Activists addressed these concerns by defending the affiliation with the UAW as a strategic alliance that would enable graduate employees to fight the costly legal battle the UC was waging. They also pointed to the UAW's reputation as one of the more democratic national unions. Perhaps the most effective means of allaying the concerns of would-be members was assuring them that the union would be run democratically. The idea that a union would bring greater democracy to the workplace, which would improve graduate employees' working conditions, and in turn improve the quality of education at the university, was a vision that most graduate employees could support.

Trust played a crucial role in developing a pro-union culture. Skeptical graduate employees were persuaded to join and participate in the union largely because they knew and trusted the people who were organizing it. Laura Holliday, an AHOC member from the English department, pointed out, "We had a real union culture ... people would know who we were and would ask us about the union."[13] When activists told friends and colleagues the union would be run democratically, they believed it because of the way activists organized. The organizing committee demonstrated that for them, talk of democracy was more than a campaign platitude. In many ways it prefigured what their union would be.

The organizing committee's commitment to building a strong base of active support was demonstrated by the way they conducted the campaign. For years, organizing committee meetings, open to all members, were held every Friday night without fail. Meeting facilitators rotated to increase participation in leadership positions. A group of activists published a regular newsletter and maintained a web site to keep members informed and to solicit feedback. Major strategy decisions were put to a vote of the membership. Even seemingly trivial matters—like how their paid organizer's time ought to be allocated—were subject to member approval. As Seth Rosenberg, an activist from the physics department, recalled: "Basically there were a number of times in the campaign where we were trying to figure out the best way to do things and inevitably the answer we came to is that we weren't really qualified to make that decision ourselves. We needed to find out what direction our members wanted to go."[14] Although their model seemed to be working, the fledgling union's methods and values were put to the test in spring 1998 as each of the UC campuses mobilized for a vote to authorize a strike to gain recognition. The walkout, which was planned for the following fall quarter, would be their most ambitious action to date. UCSB campus leaders were determined to show that a democratic, rank-and-file led union could be successful, so they began organizing for a strong turnout in the authorization vote. Santa Barbara set a quorum requiring at least half of all members to vote for the election to be valid.[15] Although the UAW constitution did not require them to do so, the AHOC felt setting the bar high was critical for two reasons. First, for a strike to be effective, it needs broad support among the membership. Therefore, allowing a potentially low turnout of mostly union supporters to determine the outcome seemed counterproductive. Second, a strong turnout would signal the union's resolve to the UC and increase the chances of bringing the UC to the table without a strike. Up until that time, the UCSB union had no elected campuswide leadership, so they used this opportunity to establish a strike committee that would be responsible for officially calling and coordinating the strike.

For strategic purposes, the UAW urged that the authorization vote be conducted in the spring. However, doing so created a problem because new grads coming to campus in the fall would essentially be asked to strike without having a say in the matter. Activists hoped the strike committee would act as democratic mechanism by which to reassess support six months hence. The organizing committee did not want to jeopardize the union and its members by following through with an ill-advised strike if support for the job action were to wane or circumstances change.

In the weeks preceding the vote, more than fifty activists worked feverishly conducting phone banks, holding meetings, and educating their fellow graduate employees about the proposed action. Their hard work paid off. Not only did they meet the quorum, but support for a strike was overwhelming. Over six hundred members cast ballots, five hundred of whom voted to strike. The activists were encouraged by the success. Joe Bandy, one of ASE's founders, characterized it as the high point of his involvement with the union: "I felt hopeful that we could illustrate to the other campuses that democracy works. No other campus had turned out such high numbers as had UCSB. I think it validated our efforts and our system."[16]

This sense of optimism was not to last. Within months, hope and enthusiasm gave way to feelings of disillusionment and betrayal. A series of events in the months leading up to the anticipated strike demonstrated to members at UCSB that they were no longer in control of their union.

THE FALL

On September 8, 1998, Mary Ann Massenburg, the UAW field representative overseeing the statewide UC campaign, called an emergency meeting of the UCSB Ad Hoc Organizing Committee. Tensions had grown in the preceding months between local activists and UAW staff involving differences in organizing style and methods. Massenburg said she summoned the activists because she was disturbed by their intentions to implement a modified version of the organizing plan that had been proposed at a coalition meeting over the summer. She began the meeting by accusing ASE activists of insulating themselves from the Coalition and its own rank-and-file members. She claimed that UCSB activists were suffering from a "dissident complex" and finished by announcing she had hired a new staff person from outside to replace the UCSB graduate employee who had been their paid organizer.[17]

Massenburg's actions blindsided activists. The charges did not make sense coming on the heels of their successful strike vote that spring and the fact that Santa Barbara's proposed modifications to "the plan" (as it would be pejoratively called) were minor—pertaining to methods of implementation.[18] The UAW plan called for organizers to arrange a single one-hour long meeting with each member to discuss the upcoming strike. They were to communicate the legal concerns related to striking, instruct graduate employees how to avoid them, and ask if they intended to strike. The UCSB modifications called for four, fifteen-minute conversations with each member over the months leading to the strike, beginning with a discussion about what it means to strike and why solidarity is crucial, and then, in subsequent contacts, discussions about the legal ramifications and their intentions to strike.[19] But most troubling to activists was Massenburg's unilateral decision to replace a trusted local leader with a recent college graduate who had no experience leading a union and was totally unfamiliar with UCSB graduate employees. It made little strategic sense to risk alienating activists who had been instrumental to building pro-union sentiment on campus. It made even less sense to do it on the eve of their most ambitious and risky action. When an activist expressed concern that this move would alienate many activists, Massenburg replied, "Too bad."[20]

In addition to the strategic concerns, this act raised a set of moral issues for activists. Massenburg's decision represented an abrupt departure from the way important decisions had been made throughout the six-year campaign. It also contradicted their assumption that local members would have control of their union. For the next few weeks, shell-shocked activists tried to make sense of what had happened and, more importantly, to figure out how to proceed with the work of organizing toward the strike. Activists soul searched as they tried to make sense of the UAW's behavior and decide what to tell members. Airing "dirty laundry" might undercut support for the strike, but not doing so would entail deceiving people who trusted them.

By October, the activists had decided to carry out their modified organizing plan. They found the new UAW staff organizer ineffectual and believed the strike would not happen without the campus activists taking a leadership role. Activists reasoned that if "they were the union" they ought to act like it, so they began organizing, aware that critical time had been lost. They established an elaborate phone-tree system to efficiently connect with each member of the union several times before the strike. As they resumed organizing, a degree of optimism was restored within the AHOC, but in a few weeks, the rug was again pulled out from under them.

On October 30, just before a scheduled AHOC meeting at the home of two lead activists, Massenburg, her lieutenant Mike Miller, and two other UAW staff members arrived early. They confiscated all union records and documents kept there.[21] Then, as the meeting began, activists were handed a letter from Massenburg in which she accused the AHOC of having "deliberately implemented a counter-organizing plan at Santa Barbara."[22] She claimed that activists refused to work with the new staffer, and by the use of the phone tree system, had implemented significant and unauthorized changes to the organizing plan approved by the UAW. The letter went on to say that if the group chose not to organize using approved methods, "they may not act, write or speak in the name of ASE/UAW, ASE or UAW, and may not use any resources, lists or other information belonging to the Union."[23]

The events of that evening, thereafter referred to as the "Halloween Massacre," had a devastating effect on activists—and the new members for whom this was their first union meeting. Several were reduced to tears. Activists were outraged. It was one thing to disagree about organizing tactics, but it was quite another to enter someone's private residence and charge the people who had built the union with "counter-organizing." Activists found it inconceivable that the UAW seemed willing to undermine all the activists had built because of a phone tree, or because they insisted on holding open membership meetings, or because they preferred to foreground the importance of solidarity during a strike rather than its legal ramifications.[24] On November 7, a week after the Halloween Massacre, delegations of activists from each of the eight campuses met in Santa Barbara to discuss strategy for the final weeks before the strike. The eighteen representatives from UCSB saw this gathering as an opportunity to tell their story and perhaps get support from other campus representatives. They were quickly disabused of that idea. Staff member Miller, who conducted the meeting, allowed only fifteen minutes for discussion of the "UCSB problem." Members wishing to speak were limited to one minute. It became clear that a story had already circulated explaining the "intransigence" of the UCSB activists. Several current and former UAW staff members again charged UCSB with counterorganizing and with jeopardizing the strike. Staffers monopolized the allotted time for discussion and then quickly moved to have the UCSB contingent barred from the remainder of the meeting.[25] The motion passed narrowly. Twenty minutes after it began, the well-orchestrated purge was complete.

Immediately following the meeting, UCSB activists spoke with representatives from other campuses. From these conversations they learned that although many of their counterparts resented them for not submitting to the UAW plan, others supported UCSB and disapproved of the way the UAW had treated local activists. Several sympathizers refused to participate in the reconvened coalition meeting held without UCSB, and at least one UAW staff member resigned in disgust.[26]

Now utterly demoralized and with the strike less than a month away, activists had one remaining reason to be hopeful that a successful strike could be pulled off. The local strike committee, composed of eleven activists from eleven different departments, had been elected to "officially call the strike and facilitate the logistics of the strike."[27] In the eyes of activists and the rank and file, this body had the final say as to whether or not UCSB would join the systemwide strike— in light of recent developments, this was no longer a foregone conclusion.

The strike committee, like the AHOC, had been told by UAW staff that it could not represent the union if it employed methods not consistent with the systemwide plan. This meant phone trees, e-mail communications, outreach to faculty, and membership meetings were prohibited. Furthermore, all documents intended for distribution were required to have Massenburg's approval. These restrictions essentially left the committee unable to perform its duties as mandated. Nevertheless, the strike committee disregarded these instructions and forged ahead in an effort to assess the level of graduate employee support for the strike. To do so, the committee relied on the results of the AHOC phone tree, which continued despite being hampered by the UAW confiscation of membership lists. They also held department-level and campuswide meetings, both to gauge the sentiment of the members and to disseminate vital information regarding the strike.

One of these campuswide meetings poignantly illustrated that rank-and-file solidarity was still strong despite the atmosphere of distrust and disillusionment. When UAW staff announced a meeting to be held at the same time and in the same building as the one previously scheduled by the strike committee, it appeared to activists that they were attempting to draw unsuspecting members away from the strike committee meeting. Despite this subterfuge, over one hundred members attended the strike committee meeting, while not a single person attended the one sponsored by the UAW.[28] During the meeting—after UAW staffers had been invited to join—several members declared they would not participate in the strike unless the local strike committee made the call. Others asked the UAW to recognize the authority of the strike committee. The room filled with moans of disgust when UAW staff refused.

The events of that evening contradict UAW claims that the Santa Barbara union had been taken over by a tiny faction of counter organizers. What the staff and members witnessed that night suggested something more dynamic was going on within the union at UCSB than a "dissident complex." That at such an historic juncture of the campaign to have over one hundred members came out in support of the local elected officers, while none identified with the UAW, suggests that the graduate employees knew that they were the union.

A week later, the strike committee officially called the strike. They knew the union was in rough shape because activist energy had been focused on the disputes with the UAW rather than on organizing. Nevertheless, members still wanted to win recognition, and this strike was seen as the best way to achieve it. The committee's decision ultimately reflected its desire to stand in solidarity with the members at the other seven campuses.[29] They reasoned that if UCSB did not walk out, it might weaken the impact of the strike elsewhere in the system.

The strike began during the last week of the academic quarter, on December 1, 1998. Despite all that had taken place, an estimated two hundred members walked off their jobs. Graduate employees formed lively picket lines at each entrance to campus, and for days, picketers received supportive honks from the stream of cars leaving and entering campus. The strong support from the campus community—especially from undergraduates who were most directly affected by the strike—buoyed the spirits of striking graduate employees. Meanwhile, legislative leaders were trying to broker a deal between the UAW and the UC for a cooling off period to suspend the strike. The USCB strikers were unaware that talks were taking place and were surprised when on the evening before the seventh day of the walkout they learned, while watching the eleven o'clock news, that the strike had been called off.

FALLING OUT

Over the next several months, union activists tried to make sense of their recent experiences and to find ways to rekindle their enthusiasm for building the union. At the beginning of January 1999, Massenburg met with UCSB members in an attempt to smooth over relations. Her tone was matter-of-fact. She began by diagramming the organizational hierarchy of the UAW, pointing out the official relationships between the international executive board, local unions, officers, staff, and the rank-and-file membership. She also informed them of the rights and responsibilities each of these groups had under the UAW constitution. As for the position of the graduate employees organizing at UCSB, Massenburg stated that because they were not yet recognized, they, in fact, were not actually members of the UAW and therefore were not entitled to the democratic rights outlined in its constitution. She suggested that this misunderstanding helped explain the problems occurring in Santa Barbara. Her analysis of the situation was that the protracted battle with the UC led local graduate employees to mistakenly assume they were full members. Massenburg expressed regret that she had not made their status more clear earlier.[30]

For the activists, that meeting was a watershed. For years, they had persuaded their friends and colleagues to join the union, to sign union cards "declaring themselves members of the ASE/UAW." They mobilized their fellow students for union elections, took to heart the assurances about "being the union," sacrificed incredible amounts of time and energy, and even risked their jobs by going on strike. After that, to hear that their own international union did not "recognize" them was too ironic, too devastating to bear. Several longtime activists resigned from the UAW, saying they could no longer reconcile their belief in democratic unionism with the UAW's actions. Although these sentiments were shared by all who had been involved, activists were divided over how to proceed. Some AHOC members wanted to break from the UAW and form an independent union, while others thought it better to stick with UAW and seek to reform it from within. Unlike earlier disagreements within the local, this one did not lend itself to compromise, let alone consensus. For the first time in the union's history, factions formed. The activists, who had derived their strength and resolve from the unity within the organizing committee, were now divided. The union was crumbling.

Activists of the AHOC, who had been the glue holding the union together, began to disassociate from the project to which they had been so committed. For these activists, it required increasingly difficult contortions of logic to reconcile the experiences of the last year with their vision of a democratic union, let alone convince others to support the UAW.

In spring 1999, PERB ruled in favor of UC graduate employees and ordered certification elections to be held at each of the campuses. Santa Barbara's turn came in June during the final days of the spring quarter. Activists had worked for years to arrive at this point, but now that they were on the brink, the mood was cynical and ambivalent. None of the remaining activists on campus were willing to publicly support the UAW or mobilize toward getting out the vote. Because most graduate employees still looked to the AHOC for leadership, they held a few meetings in which sullen graduate employees discussed how they should vote. The most visible union activity leading up to the vote were efforts of some former ASE/UAW activists who had formed a rival independent union called United Student Labor (USL). They promoted USL as a locally controlled, democratic alternative to the UAW and encouraged graduate employees to vote against the UAW by voting no in the election.

These were pro-union people—who had worked for years for the right to have this election—conflicted over whether or not to vote in favor of union representation. Many viewed it as an unsavory catch-22: vote "yes" and endorse the UAW, which had proven itself to be manipulative and undemocratic; or vote "no" and support the UC administration that had denied graduate employee rights for years.

Some of the few remaining ASE/UAW activists, who still hoped the union election could be salvaged, made a last-ditch effort to engineer a truce. They requested that Massenburg make an overture to the members that would give them some indication to believe that once officially within the UAW fold, relations would improve. Characterizing the requests as attempts to blackmail the UAW for their votes, Massenburg's staff refused.[31] After weeks of agonizing over their decision, one group of members grudgingly decided to vote for the UAW while another decided to vote no. About fifty graduate employees of both persuasions withheld their votes until the last day of voting and went to the polls together in a defiant act of solidarity. It had been exactly one year since the strike authorization vote had taken place in which five hundred graduate employees declared their willingness to walk off their jobs to gain union recognition. Now that they were in a position to achieve that goal by simply casting a ballot, fewer than two hundred felt strongly enough to walk to the polls and vote yes. The UAW prevailed: 184–135.

BIRTH OF A BUSINESS UNION

In many ways, the events after the certification election represent the final touches of a process in which the original vision that propelled the UCSB union was undermined and replaced by one nearly antithetical to it. The ironic outcome is symbolized by the ratification of a contract in the name of workers who, as far as they were concerned, were no longer a union.

A week before the results of the certification election were to be announced, UAW staff called a meeting to elect a bargaining team for the Santa Barbara campus. They did so over the objections of activists who felt that after all they had gone through, the local union needed time to regroup, heal the divisions, and restore trust in the UAW. Activists were forced to hastily mobilize in self-defense, knowing if they did not elect a bargaining team, the UAW would appoint one. Members elected eight veteran UCSB activists—essentially the only ones still willing to work with the UAW—to serve as the campus' bargaining team.

Each UC campus represented a separate bargaining unit, for which eight separate contracts would be negotiated. This fact offered some hope to the UCSB team that they would have the ability to negotiate a contract that reflected the interests of local graduate employees. Almost immediately however, the UAW began moving to centralize bargaining for the whole system. Although doing so made sense, as there were many issues that affected all campuses, it represented a loss of control of the process for individual bargaining units. Despite the repeated objections raised by UCSB, the UAW and other campus teams began acting as if the plan had been ratified. Sensing a repeat of the events of the previous fall, the Santa Barbara team balked. At a heated meeting in September 1999, they demanded the time necessary to gauge membership support for the systemwide bargaining plan before agreeing to it.

UAW staff and the other coalition teams eventually assured UCSB that any issue without unanimous agreement among all eight bargaining units would be negotiated separately at each campus. Referring to a document that specified the terms of the systemwide arrangement, Massenburg confirmed that any disputed issues would be negotiated separately by the campus units. This seemed like a workable compromise and the UCSB team agreed. For three weeks, this arrangement worked wonderfully, until a dispute arose between UCSB and the coalition over the issue of the right to strike: While the other campuses were content to follow the common union practice of giving up the right to strike in exchange for grievance and arbitration, Santa Barbara was reluctant to do so.[32] Several factors motivated the UCSB position. First, they believed that the source of union power rests on the ability of workers to withhold labor. The prospect of giving up their only leverage was unattractive enough, but to do it so early in the negotiations seemed especially unwise. Second, Massenburg had previously warned them about the UC's history of securing rigid no-strike clauses in its contracts that they used to prevent workers from participating in campus protests that were unrelated to their status as employees.[33] UCSB wanted to avoid that scenario. As their agreement with the coalition stipulated, UCSB had already started negotiating the strikes issue locally. Then, without warning, Massenburg announced that the union would give up the right to strike systemwide as a gesture of good-faith bargaining. She instructed the Santa Barbara team to change its position to conform to the coalition. When UCSB steadfastly refused to give up the union's most valuable bargaining chip as a "gesture," they were told that the coalition would proceed as if it had. The entire UCSB bargaining team resigned in protest. The resignation of the bargaining team and their subsequent withdrawal from union activism left a complete void on campus. No one remained who was willing to participate in the UAW project.

After October 1999, negotiations proceeded without elected representation for members at UCSB. The process became increasingly centralized with the statewide bargaining team hammering out the majority of issues affecting the individual campuses. In the winter, the UAW and UC negotiators reached an impasse after each side accused the other of bad-faith bargaining. The UAW called for a strike vote. For UCSB members and former activists, it seemed as if the chickens had come home to roost. After being denied a voice in the union at nearly every turn, they were being asked to walk off the job. There was little chance that UCSB members would walk the line for a contract being negotiated without them. Even worse, the strike authorization vote that took place in March 2000 was tainted by suspicions that the UAW had fixed the vote. A local team of election monitors, composed of twenty-three volunteers from the Graduate Student Association, United Student Labor, and members of the UAW, observed 185 people casting ballots in the two days of polling. The UAW, however, announced that 278 members had voted—204 in favor and 74 against authorizing a strike. This discrepancy added to the growing mistrust of the UAW, leading many members of the UCSB local to publicly question the legitimacy of the election and to refuse to honor its validity.[34] In April, when the UAW called a one-day strike, only two people walked the picket line at Santa Barbara.[35]

In May, the union and the UC reached a tentative contract agreement. UAW representatives hailed the settlement as a success and urged members to ratify it, but many at UCSB were unconvinced. Although it provided for phased-in tuition waivers, improvements in job posting and notification, and binding grievance and arbitration, it fell short in other areas: no improvement in health benefits, the most prohibitive no-strike clause the UC had signed with any of its unions, and a pay increase that was largely a chimera. The UAW had secured a 1.5 percent immediate wage increase. But the UAW also claimed to have "won" an additional 2 percent for each of the next three years, although the state legislature had already mandated that increase. In fact, the state had been giving graduate workers the annual raise for years. That the 1.5 percent increase would just cover the 1.15 percent in dues members would now pay was not lost on the graduate employees. Essentially, the contract codified existing arrangements—which in some ways was a victory—but maintaining the status quo was not what had inspired unionists at UCSB. In a vote that local members were neither allowed to conduct nor witness, the contract was ratified 146–97.

Over the following summer, the UAW announced its decision to combine all eight UC campuses into one large statewide local headquartered in Berkeley, now called UAW Local 2865. This arrangement is geographically vast, extending over five hundred miles from end to end, and numerically massive, covering more than nine thousand graduate employees. Although locals of this size and scope have become common in the United States, such arrangements inhibit rank-and-file participation. As an activist from the history department wryly observed, "I have to drive three hundred miles to attend a membership meeting."[36] By October 2000, as students were returning to campus, by-laws had been drafted and presented for ratification. Across all eight campuses, only 238 members participated in the systemwide vote to ratify this defining set of governing policies.[37] A few weeks later, a slate of union officers were "elected" by acclamation. Of the eleven local offices, not a single race was contested.

Concurrent with these developments, a new California law (SB645) established "agency shop" for all public employees in higher education. The law, which took effect in 2000, requires all employees covered by a collective bargaining agreement to pay fair share fees regardless of union member status. For most UC graduate employees who are not union members, that translates to approximately thirteen dollars a month, compared to full membership dues of eighteen dollars. Such laws are common and are welcomed by organized labor as a way to more equitably distribute the costs of negotiating and enforcing contracts. There are, however, some undesirable consequences. Fair share policies—by essentially guaranteeing a revenue stream—tend to reduce the incentive for unions to organize workers and also minimize the need for union leaders to be responsive to demands from members. This "labor-friendly" legislation, when combined with a remote and centralized organizational structure, may actually undermine union strength by contributing to rank-and-file apathy and reducing the membership base. By winter 2001, with this legislation and the governing apparatus of Local 2865 in place, the number of card-carrying union members at UCSB was fifty-three. A business union had been born.

LINGERING QUESTIONS

It is important here to ask this question: Where were graduate employee allies and comrades on other campuses when UCSB graduate activists were floundering? Although a definitive answer is beyond the scope of this chapter, I can provide some thoughts, based interviews with UCSB activists and five interviews with activists from other campuses. First, it is difficult to prove whether or not rank-and-file graduate employees at other campuses were supportive of the UCSB approach. In truth, it is likely that most of them had no knowledge of it or the ensuing conflicts. What we do know is that with a few exceptions, the graduate employees in leadership and staff positions from other campuses in the 1998–2000 period tended to support the UAW program and consistently joined them in opposing UCSB initiatives. Two of the most likely contributing factors were organizational dynamics and fundamental differences among graduate employees over the mission, goals, and methods of the union.

Organizations tend to promote and reward those who uphold institutionally dominant views while they discourage and discredit those who dissent, and the UAW is likely no exception. One UCSB activist, who was actively recruited by the UAW in an effort to usurp the AHOC as the local's leadership, described being "seduced" by the power he had been given and by the affirmation he received from staff and coalition members.[38] Additionally, the organizational structure of the eight-campus coalition required considerable commitments of time and energy, and extensive travel. If activists dissented or felt uncomfortable, chances are they would leave the union and return to their academic work rather than stay on when their presence and views were not appreciated. This process leaves only like-minded activists to chart strategy. Additionally, the centralized decision-making structure inhibited direct communication between members at different campuses. Most communication between campuses was mediated through the UAW in some way, so, for example, when conflicts between UCSB and the UAW erupted, the other campuses learned about it from the UAW, rather than from one another.[39] UCSB activists eventually recognized this structural dynamic and realized the need to reach out directly to members at other campuses, but by that time the dye had been cast.

It is also fair to ask if UCSB was exceptional in its opposition to the UAW tactics. Again, because activists on different campuses were largely isolated from one another, we don't know. Some interviewees familiar with the drives at other campuses did mention that, in the course of the seventeen-year campaign, activists at Berkeley, Davis, Santa Cruz, and Riverside fought with the UAW at one time or another over a variety of issues—including union democracy and organizing tactics. Each time those disputes became critical, the local campus leadership was forced to submit to the UAW or were replaced by more amicable activists.[40]

ANALYSIS: STRUGGLE FOR LABOR'S IDENITY

Decades of union decline have led to increasingly widespread recognition that something needs to be done to bring labor back to life, but there is intense disagreement within organized labor over precisely what corrective action to take (Nissen 1999). The events at UCSB can be understood ultimately as part of this larger struggle over the identity of the labor movement. It is a microcosm of the battle between two distinct visions for the future of labor. One orientation—business unionism—has been the dominant model of the U.S. labor movement for more than fifty years. Social movement unionism, on the other hand, draws its inspiration from the pre-World War II labor movement and seeks to incorporate many of its qualities into the labor movement of the twenty-first century.

From a business unionism perspective, the goal of organized labor is to work within existing political and economic institutions to improve working conditions and the standard of living for union members. The preferred method of achieving these goals is collective bargaining. Proponents of business unionism view securing a contract as the best way to guarantee members a voice in working conditions and a larger slice of the economic pie. For business unionists, a contract is both a goal in itself and also part of a larger strategy of establishing a baseline from which future gains can be won. In order for the collective bargaining system to function for unions, the state must oversee and enforce the laws governing the process. Therefore, one of labor's principal political interests is ensuring the collective bargaining apparatus is preserved and administered fairly. Political activity of unions is typically confined to the existing two-party system—with its support traditionally going to the Democrats—by way of endorsements, campaign contributions, members' volunteering, and lobbying for legislation favorable to unions. Business unions are characterized by centralized and hierarchical governing structures, and they rely heavily on paid professional staff to negotiate and enforce contracts, handle grievances, and conduct the day-to day-business of the union.

Proponents of social movement unionism place much of the responsibility for labor's current anemic condition on the business union model (Brecher and Costello 1999; Eisenscher 1999). They argue that organized labor's bureaucratic structure and its fixation on the narrow goals of collective bargaining, as well as its political timidity, have rendered the movement defenseless against corporate assaults on labor and have done nothing to stem the tide of membership decline. Critics argue that the business union model has fostered a dependence on professional staff, which hinders meaningful member participation and in turn contributes to workers viewing unions as little more than insurance policies—paying dues in exchange for "benefits." Finally, business unions are criticized for failing to organize new workers. Critics assert that for decades (business) unions' narrow focus on servicing existing members has contributed to the decline in union density.

As the label implies, social movement unionism seeks to reinject unions with the qualities of a social movement that once made them a powerful voice for progressive social change. The key to salvaging the labor movement is to expand its narrow focus on workplace goals and to address issues of social justice concerning the wider community. By linking the labor movement to struggles against discrimination and environmental degradation, for instance, labor can regain its relevance as a vehicle for social change. Social movement unionism requires a dramatic increase in active participation among rank-and-file members. Eschewing the rigid top-down orientation of business unions, social movement unionists seek instead to empower workers via decentralized structures that promote grass-roots activism and participatory democracy (Eisenscher 1999).

Although dividing the labor movement into business unions and social movement unions might seem simplistic, it does offer a way for us to understand the events at UCSB. The UAW executed the strategy with which it was most familiar. From their perspective, there is no union without a contract, thus, securing the contract is paramount, and all other concerns are secondary. With this in mind, it is easier to see why any opposition to a speedy acquisition of a contract might have been viewed as evidence of antiunion sabotage. Furthermore, the success of the UAW's campaign rested on waging effective battles in the courts and in the state legislature; therefore, any signs of militant or spontaneous action emanating from the rank and file that might jeopardize this strategy might have been of genuine concern to union staff.

Over the seventeen-year struggle, the UAW invested a tremendous amount of resources fighting the court battle, lobbying the state legislature, and installing staff organizers at several campuses. From their point of view, activists at Santa Barbara who demanded to have control over the union must have seemed ungrateful. During critical moments in the organizing drive and contract negotiations, UCSB activists may have struck their more seasoned counterparts as naïve, overly idealistic, or dangerously ignorant. But the overarching goal of securing a contract meant that time to discuss larger issues of union values and methods was sacrificed.

Differences in the concepts of union democracy also came into play. Stanley Aronowitz describes two models of union democracy: "democracy by consent, where the rank and file has formal, but little substantive, power over union affairs" and what he calls "strong or participatory democracy" (1999). The UAW is firmly committed to democracy—of the first type. They hold elections and allow members to ratify contracts. But the other type of union democracy—which inspired the UCSB members—demands that workers get to establish union priorities, make decisions, and determine the contents of the contract. We can see how these two distinct definitions of democracy might have led to frustrated UAW staff and workers alike. When UCSB activists demanded union democracy, UAW staff could respond "you have a democratic union." A bargaining team member from Berkeley, in trying to convince me that Santa Barbara did not need to seek direction from its members, told me, "That's what democracy is. We convince the members that our ideas are right."[41] Clearly, there were fundamental differences about the meaning of union democracy.

Despite the pain and anger expressed by many of the UCSB activists toward the UAW, there is little reason to assume that they acted with malicious intent. As loyal union staff members, they had a defined set of goals, a toolbox of trusted methods, and were no doubt armed with the confidence that they were fighting the good fight. And they probably believed the UCSB activists were taking the campaign in directions that were dangerously far afield.

Those who embrace, or are at least sympathetic to, the business union model of the labor movement are likely to view the UC campaign as a significant victory. After all, a contract has been secured, an additional nine thousand workers can be counted among union ranks, a revenue stream has been established (strengthening financial health of the organization), and the visibility of the campaign will likely increase the UAW's credibility as a legitimate union for academic workers. It is not surprising that from UAW vice president Elizabeth Bunn's perspective, it is indeed "an inspiration."[42]

But it should also be clear, despite Bunn's enthusiasm, why those who advocate a social movement approach to unionism do not share her sentiment. The graduate employees at UCSB had different expectations for their union. They cultivated a pro-union culture, characterized by widespread participation, a sense of empowerment, and pride in ownership, but instead they got a local distinguished by apathy, cynicism, and distrust of organized labor. The collective power they struggled to achieve was usurped by a bureaucratic organization intent on exercising power for them. As Corina Kellner, a long-time activist from the anthropology department, put it: "We've traded one paternalism for another."[43]

CHALLENGES FOR LABOR

In order to rebuild itself, the labor movement will need to innovate. Movement organizations unwilling or unable to learn adaptive strategies are prone to decline (Klandermans 1997; Schwartz 1976). Innovation requires a willingness to learn new approaches—even whole new orientations—to building and running unions. Yet despite AFL-CIO president John Sweeney's vision of the perfect labor movement being "one which consistently re-examines itself and corrects its own imperfections" (Sweeney 1998, 329), accomplishing change is not easy. In any large institution, efforts to implement change are almost always met with resistance (Blau 1983). Organized labor is no exception. Its failure to change can be attributed to three related dynamics: institutional inertia, the formation of a siege mentality, and the development of union staff as experts.

As union membership declines and the labor movement is under increasing attack from many sides, it is understandable that a sort of siege mentality might form within its organizations (Markowitz 2000; Sherman and Voss 2000). But that mentality makes unions reluctant to accept criticism and to treat challenges from members as disloyalty. These responses inhibit the ability of unions to adapt to changing circumstances. Furthermore, spending time and energy on new strategies are seen by many experienced labor organizers as luxuries unions cannot afford when they so desperately need immediate victories (Markowitz 2000; Sciacchitano 2000).

This organizational mentality is buttressed by the increasing professionalization of union staff. As organized labor has come to rely on grievance and arbitration, sophisticated contractual language, and labor law to exercise power, the skills and technical knowledge required to function in this arena become necessities. This leads to the view of union staff as "experts," reinforcing workers' attitudes that they should leave union decisions to the professionals. In turn, when union staff embrace this identity, they are more likely to dismiss proposed strategies and ideas from the rank and file as naïve or impractical. Together, these dynamics contribute to a type of institutional inertia that makes existing movement goals and approaches to organizing sacrosanct.

At Santa Barbara, the UAW had an opportunity to learn from graduate employees' experimentation. Students created a new union that achieved wide support. They were democratic and successful. But time and again the UAW seemed threatened by these innovations, choosing to discredit them as signs of disloyalty rather than to learn from them. Years later, the behavior of UAW staff suggests they have little interest in learning from their experience at Santa Barbara: When organizers come to UCSB, they address members' concerns about this sordid history by disparaging former activists.[44] In the sparsely attended union meetings, staff refuse to acknowledge how the UAW legacy on campus may be hampering current efforts to organize graduate employees.

The UCSB story reminds us that building unions is an inherently personal endeavor. Labor advocates frequently lament that it too often takes incredible acts of courage for people to join unions. Not only must workers overcome the negative perceptions of unions that pervade our culture, but they must also begin to think of themselves less as independent actors and more as part of a collective—no small feat in a society that celebrates individualism. For workers not already disposed to unionization, overcoming these psychological barriers involves undergoing a fundamental shift in identity. This shift is especially dramatic for white collar and professional workers—including academics—who must also overcome assumptions that unions are not meant for people like themselves.

Much of union organizing involves encouraging and facilitating these shifts in identity. Establishing trust is crucial to this process. Workers essentially take a leap of faith when joining unions and are more likely to do so if they know and trust the people asking them to jump (Klandermans 1997). Trust takes a long time to develop, which is one reason why coworkers and workplace activists prove to be the most effective organizers (Bronfenbrenner and Juravich 1998). They are able to draw on their existing relationships with fellow workers and are more likely to be seen as credible sources of information about the union. But trust operates in two directions. When workers agree to accept the risks that come with organizing, they expect the union to live up to the vision it promotes.

For years, the UAW assured UCSB activists that the union would operate democratically and be run by the members, telling them repeatedly "the members are the union." UAW staff reinforced this claim every time they insisted that activists adhere to the union's constitution, held elections, and endorsed campaign literature espousing the union's commitment to democracy. Graduate employees demonstrated how deeply they believed these promises with each of the countless hours they volunteered for the cause. As it became clear that UAW directives would usurp democracy and member control, activists felt deceived.

The experience with the UAW had an even more invidious dimension for activists. In addition to feeling manipulated by the UAW, they had unwittingly

misled their friends and colleagues who had trusted them. The comments of
Samara Paysse, a graduate activist from the English department, are illustrative:

> I had a feeling of, gosh, what have we done to these people ... who trusted us all these
> years, telling them, ... "You may have problems with the UAW, or ... you may have prob-
> lems with big labor, but we can do whatever we want, we'll have a say in the contract,
> we'll have autonomy," you know, promising them that, and then just watching that evap-
> orate was a real feeling like, "Oh my god, we've betrayed these people."[45]

If organized labor carelessly exploits this emotional commitment in the pursuit of short-term gains, the long-term effects on the movement may be difficult to overcome. At UCSB, among those I interviewed, none remain active in
the union. One former activist commented, "I don't have the stomach for it ...
I don't organize anymore because I don't believe in it."[46] These sentiments were
shared by many others. Although remarkably (and to their credit) nearly all
remain "pro-union" in principle, their support of organized labor has been tem-
pered. It is significant that among the activists who voted in the 1999 certification election making the UAW the recognized bargaining agent, only half voted
yes. Among them, all said they would vote no if the election were held today.

CONCLUSION

The struggle over the direction of the labor movement is not new. Tensions
between the interests of union organizations and the desires of local members
are a well-documented feature of the U.S. labor movement (Aronowitz 1973;
Moody 1988; Rachleff 1993). In the UC systemwide campaign, similar conflicts
between the UAW and graduate employee organizers took place at various times
during the campaigns at Berkeley, Davis, Santa Cruz, and Riverside. Furthermore, the graduate employee union at University of Massachusetts, Amherst,
was recently placed in administratorship by the UAW over related issues. These
examples are not to suggest that such problems are unique features of the UAW
and its academic unions. Rather, these are recurring patterns throughout organized labor. In our efforts to reshape labor's identity and mission, we would be
remiss to ignore the ways our traditional modes of operation perpetuate the
problems that hinder renewal.

Organizing academic workers must be seen as more than an opportunity for
unions simply to add members to their existing organizations. Graduate employee organizing represents a tremendous opportunity for unions to experiment with—and learn—new approaches to building unions. As newcomers to
organized labor, graduate employees are unencumbered by its traditional and
ineffective practices. If the labor movement embraces their enthusiasm, cre-
ativity, and idealism, the unions they build can become examples of labor at its
best. Winning recognition and contracts are tremendous achievements insofar
as they are not gained at the cost of workers' pro-union commitment. Such

Pyrrhic victories will not be enough to preserve the vestiges of the labor movement, much less contribute to its rejuvenation. The question remains: Will labor be satisfied with hollow successes, or will it support and encourage organizing efforts that seek to produce strong, vibrant, and democratic unions that have the potential to transform not only the lives of workers, but society as well? The answer, as always, is in our hands.

NOTES

I wish to thank Judith Taylor, Richard Flacks, Nelson Lichtenstein and Christopher Kollmeyer for their thoughtful feedback and encouragement on earlier drafts of this chapter. I am especially grateful to all the former activists I interviewed who gave so generously of their time and emotion. Finally, to all the people who over the years contributed their integrity and passion to the project of building a democratic union at UCSB, I dedicate this piece.

1. David Montgomery, e-mail communication to Deborah Herman and Julie Schmid, August 3, 2001.

2. See Paul Johnston's discussion of "observer as chastened participant" (1994, 48–54).

3. In this paper, the UC system refers to the eight undergraduate campuses: Berkeley, Davis, Irvine, Los Angeles, Riverside, San Diego, Santa Barbara, and Santa Cruz. There are actually nine campuses in the system. The San Francisco campus, however, is primarily a graduate and professional school with fewer than one hundred undergraduates and was not included in the unionization drive. A tenth campus is scheduled to open at Merced in 2004.

4. University of California Office of the President web site <http://www.ucop.edu/ucophome/commserv/profile/>.

5. University of California Office of the President figures for fall 1999, <http://www.ucop.edu>.

6. *ASE/UAW Union News*, "Why vote to strike?" Spring 1998, p. 5.

7. Special Issue of *ASE News*, Fall 1996; Ralph Armbruster-Sandoval, interview with author, March 29, 2001; *ASE/UAW Union News*, "Majority at Irvine," Spring 1998, p. 6.

8. *ASE/UAW News*, "CAUSE convention recommends strikes in fall," June 1996, pp. 3–5.

9. ASE/UAW web site archived at <http://www.angelfire.com/ca4/usl/MainFrames.htm>.

10. Glyn Hughes, interview with author, March 7, 2001.

11. ASE/UAW strategy primer, 1997–98, p. 1.

12. Joe Bandy, interview with author, April 28, 2000.

13. Laura Holliday, interview with author, February 28, 2001.

14. Seth Rosenberg, interview with author, April 30, 2000.

15. The UAW constitution does not stipulate a quorum requirement for such votes, requiring only a two-thirds majority of votes cast. Indeed, in previous strike votes on other UC campuses, the vote was often held during a meeting with only those in attendance determining the outcome. The low turnouts produced by this method motivated UCSB to institute a more rigorous standard.

16. Bandy, interview.

17. Author's meeting notes, September 8, 1998.

18. Samara Paysse, interview with author, February 27, 2001.

19. The differences in the two proposals were minor in terms of content, but significant in terms of logic of implementation. Based on their years of experience organizing on campus, UCSB activists felt it impractical to try to arrange a one-hour face-to-face meeting with each graduate student. Secondly, the UAW plan meant that each member would be contacted by an organizer once. AHOC felt a better strategy was to increase the number of contacts and to keep each discussion brief. Furthermore, the idea of focusing an hour-long meeting on legal ramifications would do little to inspire graduate employees to participate in the strike. Such a discussion was better to have as the action approached and workers were committed to the strike.

20. Author's meeting notes, September 8, 1998.

21. Sara Mason, interview with author, March 9, 2001.

22. Letter dated October 30, 1998, to ASE/UAW activists at Santa Barbara from Mary Ann Massenburg, UAW international representative.

23. Ibid.

24. Samara Paysse had this reaction: "The [UAW] just did everything … they could, like breaking in and confiscating all our organizing materials, databases, things like that … actively sabotaging all our organizing here. Again, it was just shocking that they would go to those lengths. It was almost like the FBI … response to Left groups in the '60s, active sabotage, active disruption, trying to discredit, personally discredit organizers here and activists here." Paysse interview, February 27, 2001.

25. Rani Bush, interview with author, March 7, 2001.

26. Michael Bourgeois, interview with author, April 12, 2001; Author's notes, November 8, 1998.

27. ASE/UAW strike authorization vote ballot instructions, 1998.

28. Bush interview; Corina Kellner, interview with author, February 13, 2001; Paysse interview.

29. ASE/UAW Strike Committee announcement to members, November 18, 1998.

30. Author's meeting notes, January 7, 1999.

31. Author's notes of conversation with UAW staff representative Mercedes Ibarra, June 7, 1999; Bourgeois interview.

32. A "no strikes/no lockouts" clause is contract language that states that no represented employee will strike or engage in work stoppages during the term of the contract and that the employer will not engage in lockouts during the term of the contract.

33. Author's notes, October 3, 1999.

34. *Santa Barbara News-Press, March 15, 2000,* "Legitimacy of strike vote at UCSB questioned," by Scott Hadly, pp. B1, B3; KEYT Television Evening News, March 14, 2000; Open letter and petition from ASE/UAW activists to campus community, March 16, 2000. After an investigation by the UCSB Graduate Student Association General Council into the complaints, they issued a policy statement condemning the UAW's recent election practices for "fail[ing] to meet basic standards of legitimacy and [being] potentially fraudulent" (full text at <http://www.gsa.ucsb.edu>). Several ASE/UAW activists sought redress from the international's headquarters in Detroit. For two months, their requests went unanswered until—the day after the contract was ratified—they received a letter from the office of UAW president Stephen Yokich informing them that since they were not officially members they could not "process an election protest from this office" (letter dated May 17, 2000).

35. *Santa Barbara News-Press*, April 19, 2000, "2 students heed call for strike at UCSB," by Scott Hadley, pp. B1, B8.
36. Mark Hendrickson, interview with author, March 19, 2001.
37. Local 2865 Election Committee, October 28, 2000.
38. Bourgeois interview
39. Hughes interview.
40. Ralph Armbruster, interview with author, March 29, 2001; Bandy, interview; Hughes, interview; Nathan Newman, interview with author, March 8, 2001.
41. Author's notes, September 19, 1999.
42. *The Chronicle of Higher Education*, July 2, 1999, p. A12.
43. Kellner, interview.
44. Erik Noonburg, interview with author, March 25, 2001.
45. Paysse, interview.
46. Kellner, interview.

REFERENCES

Aronowitz, S. 1973. *False promises: The shaping of American working class consciousness*. New York: McGraw-Hill.
———. 1999. Unions and democracy: A reply to Steve Fraser. *Dissent* 46: 81–84.
Blau, P. 1983. *On the nature of organization*. Malabar, FL: Krieger Publishing.
Brecher, J., and T. Costello. 1999. A new labor movement in the shell of the old? In *The transformation of U.S. unions: Voices, visions and strategies from the grass roots*, ed. R.M. Tillman and M.S. Cummings, 9–26. Boulder, CO: Lynne Rienner.
Bronfenbrenner, K., and T. Juravich. 1998. It takes more than housecalls: Organizing to win with a comprehensive union-building strategy. In *Organizing to win: New research on union strategies*, ed. K. Bronfenbrenner, S. Friedman, R.W. Hurd, R.A. Oswald, and R.L. Seeber, 19–36. Ithaca, NY: Cornell University Press.
Eisenscher, M. 1999. Critical juncture: Unionism at the crossroads. In *Which direction for organized labor? Essays on organizing, outreach, and internal transformations*, ed. B. Nissen, 217–245. Detroit, MI: Wayne State University Press.
Hoerr, J. P. 1997. *We can't eat prestige: The women who organized Harvard*. Philadelphia, PA: Temple University Press.
Johnston, P. 1994. *Success while others fail: Social movement unionism and the public workplace*. Ithaca, NY: ILR Press.
Klandermans, B. 1997. *The social psychology of protest*. Cambridge, MA: Blackwell Publishers.
Mantsios, G., ed. 1998. *A new labor movement for the new century*. New York: Monthly Review Press.
Markowitz, L.J. 2000. *Worker activism after successful union organizing*. Armonk, NY: M.E. Sharp.
Moody, K. 1988. *An injury to all: The decline of American unionism*. New York: Verso.
Nissen, B., ed. 1999. *Which direction for organized labor? Essays on organizing, outreach, and internal transformations*. Detroit, MI: Wayne State University Press.
Rachleff, P. 1993. *Hard-pressed in the heartland: The Hormel strike and the future of the labor movement*. Boston: South End Press.

Schwartz, M. 1976. *Radical protest and social structure: The Southern Farmers' Alliance and cotton tenancy, 1880–1890.* New York: Academic Press.

Sciacchitano, K. 2000. Unions, organizing, and democracy. *Dissent* (Spring): 75–81.

Sherman, R., and K. Voss. 2000. "Organize or Die": Labor's new tactics and immigrant workers. In *Organizing immigrants: The challenge for unions in contemporary California,* ed. R. Milkman, 81–108. Ithaca, NY: Cornell University Press.

Sweeney, J.J. 1998. Afterword. In *A new labor movement for the new century,* ed. G. Mantsios, 329–335. New York: Monthly Review Press.

Tillman, R.M., and M.S. Cummings, eds. 1999. *The transformation of U.S. unions: Voices, visions, and strategies from the grassroots.* Boulder, CO: Lynne Rienner Publishers.

Chapter 6

Unfinished Chapters: Institutional Alliances and Changing Identities in a Graduate Employee Union

James Thompson

This chapter critically evaluates the recent history of Graduate Assistants United (GAU), the collective bargaining agent for twenty-nine hundred graduate employees at the University of Florida (UF) in Gainesville. Whether union members or not, graduate employees at UF are part of the GAU "bargaining unit"— meaning they are covered by our contract with the Florida Board of Regents (BOR). As part-time researchers and teachers on short-term contracts, whose obligations include their own academic work, they function as both employees of the university and, more nebulously, as "students" and "apprentices" serving under faculty supervisors. Given that our unit operates in a southern "right-to-work" or "open-shop" state[1], UF-GAU has encountered almost the entire range of obstacles to unionism: legal constraints on organizing and bargaining, diminishing monetary resources, and, of course, challenges from within the culture of the academy and its organized labor. During recent years of rebuilding our union, GAU has also encountered roadblocks common to young academic unions and the newly organizing service sectors. Yet the peculiarities of our institutional context within Florida's open shop and alongside our parent union combines with our troubled co-identification as students, apprentices, professionals, and workers to make UF-GAU an interesting case for comparison with any union.

The peculiarities and structural features of our organizing environment are reflected in the institutional practices of GAU, its parent union, and its adversaries. It is my contention that these institutional practices operate alongside changing identities within the graduate employee sector at UF and that neither can be understood without the other. It is one thing to convince graduate "students," who obviously do much of the basic teaching and research at UF, to identify as workers, perhaps even to join a union. It is quite another matter to convince them to do so when the prospects for reform are diminished considerably by structural features that are unlikely to change in the near future. GAU organizers often ask why we have succeeded or failed at convincing workers from diverse political and social backgrounds—Republicans, feminists, Marxists, leftists, scientists, and international students, to name a few—to make these moves toward identifying with organized labor. In the case of UF-GAU, I conclude that this transformation of identity, a prerequisite to active union membership, is troubled both by Florida's open shop environment and by our unit's status as an *organizing* union in the *service* or *business* union context of our parent union.[2]

This chapter develops these themes of identity formation by addressing structural features of the UF-GAU union context. Moving from general to specific phenomena, I first examine the "Florida context" of our organizing efforts. I then analyze the more specific constraints of our parent union, especially the manifestations of discord between organizing and service unionism in higher education. Finally, I explore how these features resonate with the internal and individualized identification of many graduate employees as mere "students" or "apprentices" in the academy.

UF-GAU AND THE FLORIDA CONTEXT

Florida organizers face difficulties familiar to contingent and academic laborers in various regions and sectors across the nation. To begin, graduate employees at the University of Florida earn an average annual salary of about $9,000 in a town where the Chamber of Commerce has pegged the cost of subsistence at $14,400.[3] With these wages, even the minimal 1 percent dues are a drain on personal and family resources. The transient status of our coworkers is a problem as well; most graduate employees do not reside in Florida more than the two to seven years it takes to earn an advanced degree. Graduate assistants who join our union often leave before honing their activist skills, or even before feeling comfortable enough in their new home to set some room aside in family and personal budgets for dues deductions. Furthermore, many graduate assistants are involved in time-consuming unremunerated labor—which they feel is essential to their professional development—such as performing psychological counseling for undergraduate students on behalf of the university as part of a departmental "apprenticeship." These problems are common to many contingent labor sectors, and they often distract activists and members from the specific features of the open shop in the Florida academy. These include our institutional history, our complex set of affiliations, the "double bind" of our status as public employees in a "right to work" state, and, finally, the intersection in Florida of multiple cultures of antiunionism.

The History of GAU

Our parent union, the United Faculty of Florida (UFF), remains one of the few faculty unions in the United States that helped directly organize a graduate employee union. UF and University of South Florida (USF) graduate employees began struggling for union recognition in 1972. UFF then expended considerable resources during the late 1970s to win the legal battle that defined Florida's working graduate students as "employees" with collective bargaining rights. Confrontations with university administrators, the legislature, and the Florida supreme court finally saw USF and UF gain their first contract in 1982. Florida Agricultural and Mechanical University (FAMU) achieved the same rights in 1995. This commitment by UFF to graduate employee organizing gave rise to a sector of part-time, relatively transient, and low-paid workers within a union of mostly tenured faculty. UFF quickly became a reservoir of legal resources, money, and training for inexperienced graduate employee union activists, while our small dues inputs were entirely consumed to service UFF affiliate memberships in the National Education Association (NEA) and the newly merged Florida Education Association (FEA). UFF realizes a net loss after paying dues rebates of 9 percent to each chapter, which is our operating budget for the year.

Although UFF helped organize three GAU chapters, my familiarity with the history of the UF-GAU chapter and its recent phase of expansion leads me to focus on that organization and its relationship to external institutions. UF-GAU is actually one of three graduate employee (hereafter, "graduate assistant" or "GA") unions in Florida's ten-member State University System (SUS). Where I speak of GAU in relation to affiliates, the parent union, or government agencies, generalizations are thus entirely appropriate. Membership at UF-GAU dropped from nearly 600 during the early 1990s to a low of approximately 150 in 1997 (mostly stalwarts from the large English and sociology departments). A new high of 507 in October 2000 (17.5% of twenty-nine hundred employees) resulted from three years of organizing, the professionalization and diversification of the leadership cadre (from two or three to dozens of visible activists), and the implementation of a departmental steward structure to organize within academic disciplines. These gains appear limited, especially given that our membership rates have not yet climbed above one-fifth of the eligible employees. But the gains are relatively impressive considering the dilemmas of the GAU's institutional affiliations and the status of public and part-time employees in the Florida legislature and the federal courts.

Affiliation Overload: United Faculty of Florida and the FEA

The three GAU chapters operate under a larger parent union of faculty workers. Our sister chapters include 1,600 graduate employees at USF in Tampa, a fast-growing metropolitan campus, and 170 colleagues at FAMU, a historically black university. As of fall 2000, chapter membership stood at 507, 170, and 46 at UF, USF, and FAMU, respectively. The three GAU chapters form a GAU Bargaining Council in UFF, alongside a ten-member SUS council, eight-member community college council, and one private school (see Fig. 6.1). Because seats in the UFF Senate are assigned in proportion to union membership and not to dues income, the GAU chapters hold approximately one-fourth of the nearly one hundred votes in that governing body. Our relatively insignificant dues contribution translates into a voting power out of proportion to our financial contribution. Unlike the faculty councils, GAU senators have voted as a block in all but one minor instance in the last four years.

Higher-level affiliations have also become critical to understanding Florida union organizing. In a move toward institutional efficiency and solidarity, public education unions in Florida, including our parent union, merged under the 120,000-member Florida Education Association (FEA) in 2000. The merged organization includes multiple locals from two former adversaries in Florida union politics, the American Federation of Teachers (AFT) and the National Education Association (NEA). During the tumultuous 1970s, these institutions had competed to represent faculty chapters across the state. They now both draw dues from the merged education unions.[4] While an obviously justifiable move toward institutional solidarity, the FEA merger involves GAU in a complicated bureaucratic and political matrix. The AFT has traditionally been more active in organizing new chapters in the graduate employee sector, whereas our parent

Fig. 6.1
Institutional Structure of Florida Education Unions

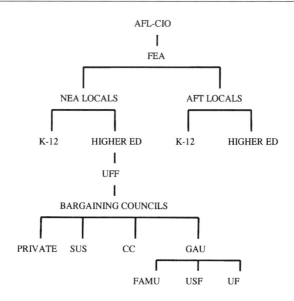

union is more closely aligned with the NEA, a historically insignificant force in graduate employee organizing. GAU is also affiliated with the National Labor Party and the national Congress of Graduate Employee Unions (CGEU). We have yet to see how this new institutional solidarity will translate into a revitalized movement culture in Florida, or which characteristics of the FEA's constituent elements will emerge as dominant. One thing is certain, few union officers, much less our general membership, understand the way money, resources, personnel, and political power circulate within these institutions. If the house of labor in Florida is a house united, its architecture is nonetheless byzantine.

A Double Bind: Public Employees in a "Right-to-Work" State

If affiliations muddy the waters of these union operations, Florida's anti-union statutes are more daunting and direct. Florida is, by law, an "open-shop" or "right-to-work" state. GAU is thus forbidden from collecting "agency" or "maintenance" fees from unit workers who benefit from the contract yet refuse to join the union. Dues are entirely voluntary. As comrades in other right-to-work states understand, the lack of an agency fee is the bane of union organizing. Simple mathematics explain the dilemma. If all employees were required to pay even half of their dues through an "agency" or "maintenance" fee, our operating budget (the 9 percent of the dues returned by our parent union) would increase from an annual $3,500 to approximately $12,000. With a larger agency fee of 80 percent, our income would be closer to $17,000, about a five-fold increase. The lack of agency fee translates into low membership among those with no collective identity or coworker solidarity. For individuals who do not identify as a labor collective, the position is obvious. It costs nothing to receive the benefits of the union, so why pay? From a market perspective, any disposable income is better invested in value-added goods and services that aid progress toward the degree. In a closed shop, one might as well pay the small difference between agency fee and actual membership dues, at least to have a voice in union affairs. But in an open shop, nonpayment is the norm, and this choice saves resources that may be applied to an ever-fleeting subsistence. The lack of an agency fee is the most tangible obstacle in the fight to build a union culture in Florida. Agency fees funds could, for example, be used to combat heavily capitalized institutions and their well-oiled public relations machines with media campaigns. Notably, our parent union does not have a public relations committee. It can barely afford one.

On top of the inability to collect dues, public employee unions are forbidden by Florida law to strike or to commit work actions such as slowdowns or sickouts. This leaves us with little leverage in stalled contract negotiations. Of course, dues from agency fees would permit units at the level of UFF or the local chapter to form a strike fund or a legal fund to defend workers challenging these anti-strike laws. As their low pay would be easy to compensate during a strike, the GA sector seems the perfect one to engage in such a tactical battle.

These antistrike laws combine with our public employee status to make collective bargaining a bit of a farce, unless it is pursued with singular purpose and aggressive tactics that simply wear management down. Decisions from the pro-states' rights bench of the state supreme court have given management (here the State of Florida) sovereign authority over the negotiated contracts of its public employees.[5] The double bind of public educators—generalized no-strike laws plus unequal protection as public employees—makes collective agency, once achieved, so much less rewarding for our sector and region than it can be for similar workers at private institutions or closed shops.[6]

The double bind means low returns on resource and personnel inputs to contract negotiations. After declaring an impasse in spring 2000 negotiations, the union won a victory during arbitration. The neutral Special Master (SM) granted GAU its first health benefits language and massive raises to the minimum stipend. But our opponents, the SUS Board of Regents (BOR), refused to accept the decision. As a public employee dispute, the matter then went before the very legislature that would have to pay for those benefits and raises. Not surprisingly, the Republican and center-Democratic legislature dismissed the SM decision and made the contract language follow the "last best" offer of the BOR: minimal raises and no health benefits. In a quarter century of public employees bargaining, the legislature has rarely done more.[7]

The BOR refers to the supremacy of the legislature to argue a "hands-tied" position, yet it practices flexibility in funding its own administrative salaries and special projects outside the appropriated limits. After proposing little or no movement on raises, minimum stipends, and health benefits, the BOR chief negotiator each year argues that, after all, the legislature may simply change the figures after the agreement is signed—so why bother negotiating? Heavy lobbying of the Joint Education Committee and more tactical lobbying of regional legislators in the Florida House and Senate will address this problem. But given our current resource base, and given the constant rearguard actions required of professional education lobbyists in a Republican statehouse, graduate employees must lobby on their own behalf. This is an exciting project, but it will require time and money that few service sectors like ours can spare.

Some recent bargaining successes have made current leadership more optimistic about collective bargaining in Florida, but structural features interfere with apparent success. In 1999 GAU negotiators won release-time positions for union workers totaling thirty hours a week at UF, with proportional increments at USF and FAMU. But it has been difficult to fill these positions, which only release union workers from a portion of their university duties. Self-identified graduate "students" find it difficult to leave their "apprentice" teaching and laboratory positions to work as employees for the union, a move that places both their career and their relationship with their advisor in jeopardy. More recently, employees ratified a 2001 contract that overhauls a management friendly grievance process, includes protocol for health benefits should the legislature allocate funds, and elaborates worker rights and privileges. Indications are that implementation will run aground against legislative fiat and administrative intransigence.

Intangible Obstacles—Cultures of Antiunionism

The lack of a union culture is an obvious barrier in explaining mergers, affiliations, negotiations, and the "open shop" to our constituents. Despite the exciting prospects of a merged FEA, Florida, as weary organizers often muse, is a southern state to the core. Indeed, the status of the South as an anti-union region is often blamed for our organizing failures. While anticommunism and a fear of "Yankee" institutions probably play less of a role in determining employee decisions now than ever before, especially since a significant portion of our unit employees are from out-of-state and out-of-country, UF nonetheless remains the largest and one of the more popular public institutions servicing Florida and the southeastern United States. The state and the region have formed an electoral axis for neoconservative and conservative political power for at least several decades. At the individual level, activists who recruit and organize employees at UF have certainly encountered the distinctive brand of southern antiunionism, but it seems to work alongside a more generalized individualism common across sector and region in the United States. The contemporary "market populism" and neoliberal identification of the general workforce is emerging as the nemesis of collective organizing. This more generalized and pervasive identification as an individual consumer-professional in an ostensibly "free" market of academic labor is undoubtedly exacerbated by any lingering southern antiunionism.[8]

For these and other reasons, no union organizer may assume that workers, professional journalists, community politicians, or even administrators are familiar with contract negotiations, collective agency, or other phenomenon common to the union environment. Local papers regularly refuse to print corrections of major factual errors and misquotes when reporting on union issues. We expend considerable time and resources explaining collective bargaining to journalists, our own activists, and our unit employees. Florida and southern residents have even fewer family, professional, and associational experience with unions than other U. S. workers. When recruiting and activating employees from nonunion cultures and backgrounds, it is not a simple matter to change identities. They must often be constructed around or over cultural contours that have become pervasive and institutionalized.

Perhaps no chapter is immune to the confusions of its affiliate structure, the barriers of legal statutes and court decisions, and the multiple cultures of antiunionism. But the overlapping barriers of the Florida context make union organizing a herculean task for GAU. As the only organized sector in Florida that is at once subaltern to multiple organizations, composed of academic and part-time labor, and encumbered with the status of public employees, the GAU case articulates all the dilemmas of Florida organizing.

GAU AND THE PARENT UNION

During the early 1990s, a new leadership cadre revitalized Florida's graduate employee organizing efforts. These activists insisted on the professionalism of graduate employees and the skilled nature of their university labor, but their collective rhetoric, tactics, and day-to-day problems resembled those of the organizing service sectors. The majority of UFF faculty, however, identified themselves and their interests as especially distinct from the industrial, service, and other nonacademic sectors. To them, organizing, aggressive propaganda, and confrontation with management seemed appropriate for marginalized farmworkers and student apprentices (graduate employees), but not for highly trained and well-established professionals. These opposing identifications led to impasse in debates about how to rekindle a faltering unionism in the Florida academy. The organizing imperative of graduate employee *activism* ran aground against the operational limits of a withering *service unionism*. What one group saw as a faulty nostalgia for a bygone academy controlled by faculty, the other group defended as "professionalism" and "collegiality" in recruitment and bargaining. As a result, few significant reforms have been made to the bargaining process, institutional practices, and organizing machinery of UFF.

GAU and Organizing Unionism: "Join or Die"

GAU is by necessity an organizing union, albeit one with an eclectic mix of political and social functions. One-fourth to one-third of our membership is lost every year to graduation, academic fellowships, and travel. Our arsenal of organizing tactics ranges from the professional and objective to the social and partisan. We provide individual departmental orientations to incoming and returning graduate employees and graduate coordinators, a source of mutual learning and strong recruiting for GAU and those faculty who supervise its constituents. Our heaviest organizing takes place at officially approved tables outside the new graduate employee orientation every year in August. At the request of outgoing associate graduate dean Richard Lutz, GAU was asked in 1999 to entirely design and operate the small-group portion of the actual orientation. All eighteen of our workers wore their union shirts and stated their job titles and union positions, but they avoided charges of "recruiting while training" by discussing the union only when new hires asked about issues related to the BOR-GAU contract. Not surprisingly, GAU still receives positive comments, even from nonmembers, about the small, intimate, and graduate-employee-led sessions that dealt with sexual harassment, human research subject protocols, ageism (against both younger and older employees, or their students), and supervisor-employee relations. Because they were more popular with graduate assistants than the yawn-producing plenary sessions led by the Graduate School, UF administrators jealously put an end to them. In designing his own program for Orientation 2000, the associate graduate dean Kenneth Gerhardt replaced all the small-group sessions with a more austere training regimen of films, mass lectures, and stilted auditorium-size "question-and-answer" sessions (assisted by a mere three "award-winning graduate students," none of whom were GAU members). Any discussion of the contract, even its existence, was deflated or avoided. Administrators even used GAU materials—designed for small interactive groups—to teach a more "efficient" factory classroom of seven hundred rookie assistants. Despite losing the implicit promotional benefits from running the small sessions, our union staged one of its most successful tabling sign-ups in years outside the "official" orientation—approximately 80 new members from 600 new hires in the first weeks of the semester. Steward organizing had increased that number to 157 by March 2001.

GAU aims to educate employees about the benefits of collective action and progressive reform, but it mostly appeals to the social and economic sensibilities of new graduate employees. While budget constraints have forced smaller outlays on food and beverages, for example, GAU socials remain the largest interdisciplinary and extracurricular events for new and returning graduate employees. Discount partnerships with local businesses, from auto repair to lingerie to books, are popular. When recounting the benefits of unionism, fulfilling the obligations of citizenship or practicing radical politics rarely make the top of the list, at least not for rookie members. Our coworkers most often mention the ability to meet people outside their discipline and department or the comfort of finding a peer group intact upon arrival in a new town. The commitment by our activists to fundamental principles of unionism is obvious. The most popular member t-shirts and posters read "Join or Die" and "Don't Be a Tool." But for many graduate employees, GAU is quite simply the best way to meet people, learn about the university, and prepare oneself for the hazards of intellectual and professional life in the academy.

UFF and Service Unionism: "To Serve and Protect"

Like GAU, the faculty chapters of UFF began as grassroots organizing unions. Given the low priority for higher education spending in this state, the unstated motto of early faculty organizing in 1970s Florida might well have been "Join or Die." Veteran faculty activists retain important positions in our parent and affiliate unions, including the presidency of the FEA, key positions in national NEA governance, and extensive Political Action Committee fund-raising and campaigning in regional politics. But the organizing tensions from UFF's early years have long been resolved in favor of service and business unionism. The maintenance of current membership services and the status quo of professionalism are the operative goals of UFF governance. UFF has effectively banned organizing by cutting funding lines that support the fieldwork and travel required for starting up new chapters. UFF guidelines for organizing new chapters require a long and evident history of organizing and solidarity on campuses before UFF will even consider a campaign for recognition. This would seem to obviate new outbreaks of activism. This preemptively curtails organizing on a campus that has become energized by recent events, in opposition to a particular administration, or by efforts on the part of UFF and GAU organizers. The union has thus been unable to make exploratory trips to nonorganized campuses interested in becoming new chapters. Closer to home, GAU has spent much of its political capital at the UFF Senate defending its $25 new-member rebate bonus—essentially an organizing fund—which nearly doubles the UF chapter's operating budget each year.

Due to no new unit additions and low interest in recruiting, UFF is in a state of decline (with a handful of community college chapters and one SUS school being the exception). SUS faculty unions now measure net annual new member increases in the single digits, and the highest dues-paying members are often near the end of their careers. UFF has had no success recruiting junior faculty at larger schools, and so it faces withering solvency as members retire or otherwise leave their unit. The UFF Senate has been forced to reduce its chapter dues rebate from 9 percent to 8 percent, further hindering any organizing efforts.

Clashing Identities and Unreformed Institutions: Bargaining and Politics in UFF

The different collective identities of the various UFF sectors are manifest in the various strategies applied at the SUS faculty and graduate employee bargaining tables. The GAU Bargaining Council now negotiates individual contracts at the three campuses, with a chief negotiator chosen from one of the three GAU chapters. Our council has had great success over the past four years in assembling aggressive, well-prepared, and professionalized bargaining teams. Predictably, the BOR argues its "hands-tied" position vis-a-vis the legislature and, when cornered, threatens to take us to an impasse hearing that will ultimately have no binding authority. The BOR offers few contract changes and little or no movement on minimum stipends (recently raised to $7,400 at UF, $7,500 at USF, and $7,000 at FAMU for a half-time appointment), health benefits, and pay. Yet GAU's combination of aggressive negotiating, legal maneuvering, and the forcing of contract issues through departmental and campuswide grievances have forced the BOR to move much further than our union's power would seem to allow. Extensive GAU research and UFF legal efforts revealed lies, malfeasance, and curious accounting practices by the BOR on a statewide basis, especially regarding its false claims to fiscal inflexibility in granting raises, benefits, or stipends beyond the limits of legislative appropriations. Confrontations have led to numerous gains, including release-time positions for union staff, a massive overhaul of the grievance procedure, the expansion of workplace rights for employees, and a "merit-only" clause governing employee evaluations (protecting workers against sexual orientation discrimination). Through it all, the union has managed to maintain small yet always uncertain raise packages (usually about 3% per year) and upward movement on minimum stipends.

Faculty bargaining within the SUS has been less successful. In the face of intransigent BOR negotiators and withering leverage against them, the less aggressive UFF teams have capitulated to almost all of the positions held by management. The fall 2000 SUS faculty negotiations resulted in no pay raise, in a state whose faculty makes less than those at all of its peer institutions. Instead, the SUS faculty Bargaining Council has committed itself to "merit" pay, which the GAU has opposed in its own contract negotiations because it places discretionary funds in the hands of administrators and their lackeys. A more embarrassing example of inconsistent tactics between GAU and UFF faculty is a 1997 memorandum of understanding between the UFF president and the chancellor of the BOR, which stated that the board had no flexibility in providing pay and benefits outside legislative appropriations, and that UFF would not pursue litigation to challenge this assertion.[9] When GAU presented overwhelming evidence of BOR spending flexibility during the April 2000 Special Master hearing, the BOR used those faculty union memorandums to imply bad faith on the part of GAU negotiators—who seemed to be contradicting the arguments of their own parent union. That was, indeed, the case. Unlike GAU, the SUS faculty are unwilling to challenge the BOR on fundamental issues such as fiscal flexibility, preferring instead to engage management on its own terms. In a classic move toward business unionism, both the BOR and UFF call this style of negotiations "collegial bargaining."

Aside from the formal environment of the bargaining table, UFF politics have at times been adversarial. In 1999, during the height of discord, the GAU chapters and like-minded faculty supported the UF-GAU copresident in a bid for the statewide presidency of UFF. The candidate was a proven organizer and negotiator from the graduate employee sector. He garnered a strong 40 percent of the combined faculty and graduate employee votes, yet did not win the election. His campaign platform centered around making the parent union more proactive in organizing, more confrontational when negotiating with the BOR, and more visible to the public. Certain officers and leaders within UFF had "adopted the conceits of management," claimed one of his campaign flyers. UFF was executing an unwarranted strategy of retreat in a situation that required forward movement.

The obvious question of qualification—whether a graduate employee could run a predominantly faculty union—was raised in passing during the campaign, but few people denied the candidate's basic capabilities. Rather, opposing faculty were concerned that a subaltern, an "apprentice scholar," would be unable to properly fill an office designed to serve and represent a class of "professionals" above his own. Opponents further argued that to put someone into office whose career trajectory tended toward politics and labor organizing would derail a successful tradition in UFF. Its elected officers, so the argument went, had almost always been committed first to higher education and to unionism only as an afterthought. Considering the state of the union, faculty opponents should have known better than to pass up the opportunity to have a recognizable unionist at the helm. But they continued to see the candidate and his graduate employee peers as "students" or "apprentices," energetic youngsters playing at unionism before "moving on" the career path to fully professional status. For graduate employees who performed highly skilled teaching, grading, and research tasks on a daily basis, the choice was obvious. Faculty had only to ask whether they wanted a new style of leader: an executive identified with proactive policy, organizing, lobbying and public relations at the helm of what had become a defunct service union. It soon became clear to many GAU organizers, and ever more obvious to supporters among faculty, that such activism as the candidate promoted was valued only insofar as it did not interfere with the institutionalized status quo at UFF. The rhetoric and promises of a self-identified "labor organizer" and "worker" fell on deaf ears to an audience of "professional" academics.

The new possibility of affiliating with Miami-Dade Community College is a more recent and equally disturbing index of UFF's position within the Florida academy, and its distance from GAU organizers and the *activist* identity. As an AFT local in a state dominated by NEA unions, Miami-Dade and UFF had no formal working relationship with each other in the past. But under the protocols of the FEA merger, Miami-Dade has an opportunity to contribute its stellar 70 percent membership rate and high media visibility to the UFF. However, UFF's record as a nonorganizing service union has led the dues- and activist-rich Miami-Dade chapter to avoid affiliation with UFF. The hope of GAU organizers was to construct a voting block, composed of the former supporters of GAU's UFF presidential candidate and of Miami-Dade progressives. This would have constituted well above a voting majority at the UFF Senate and would have fundamentally altered the identity of the union. But the possibility of a Miami-Dade/GAU organizing axis appeared as a flash in the pan. After delivering a rousing union-hall speech to the spring 1999 UFF Senate, a Miami-Dade representative was greeted with a mixture of fascination and bewilderment. Things had not been so loud at UFF for quite some time, nor did it seem that they would be in the future. Service unionists cheered for Miami-Dade speeches just as they did for GAU chapter reports, but they wanted no part of Miami-Dade's successful organizing methods—work actions, public confrontations with administrators, and one-on-one shop floor organizing. Things are different "down there," said one UFF faculty, as if Mami-Dade were an aberration, instead of a model for reform. GAU was disappointed by the failure of a Miami-Dade affiliation, for it meant that our progressive UFF voting block remained a minority. Likewise, the fallout from the presidential campaign is still receding. But I should mention the renewal of camaraderie and mutual respect between faculty and graduate employees in UFF, especially during the evolving crisis of the legislative dissolution of the Board of Regents. Neither can one discount the excitement surrounding the FEA merger. GAU activists do recognize that many faculty have worked lifelong for social justice and are committed to progressive unionism. Furthermore, we were recently given full NEA and FEA voting status by a surprising and unanimous vote of the UFF Senate (we had only been "student" members before). This vote encumbers even more graduate employee dues input as membership fees to national organizations. For the time being, the desire for solidarity with faculty comrades, the loyalties of stalwart faculty activists and a devoted UFF staff, and the need for legal and other services, have kept the GAU close to its parent union. As the BOR has recently been abolished by the legislature in a massive restructuring of education governance, and since UFF continues to decline, GAU must responsibly consider the option of reaffiliation with another parent union if the opportunity arises. But with our futures uncertain, the GAU and the UFF stand united—service or organizing union, no matter.

CHANGING IDENTITIES—WHY JOIN?

The institutional problems just discussed, both external and internal, are considerable but not overwhelming. They will require new efforts in lobbying, in obtaining pro-union court decisions, in organizing current and new chapters, and in helping faculty and graduate employees identify, or reidentify, themselves as organized labor. But within the structural limits of the Florida open shop and the service unionism of UFF, how will this be possible? Why have we seen even moderate success, given that we have so little to offer in bread-and-butter contract gains (health care and pay)? This begs the question of the relationship between institutional affiliations and practices and the formation of identity as activists and organized labor inside those structures. The GAU is forced to answer that its members are probably unlike those who would join in other environments, where political action, collective agency, and shop floor solidarity are the means, not the ends, to building a union.

Who Is GAU?

So who are our graduate employees? Who becomes a GAU member, and why? Given our fledgling communications and steward apparatuses, it is difficult to answer these questions with the kind of statistics that satisfy the social scientist. Only 113 of 2,900 bargaining surveys were returned to the GAU office via campus mail in September 1999, probably most of them by union members. Electronic communications have proven unreliable for volunteer operations and even less so for gathering information. A revamped web site takes us further into the electronic age, but in this area results have only been seen in operations efficiency among those already organized. We are dealing with a literate, highly educated, and text-oriented workforce, people who write reports, exams, essays, and technical papers on a regular basis. Yet even our cadre of approximately forty UF-GAU activists and stewards are often poorly informed about workplace issues, state politics, and the institutional dilemmas described in this chapter.

Even without individualized data, some reliable generalizations about our bargaining unit can be put forth. We are a highly skilled workforce; everyone arrives at our bargaining unit with at least a bachelors or equivalent university degree in hand. Most are committed to some kind of work in public education or scholarly research (professional and medical schools are excluded from our bargaining unit). It should noted, however, that the actual College of Education, which produces K-12 administrators and teachers, is one of our least organized. Most of us are poorly compensated workers who subsist with the aid of loans, scholarships, partner income, or family contributions. The problem of poor pay at UF is exacerbated by an extreme wage disparity unlike that at most large public institutions. The top quartile of the graduate employees make an average 160 percent more than the bottom quartile.[10] International workers, for their part, share a generalized constraint on income because of legislated out-of-state fees, the requirement that they purchase their own health care, and the extra costs of communications and travel. Imagine living below a subsistence wage at all, much less in a foreign country.

But the most striking commonality apparent to recruiters and organizers remains this: The overwhelming majority of graduate assistants, even many within the GAU, find it difficult to publicly commit themselves to the notion of their status as "workers" and not merely "students." This conceptual dilemma is the single most pressing internal issue confronting GAU, mainly because of our voluntary dues system in the open shop environment. In a closed shop, a worker who is not union-identified may purchase voting rights with an insignificant increase from agency fee to full dues, and most will do so. Identification with a movement culture or with unionism is not mandatory—the union will take its dues whether one joins or not. But with low pay, an open shop, and only a weak promise of future employment in the academy, the incentive to join must center around identification with the professional, social, intellectual, or political mission of the union. One must think and feel a certain way about one's status as an employee to "make a donation" to GAU, as a recent new member termed it. No doubt many of our members feel content that they have "volunteered" their dues in a situation in which the vast majority of employees do not pay, never mind that they might become activists and give up time they could spend in developing their professional skills.

Organizing the Humanities and Sciences

The antiunion attitude would not seem to constitute a general malaise among the UF's graduate employee ranks. In sheer numbers, membership and volunteer hours are currently higher in the humanities and social sciences than in the natural sciences and engineering. Indeed, in the most organized sectors in the humanities, it has been argued that getting volunteers is a simple case of convincing politically minded or progressive intellectuals to step into the world of cold calls on the telephone, stapling and folding sessions, and old-fashioned bargaining research. The argument goes that left-leaning scholars need merely to be shoved gently from the rarified yet inherently politicized world of criticism and the seminar into the mundane world of politics and shop floor organizing. The companion argument is that the natural sciences and engineering present an altogether different dilemma than the humanities and social sciences, since their career trajectories tend toward higher pay and a more corporate environment. Indeed, certain employees may feel their channels of advocacy are best pursued in flush science and engineering departments rather than in the resource-poor GAU chapter.

But the task of organizing the humanities is more daunting than it would seem, and the sciences are not so terribly antiunion as one would imagine. In the first case, radical "Marxists" and students of culture are hardly immune to antiunionism, careerism, and disciplinary myopia. Only a handful of GAU members attended the spring 2000 "Labor Forum" of the annual Marxist Reading Group Conference. This interdisciplinary event is organized by graduate student scholars in a heavily unionized department, English, which has 86 percent of its 127 workers paying voluntary dues. At the forum, one counted more visiting private and public sector organizers (about eight) than graduate employees. Now is a critical period when the graduate employees at UF desperately need to identify as labor, and with "traditional" labor sectors, especially as an example to faculty colleagues in the parent union. Yet the most outspoken, radical, and progressive members of GAU fail to attend events designed to do just that. In the second case, and contrary to the prejudices of many academic labor organizers, scientists have eagerly joined UF-GAU. About one-third of the new sign-ups in fall 2000 were from the sciences, not including additional members from management, engineering, and other fields such as mathematics. How do we explain this?

First of all, the myth of high pay and comfortable corporate careers is just that, a myth. Upon closer discussions with scientists, it is obvious that their career paths are every bit as fraught with economic uncertainty and constitutional unease as are those of humanities scholars. While future teachers and social scientists might trouble over the complicity of their labor in abetting the degree-mill culture of the corporate university, scientists must often pursue jobs at unpardonable firms such as Monsanto or Exxon. Moreover, economic uncertainties have led many hard scientists in the direction of the American Medical Association and other nontraditional labor sectors in discussing unions as an option. A history lesson helps explain the science recruitment as well. Activists from the natural sciences (zoology and biology, for example) and the College of Engineering organized and ran UF-GAU in the first and formative decade. The initial organizing drives at FAMU-GAU were activated by chemists, and current FAMU leadership hails almost entirely from pharmacy.[11]

Despite being the most obviously overworked sector (given their required hours in the lab and high frequency of unpaid labor), scientists and nonhumanities scholars now work on the UF-GAU bargaining team, support the general activist cadre, and are among the most diligent stewards and officers. This suggests that the tendency to organize the humanities before other sectors is unwarranted. If humanities are over-represented currently, it is only an aberration from a historical trend of science involvement. We must address the traditional aversion by unionized humanities scholars to engage and organize their science comrades. It will then surprise us less to note that our most successful steward during the 2000–2001 term hailed from the Department of Geology, where fourteen of twenty new hires were recruited in five months time. The ability to shift to union membership and activism seems possible given a variety of disciplinary and intellectual starting points; the key seems to be individual leadership among the steward cadre, not radical politics or pedagogy.

WHERE GOES THE UNION?

Regardless of discipline, all graduate employees struggle with their identification as intellectuals and students, on the one hand, and as workers and organizers on the other. Choices have to be made that will undoubtedly affect one's status in the very academy that one seeks to reform. Disciplinary conferences and professional obligations, for example, have become a canker on the body politic of the academy, with Florida GAU being no exception.[12] Even our union affiliations are a case in point. Because of our new status as full voting members in the FEA and NEA, UF-GAU must send delegates to their conventions in addition to those sent to UFF Senate meetings; that is, if we are to point these institutions in the direction of organizing. UF-GAU's new membership in the AFL-CIO North Central Florida Labor Council creates new duties in canvassing and candidate selection, duties that must be upheld if academics and intellectuals are to regain legitimacy and respect from organized labor outside the academy. Attending all of these events is impossible, and yet as representatives of the academy, of graduate employees, of campus activism, of organized labor, and of organizing professionals, our failure to be active at these events has dire consequences for our legitimacy within the larger movement culture. This movement-level solidarity with Campus National Organization for Women, the UF chapter of the American Federation of State, County and Municipal Employees, the legislative Black Caucus (to preserve affirmative action in Florida), Gainesville Civic Media Center, or with local environmental groups are but a few of these "unfinished chapters" in GAU organizing at the University of Florida. Whether to finish these before we complete those other chapters—in our theses and dissertations—will be the key decision for many incoming graduate employee activists.

UF-GAU has had mixed success in overcoming the obstacles presented by contrary institutions and identities. On the one hand the executive, steward, and activist cadre has expanded from three or four visible leaders in 1997, and a membership of 150, to a diverse organization with a professionalized executive committee and over 500 members. There are now thirty-six stewards in almost as many departments. Two former chapter presidents have moved on to high-level organizing jobs within public education. But the GAU is still poor in terms of remunerated personnel, real membership, and affiliate strength. Financing is always a problem. More cash is needed to develop effective communications networks, to lobby as public employees, to hire professional staff, and to run grievances and bargaining more effectively. The GAU still relies on a handful of outgoing and recently trained officers to transfer institutional knowledge and bureaucratic technology to a revolving leadership and activist cadre. If GAU is a rainbow organization of Republicans, gay and lesbian workers, feminists, sports fans (Gator sports transcend politics and the disciplines as unlike any in my experience), scientists, humanities scholars, parents, leftists, and international students, the problems of organizing these workers seems nonetheless to fall away no more than one member at a time.

If this analysis has yielded no philosopher's stone for organizing such a diverse constituency, that is the point—people seem to join because of interpersonal contacts and because they feel alone at the corporate university. Politics and organizational skills come later, and with further educating. By attending, sometimes first, to the social and personal needs of our demographic, and by asking the already converted to turn words into actions, the social and political functions of the union combine in a powerful mixture. In no case has an active and friendly steward failed to double, triple, or quadruple membership in a department, be it a science, humanities, or other discipline. First we create a community of working academics and then, based on the strength of this community, we push bargaining and grievances to its limits in the context of our parent union and the open shop. Organizing is always our first imperative, even if it runs aground against service unionism and the open shop.

The relationship between identity and institutional features in Florida graduate employee organizing is, in the end, one of contradiction. To wit: those stewards and other activists who are most inclined by identity to organize in the academy will often find it difficult to pursue an academic career in the face of institutional barriers. Indeed, the loss of academic activists because of sidetracked careers, poor resources, and the frustrations of conflicting identities in the academy is a serious casualty of the renaissance in graduate employee organizing. Advisors, hiring committees, and fellowship committees rarely consider union activism as progress toward the degree. The putative role of graduate employees as upwardly mobile "apprentices" in the ivory tower is a guiding myth within the culture of the academy. If we are to move on to the next chapter of academic unionism—the part of the story where labor wins—we must overcome such biases in our institutions, our constituencies, and ourselves. While it is pretty to imagine that our energy and institutional solidarity will inspire this expanded sense of collective identity among our comrades, the GAU case proves otherwise. To offer something beyond community to the union's constituents, we must challenge the open shop and our status in the courts and at the statehouse. This will require escaping our withering financial solvency and political irrelevance—perhaps by way of a commitment to lifelong financial and intellectual support from our affiliates, faculty supervisors, faculty union comrades, and graduate employee union alumni.

NOTES

The author wishes to thank Aline Gubrium, Erika Gubrium, Steve Hach, Marcus Harvey, María Martínez, and Dina Richman for comments and support. This chapter is lovingly dedicated to the memory of Ruth "Ma" Young.

1. In states with "right-to-work" or "open shop" laws, members of a bargaining unit, while protected by the union grievance procedure and other benefits of the contract, are not required to join the union. Such laws prohibit the union from assessing "fair share dues" to such nonmembers.

2. An *organizing* union is committed to recruitment and mobilization of membership, as well as organizing new chapters and bargaining units. A *service* union allocates its resources primarily to maintaining the benefits and status of its current members, and it may even be hostile to accepting new members or chapters. A *business* union often adopts the operating styles and political program of management, even if it has not incorporated management into its executive cadre. The categories are not mutually exclusive. For an elaboration of this taxonomy and an excellent review of the relevant literature, see M.F. Masters and R.S. Atkin, "Union strategies for revival: A conceptual framework and literature review," In *Research in personnel and human resources management*, ed. G.R. Ferris (Stamford, CT: JAI Press, 1999), 283–314.

3. During contract negotiations, the University of Florida inconsistently reports a much higher average salary of anywhere from $10,000 to $11,000. This fiction is achieved by calculating salaries at a half-time rate (twenty-hour work week) for all workers, whereas few employees in the UF-GAU unit have half-time contracts. The current average appointment is 37 percent of full time, about fourteen hours a week.

4. Since the AFT was already under the AFL-CIO umbrella, the FEA merger was contingent upon AFL-CIO affiliation. All FEA units may now pay dues to the important and politically active regional councils (in GAU's case the North Central Florida Labor Council) on top of their national dues to AFT or NEA.

5. On the effect of states' rights decisions, see H. Schwartz, "States' rights rise again," *The Nation*, October 9, 2000, 28–29. Also see T. Geoghehan, "No love lost for labor," *The Nation*, October 9, 2000, 35–36.

6. This argument is based on the assumption that a binding decision by the National Labor Relations Board, which governs private sector employee-management disputes, would be preferable to that of the partisan and pro-business Florida legislature. For a more critical evaluation of the NLRB and one of its Democratic appointees, see S. Early's review of *Labored relations: Law, politics, and the NLRB* by W.J. Gould ("How stands the union," *The Nation*, January 22, 2000).

7. The BOR also negotiates with nurses, police, and service sector unions in the State University System and community colleges of Florida.

8. An excellent critique of the new ethos is T. Frank, *One market, under God: Extreme capitalism, market populism, and the end of economic democracy* (New York: Doubleday, 2000).

9. Brian Nelson, UFF President, to Charles Reed, chancellor of the Board of Regents, memorandum, July 9, 1997, UF-GAU Bargaining Files, Gainesville, Florida.

10. UF payroll data, October 13, 2000, UF-GAU payroll files, Gainesville, Florida. This information is reported to the union per contract stipulations.

11. An eleventh hour historical study by UF-GAU co-president Erika Gubrium made this section possible.

12. For a valuable critique of the way professional associations hamper efforts to organize academic labor, see M. Harvey, "Between discipline and profession: Conceptualizing labor in the academy" (paper presented to the 2001 Annual Meeting of the American Historical Association, January 6, 2001). The trend, as Harvey notes, is not a new one. See B.J. Bledstein, *The culture of professionalism: The middle class and the development of higher education in America* (New York: Norton, 1976).

Part III

New Tactics, Old Battlegrounds

Chapter 7

Shutting Down the Academic Factory: Developing Worker Identity in Graduate Employee Unions

Eric Dirnbach and Susan Chimonas

It has been an open secret on college campuses for years that the majority of teaching is performed by graduate employees and part-time, nontenured faculty.[1] In this context of an increasingly disempowered academic labor force, working within universities that are guided by corporate priorities, unionization becomes essential to address the lack of institutional voice and improve compensation and working conditions. Hence, graduate students who are employed to teach or perform research at universities across the country are exercising their right to organize unions and bargain collectively with university administrations.

There are currently over two dozen established graduate employee unions in the United States, until recently all located at public universities.[2] The groundbreaking success of the new graduate employee union at New York University will bring about the long-delayed expansion of unionization to private universities (for more details on this development, see Arenson 2000a, 2000b; McQueen 2000). By unionizing, graduate students are rightfully asserting their identity as crucial academic workers, alongside their more accepted roles as students and professionals. The formation of a union is, however, only the first step toward better compensation and working conditions for graduate employees. The ongoing challenge facing unions is to forcefully articulate and defend the rights of graduate workers by winning contractual improvements from administrations that continue to resist graduate employees' collective demands. As with traditional corporate management, university administrations that fight the formation of graduate employee unions will generally maintain a hostile position in ensuing contract negotiations.

To this difficulty are added the structural problems inherent in graduate employee union organization. Established graduate employee unions face many continuous and formidable challenges, including high membership turnover, transient leadership, poor historical memory, and an almost exclusive reliance on volunteer labor from a pool of stressed and notoriously busy members. A primary contributor to these problems are the multiple identities and commitments of graduate students that compete with active union involvement. Each new generation of graduate students must come to recognize that their roles as students or professionals offer no effective means to ensure their rights as workers. In contrast, a successful challenge to their administration can only be accomplished by demonstrating their collective power as academic workers who can withhold their labor. This will present a problem for graduate employee unions that do not have the legal right to strike, though a creative union can still take necessary job actions. The union must facilitate this identity shift by creating and sustaining a serious union culture that discursively focuses on graduate students' role as workers, the crucial contributions they make as employees of their universities, and their corresponding rights to fair compensation, benefits, and working conditions. Most importantly, during contract negotiations the union must develop this worker consciousness through organizing events that enable members to recognize this identity and solidify it through actions that can lead to an effective work stoppage.

How can unions accomplish this identity shift? How can they convince their members to set aside traditional student protest methods (rallies, petitions, etc.) and illusions of professional collegiality in favor of work stoppages that raise the social and economic costs of administration intransigence? To address this issue, we will draw upon the contract negotiations of the Graduate Employees Organization (GEO) at the University of Michigan in 1995–96 and 1998–99. GEO was certified in 1974 as the official bargaining agent for graduate employees at the University of Michigan. GEO currently represents approximately fifteen hundred graduate employees who perform teaching duties, called Graduate Student Instructors (GSIs), and those who perform administrative and clerical tasks, called Graduate Student Staff Assistants (GSSAs). We will analyze how GEO used the negotiation process and other organizing methods to call members' attention to the inadequacies of the traditional roles of student and professional. The analysis will first examine the challenges facing graduate employee unions as they confront the problems associated with the multiple identities of graduate employees. We will then outline the experience of GEO during two contract campaigns in bringing attention to the problems associated with nonworker identities, thereby allowing their members to realize their worker identity through collective action. As the experience of GEO illustrates, a meaningful and successful challenge to the administration is only possible when a union establishes its own power by discursively and materially reinforcing members' collective identity as academic workers.

UNIQUE CHALLENGES FACING GRADUATE EMPLOYEE UNIONS: MULTIPLE IDENTITES, MULTIPLE BARRIERS TO SUCCESS

Graduate employee unions face many difficulties not usually experienced by traditional labor organizations. There is a continuous danger of disorganization and weakness due to high membership turnover from year to year (though this is also true of many traditional unions, such as retail workers). At Michigan, graduate students who teach may do so for only one or two semesters (engineering and natural sciences), or for as many as ten (humanities and social sciences). The union consequently suffers a continual loss of experienced members as they stop teaching or graduate. The union leadership is transient as well. The elected leaders of GEO generally serve for only one or two years. Unless well documented and discussed, important debates, issues, and events from the past will be lost to the current membership. As such, the union has a poor historical memory and has to constantly relearn how to function. Moreover, the reliance almost exclusively on volunteer labor from a membership with many other academic commitments guarantees that much needed union work will be left unfinished. Most of the work is typically performed by a relatively small core of union activists who are overburdened and susceptible to burnout. Accordingly, alongside the challenges commonly faced by all labor organizations, graduate employee unions encounter a number of additional structural problems.

Primary contributors to these difficulties are the multiple identities and commitments of graduate employees that often compete with active union membership. Classwork, teaching, research, departmental responsibilities, and other academic duties drain the membership of time and energy to contribute to the union organization. Moreover, these duties reinforce the disempowering roles of student and professional. The ideology of academia emphasizes hierarchy, apprenticeship, and individual excellence. Dissent and collective action are discouraged as unprofessional, uncollegial, and inappropriate. Indeed, when graduate employees organize, the administration employs rhetoric about the graduate student "apprenticeship" and the special "collegial relationship" between professors and graduate students, which would be forever compromised with the intrusive presence of a union. The code words "apprenticeship" and "collegiality" serve an important role in reinforcing academic ideology and, in an Orwellian manner, take on opposite meanings. Regardless of whether the apprentice model ever applied to graduate students in the past, it certainly is used today to mask their labor contribution and highlight the student/professional-in-training role (Watt 1997). In truth, beneath the "collegial" relationship is a rigid academic hierarchy, in which administrators and professors dictate terms, and graduate students take orders. In this way, common assumptions about the academy as a special place of scholarship hide what is increasingly a boss-worker relationship. This academic ideology was clearly visible in the response of the faculty and administration of Yale to the graduate employees' grade strike in 1995 (for details on the Yale case, see Lafer 1997; Nelson 1997a; Bérubé 1997). The majority of the professors in that confrontation sided with the administration, unable and unwilling to see workers engaging in collective action for union recognition.

As this chapter will explore, this academic ideology, aggressively expressed during initial graduate employee organizing, persists after the union is recognized. Therefore, even where graduate employee unions exist, administrators, faculty, and even many union members identify graduate workers primarily as students and professionals-in-training. The identity of an academic worker, who makes a labor contribution that is vital to the functioning of the university, is never fully recognized or approved in the academic environment. Furthermore, academic ideology forms the basis and rationale for continued administration resistance to graduate employee contractual gains.

Thus, unlike traditional labor unions whose members are unlikely to question their role as workers, graduate employee unions must constantly work to dismantle this extra ideological barrier constructed by the academic setting. The union must facilitate an identity shift by creating and sustaining a visible and uncompromising union culture on campus. This culture contributes a counter-hegemonic discourse centered on the labor of graduate employees as crucial to university functioning and their corresponding rights to fair compensation, benefits, and working conditions.

For example, GEO has long organized around the concept of a living wage that takes into account the high cost of living in Ann Arbor. Unlike the concept of a stipend or fellowship, which emphasizes the student identity, the living wage focuses discursive attention on the role of members as workers and wage earners. Likewise, organizing around grievances as violations of working conditions serves the same purpose. These tactics, which allow the union to develop worker consciousness among its membership, are essential tools in establishing the collective power necessary to match the university administration, which can draw upon its expertise and vast resources to manipulate the negotiation process and thwart union demands. Only through the collective expression of worker identity, via an organized work stoppage or strike, is the union likely to be successful.

Moreover, in building a worker identity within graduate employee unions, the membership needs to explore and exhaust the potential of graduate employees' other, less controversial identities as students and professionals. Rather than simply dismissing the powerful academic ideology, which encourages graduate employees to embrace and act within these roles, graduate employee unions must exploit this ideology. The union must provide organized opportunities for members to engage the administration as students and professionals, if only to illustrate the powerlessness of these roles. Once members come to see for themselves how the administration simply ignores their requests as students and professionals, they become more willing and able to contemplate defying the administration by embracing their worker identity and the real power it offers. Thus, during a contract campaign, the union must utilize the negotiation process and organized mass actions to demonstrate to the members the ineffectiveness of the professional and student roles in bringing about contractual progress.

THE "NEGOTIATIONS": GRADUATE EMPLOYEES AS PROFESSIONALS

In a sense, the negotiations represent the union members in professional mode. Contract talks involve only discussion, which does not threaten to disrupt "collegial" relations with the administration or impede the functioning of the university. This type of activity can and will be dismissed by the administration, but it does have much value in demonstrating to union members its utter ineffectiveness.

The contract negotiation process, in GEO's experience, does not involve actual negotiation in any meaningful sense of the word. Inexperienced members of GEO, upon attending their first bargaining session, often expect to witness a process of intelligent debate, with fair compromises reached on proposals. In reality, however, GEO has found that negotiations rarely involve any substantive discussion or compromise. In 1995 and 1998, GEO's major proposals were to increase wages to a "living wage" level, to identify and eliminate discrimination in hiring, and to compensate mandatory training required of international graduate student instructors (who make up 25 percent of the bargaining unit).[3] At the beginning of the contract talks, GEO and the administration agreed to participate in "interest-based bargaining," a process intended to facilitate agreement by encouraging both sides to explain their interest in an issue, rather than simply stating a firm position. To this end, GEO would spend considerable time researching issues and presenting them in detail during the negotiation session. Unfortunately, GEO's good-faith efforts were seldom reciprocated by the administration. The university's response to most of GEO's important proposals was a refusal to discuss them, claiming they were irrelevant to the contract, or flatly rejecting them in favor of current contract language (Berg 1998b). Decisions on some issues, such as class size limits, were declared matters of academic policy and, as such, the exclusive domain of the administration. Compensation for international GSIs for their mandatory training was delayed by the administration for years, with the claim that they were not employees at the time of the training and, consequently, were not covered by the contract. The union's effort to implement effective affirmative action policies that reduced discrimination in the hiring of women and GSIs of color ran into similar trouble, where the administration would agree only to the establishment in 1996 of a committee that would investigate the matter. One astonishing example of non-negotiation occurred during the 1995–96 contract talks. After months of silence on GEO's wage proposal, the administration counter-proposed a wage package that would give GEO members the same percentage increase as faculty, with a guaranteed increase of 2.5 percent. While the administration argued that the proposal showed fairness and respect, GEO recognized that they would be giving up the right to negotiate meaningful wage increases and would, instead, be allowing the administration to decide the matter unilaterally, based on what they believed the faculty, a non-bargaining unit, deserved. The administration held to this position for the remainder of those negotiations. After several months of this kind of "negotiation," the administration in both 1996 and 1999 proposed outside state mediation, which generally works in their favor. Experienced members of GEO have come to see that the interest of the administration is not to negotiate but to make no meaningful changes to the contract.

Consequently, throughout the 1990s, GEO has demanded that negotiating sessions remain open for all GEO members to attend. This was to encourage transparency in the contract process and provide an avenue for members to get more involved. Most importantly, the bargaining sessions have proven to be one of the most effective organizing tools for mobilizing members. To sit through several fruitless hours—even months—of talks, composed mainly of GEO arguing its case to a silent administration team, had a profound emotional effect on the members who were in attendance. It unmasked "negotiations" as a charade constructed and controlled by the administration, a process that many people must observe directly to believe.

In 1998, the administration requested at the outset of contract talks that the bargaining sessions be closed to GEO members, which they argued would facilitate more productive discussions. This request showed that they were clearly uncomfortable having members in attendance. To the surprise of most of the GEO leadership, the GEO bargaining team also argued for closed sessions, but for a different and interesting reason. They had no illusions about productive discussion, but instead felt that with closed sessions the administration would cease their typical stalling and delaying tactics and simply turn down GEO proposals *faster*. This illustrates that negotiations are merely part of a larger, more important process. The bargaining team recognized that the administration was likely to reject nearly all of GEO's proposals anyway and wanted to reach a point of impasse sooner rather than later. Dragging out negotiations is an effective tool of the administration. It serves to drain the union of energy and bring the process closer to the end of the semester when organizing becomes difficult if not impossible. In contrast, allowing the negotiations to deadlock sooner creates the crisis that is necessary for further mobilization by the union. The GEO Stewards Council[4] struck a balance in 1998 by voting to close the bargaining sessions for a limited time and reopen them after a month. This allowed the contract process to speed up in the way the bargaining team argued, yet captured the benefits of open sessions as an organizing tool for members.

Consequently, GEO has found that the principle value of "negotiations" is to educate members on the contested issues, to provide an opportunity to observe administration intransigence, and, in turn, to organize members to actively support the contract campaign. While negotiations alone seldom produce contractual gains for the union, the unequal power relations revealed by the negotiation process can be used by the union to educate and radicalize the membership. Observing the negotiation process allows members to see that the "professional" mode is an ineffective means of asserting their collective concerns. In this way, the negotiations are a crucial organizing tool.

RALLIES AND DEMONSTRATIONS: GRADUATE EMPLOYEES ENGAGING IN STUDENT PROTEST

In response to the administration's unwillingness to make contractual concessions, GEO has developed a strategy of an escalating series of actions designed primarily to raise awareness of the stalled negotiations and bring more members actively into the contract campaign. The series typically consists of rallies, sit-ins, mass meetings, petitions, leafleting, and attendance at negotiation sessions. It is tempting to think that such actions, typical of student protest tactics, might bring pressure to bear on the administration and possibly force a settlement. More realistically, this phase of the contract campaign represents the union in "student mode," which involves relatively unthreatening activity that will in most circumstances be ignored by the administration.

In effect, these mass displays of protest are a public challenge to the administration, bringing the private negotiating process out of the bargaining room and into the open on campus. These actions are by their very nature designed to attract the attention of the campus community and the media and publicly demonstrate to the administration the solidarity and strength of the graduate workers. They are symbolic acts of protest, in that they imply a threat of growing dissatisfaction and impending disruption, but in themselves actually disrupt nothing. Thus, these acts alone, unless carried out on a truly massive scale, are unlikely to move the administration at the bargaining table. Over the years, GEO has been successful at holding mass meetings and rallies of between two hundred and three hundred members and supporters, representing at most approximately 20 percent of the bargaining unit. An honest assessment would indicate that such turnout is unlikely to impress the administration or cause them much concern. Why then is it helpful to carry out these actions?

In GEO's experience, these events have little or no value in moving the administration but are essential in mobilizing members toward a possible work stoppage. The majority of members will not be ready to engage in a strike until they realize that no other course of action will be effective. In other words, the members must exercise and exhaust the possibilities of their student identity through these mass actions, just as they exercise and exhaust the possibilities of their professional identity during negotiations. Only through this process, which may take many months, can the membership come to the understanding that more radical action such as a strike is needed. The worker identity consequently emerges as the only remaining viable option.

THE STRIKE: GRADUATE EMPLOYEES REALIZE THEIR POWER AS WORKERS

A work stoppage or strike is perhaps the most difficult action a union can perform. As with more traditional unions, a graduate employee union strike is the ultimate expression of strength in a labor dispute and the clearest way to demonstrate to the administration the members' central role in academic production. What is unique about a graduate employee union strike is that it depends crucially on how well the union has been able to facilitate the identity shift to worker consciousness among its members. It also acts to further reinforce and solidify this worker identity through the powerful experience of withholding labor.

The goal of the strike is to stop or reduce the important teaching and/or research work performed by the union members and preferably other academic workers such as lecturers and professors. This goal is extremely difficult to achieve, as it is a tremendous task merely to bring the majority of union members onto picket lines. Added to this is the challenge of gaining support from professors, lecturers, and nonacademic staff members. Against these obstacles, most graduate employee unions rarely find themselves in a position to perform an effective work stoppage, yet it is absolutely crucial in winning concessions from the administration.

The early history of graduate employee unions shows the importance of withholding labor during contract disputes. GEO staged a successful month-long strike in 1975 during the negotiations for its first contract. This action followed eight months of bargaining and brought a quick and favorable resolution of the outstanding issues, including nondiscrimination and affirmative action policies, wages, the establishment of an agency shop, and improvements to the grievance procedure (for an account of GEO's history through 1998, see <http://www.umich.edu/~umgeo/archives/history>). Similarly, the oldest graduate employee union, the Teaching Assistants Association (TAA) at the University of Wisconsin-Madison, struck for twenty-four days during their first contract negotiations in 1970. This action followed eleven months of bargaining and resulted in a contract resolution with important gains for the union on the grievance procedure, health insurance, class size limits, and fair disciplinary procedures (for more information about the formation of TAA, see Czitrom 1997).

Fortunately, while these incredible accomplishments are difficult to match, a union can achieve a victory even with a much shorter work stoppage, as long as it can create a crisis point that brings many elements of pressure to bear on the administration. Through the work stoppage, the union raises social and economic costs to the administration such that it would be advantageous to settle the contract. The social costs to a university are raised if there is damage to its public image and reputation through negative publicity arising out of the strike. The economic costs are raised if the university is forced to spend more money dealing with the strike. It is these indicators, rather than the conversion of individual administrators to the union's cause through moral or intellectual persuasion, that will determine a contractual victory.

GEO's contract campaigns of 1995–96 and 1998–99 followed a similar process, but with different outcomes.[5] In both campaigns, after approximately four months of negotiations and mass actions, GEO tested the willingness of the membership to take more serious action by stopping work. In the ensuing month, the union attempted to measure accurately the sentiments of the membership and make the process as democratic and transparent as possible. Two strike authorization votes were taken, the first at a membership meeting and the second through the mail to the entire membership, as demanded by the GEO constitution (the constitution is available at <http://www.umich.edu/~umgeo/contract/constitution>). The strike votes passed overwhelmingly, giving the GEO leadership the authority to call a strike if necessary (Falzone 1999a). Further mass meetings and Stewards Council meetings were held to determine the form and timing of the job action.

GEO's approach has evolved over the years to strike a balance between efficiency and democratic participation of the membership in decision making. Due to the academic semester timeline, the union cannot take too long to determine its course of action or the negotiations may run into the summer when many members are absent and organizing dies off. However, the union must make every effort to maximize the exposure of the membership to important debates and decisions. In 1996, GEO decided to hold a two-day work stoppage at the beginning of April right before heading into state mediation. In 1999, a one-and-a-half-day work stoppage was planned for mid-March, to be followed by an extended strike the next week if negotiations were still unsatisfactory.

It is not easy to assess the impact of these work stoppages on the university (Falzone 1999b). In both 1996 and 1999, GEO brought approximately 20 to 30 percent of the bargaining unit out onto picket lines around key buildings on campus. The number of graduate employee-taught classes canceled is difficult to estimate, due to incomplete data, but a reasonable estimate would be 10 to 20 percent for both contract campaigns. GEO members teach approximately 50 percent of the undergraduate contact hours, so this is a considerable amount of stopped production. In both work stoppages, there were a small number of sympathetic professors who cancelled their classes or moved class off campus. Large numbers of undergraduates stayed away from their classes, and the campus looked relatively deserted. Despite these accomplishments, it can hardly be said that the university was brought to a halt. There are any number of reasons why it is an extremely difficult task to organize the majority of graduate employees to stop work. Primary among them are the conflicting identities that they must resolve when preparing for a work stoppage. Many feel that to go on strike is in direct conflict with their professional role of teacher, and many graduate employees experience a real and compelling obligation to continue to teach their students. A work stoppage also conflicts with the student identity, as the striker may be missing class to walk a picket line. A violation of either of these identities may lead to a reputation in their department as an unprofessional troublemaker, a fate that many wish to avoid. This is in addition to the real (and probably illegal) disciplinary sanctions that may result from strike participation. These difficulties affect the number of graduate employees who are full members of the union and would be candidates for serious participation in work stoppages. At Michigan, which has agency shop or fair-share dues, a relatively constant two-thirds to three-quarters of the bargaining unit have annually signed up as members of the union, which primarily gives them the right to vote on union matters. The remainder are represented by the union but do not have voting rights. Thus, work stoppage participation would be expected to occur only among the actual members who believe that the union is an organization worth joining. Many of these members, though officially supporters of the union, will still find it extremely difficult to participate in a strike. To the extent that the union can deal with the multiple identities problem, it will build a stronger organization with more members and have larger participation in work stoppages.

Added to the difficulty of bringing a large percentage of graduate employees out on strike is the nature of the stopped academic production. Although the strikers stopped teaching and grading during these brief work stoppages, the administration could count on many of them to make up most of the work afterwards. An obviously more compelling and threatening work stoppage would take the form of withholding class grades, the final product of academic work. This is the job action that the Yale graduate employee union attempted in January 1996, which they were unable to sustain successfully (see the essays in Part I of *Will Teach for Food* [Nelson 1997b] for more information about the Yale case). In recent years, GEO has not felt strong enough to attempt a work stoppage at the end of the semester, where the disbursement of grades would be interrupted.

GEO has carried out these work stoppages despite the fact that the right of public school teachers to strike is not protected in Michigan. Many officers and members of graduate employee unions will find themselves in similar legal circumstances, facing potential heavy fines or possible jail sentences for organizing strikes. In this legal climate, it is still possible to organize effective job actions. GEO's work stoppages that are discussed here were very brief, lasting only two days. In general, it will be very difficult for university administrations to obtain an injunction against a graduate employee union strike that is short, and many administrations, as with Michigan, will never attempt to do so. Aside from strikes, creative graduate employee unions can employ a number of job actions, such as "work to rule," where job descriptions are followed to the letter, or a "sick out," where graduate employees call in sick on agreed upon days.

After the 1996 work stoppage, GEO and the administration went immediately into state mediation, with disappointing results for the union. GEO was pressured by the mediator to accept the administration's last best contract offer, which included the linkage of percentage wage increases to faculty, as discussed earlier. GEO agreed, since the union was unable at that late point in the semester to mount another work stoppage. After learning this important lesson in timing, in 1999 the union held a work stoppage earlier in the semester, refused mediation entirely, and threatened a prolonged strike for the next week if contractual progress was not made. In this case, after the short work stoppage and two days before the extended strike was scheduled to begin, the administration ultimately conceded nearly all of GEO's major demands. With regard to the wage issue, GEO secured a guaranteed increase of almost 11 percent over three years. Most significantly, the teaching assignment system was changed dramatically. The most common teaching assignment category had been the 0.40 full-time equivalent (FTE), which represented an expected 16 to 20 hours per week of work. This fraction was eliminated, and those GSIs were reassigned to the next higher level, which is the 0.50 FTE, with an expected work level of 16.5 to 22 hours per week. This resulted in a 25 percent wage increase for those GSIs and a negligible increase in workload. Consequently, at the start of the 1999–2000 academic year, the average teaching appointment paid almost $1,500 per month, which is a living wage for most graduate employees in Ann Arbor. The new contract also had strong language on compensation and health care benefits for international GSIs taking the mandatory three-week summer training, an issue that had been in dispute for years.

How was GEO able to achieve its major contract goals in 1999 after having less success in 1996? Most importantly, GEO demonstrated with the two-day work stoppage a meaningful threat of an extended strike. A brief work stoppage alone, without the possibility of more work disruption in the future, is unlikely to be enough of a cost to force the administration to move. GEO also generated tremendous media publicity, with several local television stations broadcasting live from the picket lines. Universities will generally try to avoid this kind of publicity and its corresponding social costs. Furthermore, GEO obtained promises from the construction unions and the Teamster delivery drivers to stop work if the extended strike occurred. This assistance from other campus unions is essential, for it increases the economic cost to the university. GEO has been a participant in the All-Campus Labor-Council and the Huron Valley Labor Council, which seek to foster solidarity and cooperation among campus and local unions. GEO must continue to strengthen these relationships to campus and local unions, engaging in regular mutual support and assistance during contract negotiations and work stoppages. Graduate employee unions in general should work closely with other campus unions, assisting in new union organizing and possibly implementing coordinated contract bargaining in order to confront the administration from a maximum position of strength. In 1999, this convergence of many points of pressure raised the social and economic costs of the negotiations for the administration to an intolerable level. Rather than face an increase of these costs, the administration decided to conclude negotiations and avert a continuation of the strike.

CONCLUSION

In summary, in order to successfully challenge the administration during a contract campaign, a graduate employee union must facilitate the identity switch of the membership from student and professional to worker. The union must help the membership explore and undermine the pervasive academic ideology that assigns to graduate employees a position that lacks meaningful voice and agency, along with avenues of dissent that lack power and effectiveness. The contract campaign is the ideal process to achieve this understanding, as it has elements that incorporate all the roles of the graduate student/professional/worker. The experience of GEO from the past two contract campaigns indicates that contractual progress can only be achieved when the union comes to see that professional "negotiations" are not a meaningful process and that student protest methods are an ineffective means of asserting their collective power. As long as the union membership thinks and acts as an organization of students or professionals, treating negotiations as an opportunity to convince the administration of the validity of a proposal, or placing faith in traditional forms of student protest, their efforts will be frustrated and thwarted by an administration that does not share their interests.

In contrast, a graduate employee union that builds and maintains a worker consciousness in its union culture will unmask any illusions about negotiations and prepare its membership for other actions necessary to make meaningful contractual progress. In many cases, nothing short of a work stoppage or strike will create the necessary crisis that raises social and economic costs for the administration that will lead them to settle the contract dispute. The futility of professional and student modes of action must be demonstrated by the union during the contract campaign in order to foster and solidify the worker identity upon which a successful work stoppage depends.

NOTES

1. See *Casual Nation*, a report by the Coalition of Graduate Employee Unions (2000; CGEU). The Graduate Employees Organization (GEO) at the University of Michigan estimated in 1998 that graduate employees taught approximately 50 percent of all classroom contact hours at Michigan. This included primarily laboratories, discussion sections, and some lecture classes.

2. See <http://www.cgeu.org/contacts.html>, "CGEU Contact List."

3. See Berg 1998a, 1998c, 1998d. Prior to the contract signed in 1999, the wage for an average teaching appointment (twenty hours per week) was approximately $1,100 per month, and GEO calculated that on average, over 40 percent of this wage went to pay for rent in Ann Arbor, a college town with notoriously high rents.

4. The GEO Stewards Council is composed of all the academic department representatives and is responsible for setting all union policy and strategy.

5. For more detailed accounts of the 1995–96 contract campaign, see Dirnbach 1997. The 1998–99 contract campaign is discussed in Dirnbach 1999.

REFERENCES

Arenson, K.W. 2000a. Board allows graduate students to unionize. *New York Times,* April 4, p. B1.

———. 2000b. U.S. panel allows union organizing by postgraduates. *New York Times,* November 2, p. A1.

Berg, P. 1998a. GEO begins contract bargaining. *The Michigan Daily,* October 22. <http://www.pub.umich.edu/daily/1998/oct/10-22-98/news/news1.html>.

———. 1998b. GEO unhappy with contract negotiations. *The Michigan Daily,* November 2. <http://www.pub.umich.edu/daily/1998/nov/11-02—98/news/news2.html>.

———. 1998c. GEO proposes wage increase to 'U.' *The Michigan Daily,* November 12. <http://www.pub.umich.edu/daily/1998/nov/11-12-98/news/news1.html>.

———. 1998d. Wage concerns rile GEO members. *The Michigan Daily,* November 19. <http://www.pub.umich.edu/daily/1998/nov/11-19-98/news/news5.html>.

Bérubé, M. 1997. Blessed of the earth. In *Will teach for food: Academic labor in crisis,* ed. C. Nelson, 153–180. Minneapolis: University of Minnesota Press.

Coalition of Graduate Employee Unions. 2000. *Casual nation.* Available online at <http://www.cgeu.org/Cnpressrelease>.

Czitrom, D. 1997. Reeling in the years: Looking back on the TAA. In *Will teach for food: Academic labor in crisis,* ed. C. Nelson, 216–228. Minneapolis: University of Minnesota Press.

Dirnbach, E. 1997. Graduate union activism. *Z Magazine* (January):15–17.

———. 1999. Graduate union activism. *Z Magazine* (July/August):25–28.

Falzone, N. 1999a. Vote shows inclination to strike. *The Michigan Daily,* February 22. <http://www.pub.umich.edu/daily/1999/feb/02-22-99/news/news2.html>.

———. 1999b. GEO members unite: Results of walkout debated. *The Michigan Daily,* March 11. <http://www.pub.umich.edu/daily/1999/mar/03-11-99/news/news3.html>.

Lafer, G. 1997. Yale on trial. *Dissent* (Summer):78–84.

McQueen, A. 2000. Fed board backs grad student unions. *Associated Press,* November 1.

Nelson, C. 1997a. *Manifesto of a tenured radical.* New York: New York University Press.

———, ed. 1997b. *Will teach for food: Academic labor in crisis.* Minneapolis: University of Minnesota Press.

Watt, S. 1997. On apprentices and company towns. In *Will teach for food: Academic labor in crisis,* ed. C. Nelson, 229–253. Minneapolis: University of Minnesota Press.

Chapter 8

Are You Now or Have You Ever Been an Employee?: Contesting Graduate Labor in the Academy

William Vaughn

Tortuous though this account may become, it bears a simple moral: If, as a graduate student, you seek employee status, do not wait for the legal system to acknowledge you. If you work—and teaching a class, running a lab, or staffing an office all count as work—you are, de facto, an employee, unless you happen to *own* the school where you teach, research, or manage. Should that be the case, though, you probably would not be concerned about securing formal[1] collective bargaining rights, one prelude to which, at most public universities, entails establishing status as an employee *eligible* for such rights. Depending on the relevant agency, your state may opt to define *employee* in all sorts of ingenious ways, and by emphasizing the legal negotiation of that term—so clear in its practical experience, so jesuitically inviting to analysis as an item of public policy and case law—you risk ceding your union's organizing initiative, and almost guarantee that even should you "win" your legal battle, those who began your campaign will be long gone by the time that first contract gets hashed out.

If you work, you are an employee. If you teach, or do research, or run an office, you can organize. If you can organize, you can make a union. If you can make a union, you can bargain a contract. Too often, the law just gets in the way; and even when it is not designed to do so, employers will manipulate it to achieve their desired effects. As one labor lawyer I know puts it, "Don't worry about the law—worry about your organizing strategy. The law will come around some day." At the very least, legal battles take time, and time is the employer's ally, not yours. Your allies are your fellow employees and the undeniably practical effect of their work, whether it be performed or withheld. Know your work, recognize yourselves as employees, and you can compel your employer to recognize your union, no matter what the law says. This is never easy, but it is rather simple.

More difficult are the negotiations of identity necessitated by both organizing and legal wrangling. To begin with, there are the purely linguistic dimensions. As academics, especially in the humanities, we are sensitive to language. We enjoy word games but also appreciate the power words possess. A word such as *employee*, or, in the story I am about to relate, *student*, may also disempower. As a member of a union that has been forced to play word games now for five years, I know all about the disempowering capacities of language—along with the dissipating powers of time and the disenabling structures of labor law. Our union, the Graduate Employees' Organization, IFT-AFT/AFL-CIO—known simply as GEO—affiliated, ran a card drive and won a third-party monitored election in less time than it has spent fighting to overcome the legal barriers the state and university have used to deny the validity of that drive and victory.

Nevertheless, even without a recognized bargaining unit, the GEO has secured significant benefits for its members (among other things, eye and dental care and substantial raises) because, as is often the case, the mere threat of a union prods an employer to respond to demands. Marshaling such a threat entails organizing at multiple levels: professional, public, and legal. It means recognizing how one talks to colleagues in the humanities may differ from how one converses with those in engineering and that the sciences may require their own distinctive approaches.[2] Enlisting the aid of professors is different from garnering student support, and each of these efforts is distinct from how one connects with other, unionized workers on campus. At times you may find yourselves demonstrating raucously outside a trustees' meeting, while on other occasions, you may quietly but publicly hold a work-in—teaching, grading, holding office hours—inside and around the administration building. All the while, as this account will disclose, you may operate in two distinct arenas—your workplace and the legal realm—which require entirely different mindsets. I hope here to give some sense of why and how the latter arena can prove so frustrating and, thus, why those interested in organizing should devote their energy to on-the-ground campaigns, rather than legal squabbles. When you organize, *you* define the terms of the debate. When you litigate, you do not.

Organizing and litigation converged for us in April 1996, when the GEO submitted 3,226 petition cards authorizing it to be the sole representative for graduate employees at the University of Illinois, Urbana-Champaign (UIUC). Such authorization gives the union the right to bargain collectively over wages, benefits, and terms and conditions of employment. Filing authorization cards is a nearly universal requirement for calling a formal union election. For public universities, the cards are counted and validated by the relevant state labor agency; for private schools, the responsibility resides with the National Labor Relations Board. In Illinois, before an election can be called, the petitioner must establish that at least 30 percent of those seeking representation indicate so. In all cases, though, a union typically aims for and needs twice that level of endorsement, primarily because support tends to dwindle from filing date to election. The GEO's 3,226 cards represented about 60 percent of its proposed unit—a less than ideal percentage, but a solid achievement nonetheless, for at least two reasons. First, a plurality of the unit consisted of research assistants. Many research assistants, because they are essentially paid for working on their dissertations—rather than for staffing an office or teaching a class only marginally related to the area of their scholarship—are less likely to understand themselves as employees. Second, the GEO used what is known as a "strong" card—one that not only calls for an election, but also authorizes the petitioner to be the signer's bargaining agent. In a better world, an employer would recognize and bargain with a union once a majority of the unit's prospective members identified the union as their desired bargainer. The GEO clearly met that threshold, and both the union and the university could have saved hundreds of thousands of dollars in legal bills had the latter been willing to respect the clear wishes of its employees.

How do 3,226 individuals come to authorize a union to represent them? The GEO's campaign began in the fall of 1993, when early activists in the English department were struck by two aspects of their working circumstances: the magnitude and the formal invisibility. A standard assistantship in English entailed the same amount of teaching as a faculty appointment, and overall, teaching assistants taught two-thirds of their department's classes. Yet from the perspective of the institution that employed them, such teaching was not recognized as labor—rather, it was considered a species of training (even when, as in almost all cases, no faculty supervised this preparation), or just a kind of financial aid that required work, but not work itself. Students in English quickly learned their circumstances were not unusual—that similar conditions obtained elsewhere on campus and on campuses nationwide.

Self-recognition, then, was the first stage of their campaign, as it must be in any such endeavor. From the moment the campaign at Illinois formally began, in the spring of 1994, the GEO's efforts have been sustained by conversations in which colleagues define and contextualize the work they do. Indeed, for many early activists, the most invigorating aspect of their union work stemmed from the sense they earned of the common enterprise their jobs entailed. Their experience describes a trajectory from sociality to responsibility, in which graduate employees may become involved in a union due to a simple social appetite, but then discover that in reaching out to peers across departments, they come to understand the larger community they constitute. Having made that social and intellectual leap, they begin to feel obligated toward that new community,[3] especially as a way of overcoming the sense of alienation from which many start out, structurally isolated as they are in individual labs, offices, and departments.

Unions are oftentimes the only collective institutions available to graduate employees, and specifically so with regard to their employment status. As such, they function as a locus for many of the identities occupied by those working in the classroom factory. One may enter graduate school as a *student* and fund one's education as a *teacher*. By recognizing one's status as an *employee*, and hoping to improve the circumstances of that teaching job, one becomes a *colleague* by realizing improvement is a necessarily collective effort. In reaching out to other colleagues, one may do so in the capacity as a fellow *professional,* whose interests are informed by disciplinary or institutional—rather than merely personal—motivations. *Activist, organizer,* and *unionist* are further roles one might play in collective efforts as a colleague or professional. These differences, even with regard to the last three terms, are more than semantic. They describe both an evolution in identity and the range of choices one has in shaping that evolution. Unions both sustain themselves and sponsor other species of activism; and those trained in organizing may translate their union-honed skills to purely academic scenarios as well. Yet it is the climate of academic labor and the culture of organizing its effects that tie together the many roles just enumerated. Read one way, the academic labor movement is the consequence of generically poor working conditions. While recognizing that stimulus, we would do well to also acknowledge the opportunities made visible by a union consciousness, the most important of which is precisely our enhanced sense of a profession that has always combined scholarly research with classroom instruction, individual and collegial responsibilities, and professional and activist impulses. Unions clarify the roles we already perform.

But knowing oneself to be an employee and proving employee solidarity do not, by themselves, satisfy the legal requirements for recognized bargaining status. To count as employees for the state's purposes, and thus be eligible to bargain collectively, the GEO had to satisfy the definition of "professional employee," as laid out in the Illinois Educational Labor Relations Act (IELRA). This act "establish[es] the right of educational employees to organize and bargain collectively, [and] to define and resolve unfair practice disputes." Furthermore, it "establish[es] the Illinois Educational Labor Relations Board to administer the Act" (Illinois Educational Labor Relations Board [IELRB] 1999, 3). The act authorizes the labor relations board to oversee the means by which unions of educational employees petition for and hold union elections. The validity of such a petition, which could then trigger an election the results of which the university would be obligated to honor, hinged on the following 31-word passage from Section 2, paragraph (b) of the IELRA:

"Educational employee" or "employee" means any individual, excluding supervisors, managerial, confidential, short term employees, student, and part-time academic employees of community colleges employed full or part time by an educational employer. (IELRB 1999, 4)

Over the next five years, lawyers and witnesses for the GEO and UIUC, along with hearing officers and judges for the state, argued over the punctuation, spelling, and semantics of this passage. The key term is *student,* and the crucial issue is how broadly it excludes those with student status from organizing under the act. Hoping from the outset that it had an open and shut case— everyone in the GEO's proposed bargaining unit was clearly enrolled at UIUC— the university, in May 1996, filed a motion to dismiss the union's petition. They offered the following reasons why graduate assistants were clearly "students":

1. The money assistants earn is actually financial aid.
2. Assistants "do not participate as 'employees' under the State Universities Retirement System" (Motion to Dismiss 1996, 2).
3. Assistants do not receive employee insurance.
4. Students as such were clearly excluded from the IELRA by the language of Section 2, paragraph (b).
5. The IELRA fails to define any student bargaining unit.
6. It would be both costly and a waste of the board's time to hold hearings to establish the validity of the union's petition.

That same month, the union filed its response, calling for either an election or a hearing by the board to determine the employment status of petitioning for employees. It challenged the university's reading of the act, claiming that (1) the student exclusion did not apply in this case; (2) GEO members were obviously employees whether or not they were also students; (3) to deny them collective bargaining rights would violate state and federal equal protection clauses; and (4) "collective bargaining with Assistant employees [would be] an advantageous method of furthering employment relations between the parties that furthers the purposes of the IELRA" (Graduate Employees Organization 1996a, 2–3).

The union then took up the tricky matter of Section 2, paragraph (b). It pointed out that the act nowhere mentions UIUC students, and that furthermore, "the legislative history is completely devoid of any discussion regarding the inclusion of the word 'student' in [the IELRA's] definition" (Graduate Employees Organization 1996a, 4). Calling Section 2, paragraph (b) "a poorly-worded, unclear list" (Graduate Employees Organization 1996a, 3), the union suggested it might even be construed to exclude from coverage public high school teachers taking evening courses—a reading the union found only slightly more implausible than that offered by the university in hoping to exclude graduate assistants. "A more reasonable reading," it went on to argue, "is that the exclusion was intended to apply to students working for educational credit rather than to traditional employees providing services for remuneration who are also students. Moreover, the exclusion list is confusingly worded and is not at all clearly applicable to anyone other than community college employees" (Graduate Employees Organization 1996a, 4).

If the university were correct, the union argued, and *student* were its own category—like *supervisors* and *employees*—then it should be written as the plural *students*. Since it is not, the word is most likely part of a modifying clause, such that the proper reading would not be "student[s]," as the university proposes, but "student and part-time employees of community colleges." "The problem," the union acknowledged, "is that both interpretations have glitches; either 'student' should be plural or the comma should not be there" (Graduate Employees Organization 1996a, 5–6). The university would prefer to see an "s"; the union would hope to overlook a comma. Matters many composition instructors are now trained to de-emphasize compose the core of a legal dispute over bargaining rights for thousands of workers!

The union then pointed out that "although the Act defines all of the other exclusions—supervisors, managerial employees, confidential employees, and short-term employees—there is no definition of the 'student' exclusion" (Graduate Employees Organization 1996a, 6). Thus, given the various ambiguities of Section 2, paragraph (b), along with the absence of any relevant legislative documentation by the act's framers to guide subsequent readers, the union held that the board be obligated to adopt the narrowest interpretation possible. "An unbounded student exclusion," it declared, "would deprive clear employees of bargaining rights simply by virtue of their concurrent status as students, no matter how unrelated that student status is to their employment" (Graduate Employees Organization 1996a, 6). If that were what the legislature wished, the union argued, it would have defined *student*. "The most reasonable reading of the statute therefore would exclude student employees of community colleges, not all student employees" (Graduate Employees Organization 1996a, 7). Indeed, the only previous instance when the student exclusion came up before the board involved student security workers at a community college.

The union further pointed out that administrative employees at UIUC could enroll free in classes there. Were one to construe the act as broadly as the university now wished, such employees would be similarly excluded from coverage under the act. Addressing next the possibility that the act's authors simply forgot about graduate assistants, the union argued this omission in and of itself could not justify excluding them. It then cited a case involving Northern Illinois University (NIU), where students who were also employees were distinguished from "students" per se. "An exclusion," the union argued, "must be clear. As the NIU case demonstrates, the presumptively appropriate units established by the Board do nothing to clarify this patent ambiguity" (Graduate Employees Organization 1996a, 13). The union also cited a similar dispute at the University of Florida, which led to the Florida Court of Appeals finding that an explicit student exclusion violated the right of equal protection. Thus, "a statute capable of more than one interpretation should be interpreted so as not to work a constitutional violation," and in this instance, "the burden [was] upon UIUC to demonstrate that the General Assembly intended to exclude this class of employees" (Graduate Employees Organization 1996a, 17, 18).

The union response concluded with a list of other states that have determined graduate employees to merit bargaining rights and argued that in exercising such rights, employees across the country have in no way damaged the academic climates of their employing institutions. It appended nearly fifty affidavits, the majority from UIUC graduate employees who described the nature of their work *as* work. As the union pointed out, "the University's own documentation indicat[ed] that the Assistants teach roughly 35% of all undergraduate instructional units" at UIUC (Graduate Employees Organization 1996a, 32). "The Assistants," it went on to say, "are employees performing the essential business of the Employer" (Graduate Employees Organization 1996a, 33). What would be the effect of dismissing the union's petition? "The primary thrust of UIUC in this proceeding," the union contended, "is to advance an interpretation and application of the word 'student' which, in effect, would exempt, at least, one-third to fifty percent of the professional services provided to the undergraduate student body at UIUC and a substantial component of the professional administrative and research functions of the academic departments" (Graduate Employees Organization 1996a, 20).

At this point, only three major documents into the dispute, it may help to pull back and contextualize matters. The petition that triggered the Motion to Dismiss and Response to the Employer's Motion grew out of a six-month campaign, involving dozens of organizers and thousands of conversations. During the summer of 1996, as the GEO and UIUC traded opening salvos in the legal battle, the union was mapping strategy for another six-month campaign to culminate in an election the following spring. This entailed further thousands of contacts both across the campus and into the community, as graduate employees were recruited on the job, at union events, and at home. There were face-to-face meetings in offices and labs; union appearances at department functions; flyers, newspaper ads, and radio pitches; sign-up opportunities at tables in building lobbies; appeals over e-mail, on the union's web site, and through campus mail; general meetings of the union; phone calls; and countless chance encounters and casual exchanges. Like any union, the GEO would have preferred to achieve bargaining rights in such a way that the university would be legally required to acknowledge. But they could not be confident this would happen soon or ever. They made the best case they could at both the legal and member levels, hoping for success at the former, and building momentum with the latter.

It is difficult to overestimate the value of building such membership, both for those doing the organizing, and those being recruited. If the state of academic labor is more dispiriting than ever, it is all the more imperative to overcome such malaise by defining roles for ourselves that lift us out of despair, routine, and the kind of narrow self-focus that denies any larger and more meaningful nature to our profession. Roles such as colleague, professional, activist, and organizer reclaim the value of the university; they constitute acts of self-definition made all the more necessary by the kind of externally generated definitions of academic work and workers illuminated by the GEO's legal struggles.

The next salvo in that legal fight came from the university, which, in what after only a month and a half had begun to seem like an endless tit-for-tat dispute, issued a Reply Brief in Support of Motion to Dismiss. "The Union's petition," the university reiterated, "must fail as a matter of law for the simplest of reasons. Under the Illinois Educational Labor Relations Act … a 'student' may not be a member of a bargaining unit for collective bargaining purposes, and the assistants who would compose the proposed unit in this case are, first and foremost, *students*" (Reply Brief, 1, emphasis in original).

The university principally contended that whatever facts the union might marshal, the clear language of the act trumped these, such that the union's only response was to monkey with the act's language:

Even though the Union submitted a 43-page Response to the University's motion to dismiss, it devotes relatively little attention to reconciling its petition with the plain language of the Act. Instead, it literally asks the IELRB to *change the punctuation and plain language of the IELRA* so that its square-peg petition can fit into the round-hole statute. The Union devotes most of its brief to vague constitutional arguments and lengthy discussions of extra-jurisdictional case law, trying to ignore the clear language of the IELRA. The IELRB should reject this theory, and the Union's attempt to nullify legislation, and dismiss the petition. (Reply Brief, 2, emphasis in original)

The university granted the facts put forward by the union in its brief, affidavits, and exhibits. "However, none of the facts submitted by the Union matter," save for one: "that the assistants sought to be represented must be admitted and enrolled as students in a graduate program at the University.... This simple undisputed fact is dispositive of the University's motion to dismiss, and obviates the need for a hearing" (Reply Brief, 2). Claiming the language of the act was plain, simple, and unambiguous, the university then employed one of the hoariest maneuvers from first-year composition. "The American Heritage Dictionary," they pointed out, "defines 'student' as 'one who attends a school, college, or university'" (Reply Brief, 4). Given such an obvious meaning of the term, the university argued, "the Union concedes that the comma following the word 'student' destroys its principal argument." Thus, "faced with this seemingly insurmountable hurdle, the Union asks the IELRB to do something which it could not do even if it were so disposed: ignore the comma because 'it should not be there'" (Reply Brief, 6).

The university then proceeded to dispense with the rest of the union's arguments. They labeled erroneous the union's other examples of student employees who might be excluded by the act. For example, a secretary who took classes would not lose her job if she stopped taking them (as would the equivalent graduate assistant). The university also found it "inconceivable" that the IELRB could have overlooked a bargaining unit comprising graduate assistants. In addition, they argued that the union misrepresented the NIU case, and that, regarding cases from other states, "the fatal problem for the Union is that *none* of these decisions involves statutory language even remotely similar to the language in the IELRA" (Reply Brief, 10, emphasis in original). Ultimately, "the Union's argument boils down to this: set aside the plain language of the IELRA and conclude, based on extra-jurisdictional case law interpreting different statutory language, that student-assistants may constitute a collective bargaining unit" (Reply Brief, 10).

In June, the union issued its Sur-Reply on Employer's Motion to Dismiss, chiding their opponent for spending "pages banally asserting the undisputed fact that the petitioned for Assistants are students at the University of Illinois." Yet "no matter how many times the Employer repeats its mantra that the statute unambiguously excludes the Assistants, it cannot avoid the abstruseness of the student exclusion" (Graduate Employees Organization 1996b, 2). Indeed, the university, far from offering a straightforward definition of the word *student*, instead generates its own favorable interpretation of the act, which is that the exclusion concerns students whose jobs are contingent upon their student status. "Either the statue [sic] is clear on its face," the union claimed, "or it requires interpretation. By the Employer's own argument, interpretation is necessary to avoid a result that would cause too large a class of employees to forfeit their bargaining rights. This is precisely the argument the GEO makes, only its interpretation would deny bargaining rights to a smaller, more reasonable class of employees"(Graduate Employees Organization 1996b, 4).

The union maintained student status did not qualify as a per se exclusion—the real issue was functionality, and the consequent relation between studentship and employment. Here the union reiterated that graduate assistants of all categories meet the act's definition of a "professional employee."

The next union move was to delve into the legislative history of the student exclusion, which came about as "the result of the Governor's Amendatory veto, not the result of the legislature's deliberative process... The reason why the legislature did not expound on the exclusion is that it was added by the Governor and, without further legislative deliberation, passed as such" (Graduate Employees Organization 1996b, 21). Neither then nor since has "the State of Illinois ... articulated a legitimate State interest in excluding Assistants from coverage" (Graduate Employees Organization 1996b, 24). Finally, the union addressed concerns about how a graduate employee union might impact the purely academic dimensions of those employees' lives. "The employer," it pointed out,

accepted as true for the purposes of this Motion to Dismiss the GEO's extensive evidence that the Assistantships are not part of the Assistants' educational programs. They are not degree requirements, there is seldom any relationship between the subject of their Assistantship appointments and their dissertation, they receive no course credit for their Assistantships, they have little or no faculty supervision, and they are treated as employees in that capacity rather than students. It is therefore a mystery what learning process would be disrupted by collective bargaining or necessitates unequal bargaining power. (Graduate Employees Organization 1996b, 26)

Finally, after almost three months of steady, back-and-forth niggling, mudslinging, and grammatical nitpicking, the executive director of the IELRB issued his decision. "After careful consideration of the parties' arguments," he declared,

I deny the Employer's motion to dismiss. I find that the issues presented require a hearing to develop an evidentiary record of student status. A factual determination, in this case, must be made as to whether the employees in the petitioned for unit are students. In addition, a question of law exists as to whether an individual that has dual status as both a student and as an educational employee may or may not be excluded from coverage under the Act. For the reasons that this case presents material issues of fact and questions of law I direct that a hearing be held before an Administrative Law Judge. (Illinois Educational Labor Relations Board (IELRB) 1996, 2)

This hearing would prove almost superfluous. Indeed, the structure of the legal dispute between UIUC and its graduate employees would come to resemble that of the First World War, in which a flurry of activity at the outset laid out the basic terms and terrain of the conflict, after which the two sides engaged in a seemingly interminable stalemate. If I dwell on these first few months, it is because that period saw the basic dimensions of the argument established. Both sides acknowledged some indisputable facts about how work got done at UIUC but differed over how to interpret that work in terms of the only relevant statutory language, which language determined whether graduate employees at public institutions in Illinois could organize unions under the aegis of state law. All of the back and forth name calling served to influence a relative handful of individuals empowered to adjudicate that law: first, an administrative law judge, or hearing officer, of the IELRB; then, the full board; and finally, the Appellate and Supreme Courts of Illinois.

Of course, there remained those thousands of graduate employees to be organized, and indeed, the union proceeded with an election—monitored by an association of local religious groups—during the very year the legal battle was first engaged.[4] The contrast between these halves of the campaign is instructive. In the legal arena, an audience of one, the law judge; on the ground, an audience of fifty-six hundred. In the legal arena, pages and pages of briefs and replies; on the ground, hours and hours of meetings and conversations. In the legal arena, the language of policy and precedent; on the ground, the facts of the workplace. Of course, it took meetings and conversations to prepare those legal documents, just as the union, to facilitate conversation and motivate action, prepared all manner of paper argument: flyers, charts, ads, newsletters, and press releases. The legal and organizing efforts did overlap, perhaps most concretely in the affidavits and testimony of the witnesses for the hearings. Here, the ultimate setting was the legal realm, but recruiting witnesses in the first place is a species of organizing, and the stories they told to the hearing officer mapped experience onto policy matters. The overall question, though, remains one of efficacy. The most well-argued case still depends on the favor of jurists and the letter of the law, however biased the former and sloppy the latter. Organizing, it is true, requires a greater volume of consent, but the favor you earn is yours to deploy, and you shape the language that earns and deploys it.

To appreciate what it means when the employer shapes the debate, consider one instance from the evidentiary hearings. The union's first graduate employee witness was Dave Breeden, a PhD candidate in philosophy. Breeden was then employed as the director of the university's radioisotope lab, and because his dissertation research involved the philosophy of science, he was pressed by the university's lawyer to admit his current job did serve a relevant educational purpose.[5] (Earlier, when asked by the union's lawyer why he had applied for the position, he responded, "Quite frankly because it pays really well for graduate employee work" [Testimony of Dave Breeden, 682].) As the university's lawyer continued to press Breeden, it became clear he was invoking statements from Breeden's graduate school application materials. Such documents are part of a student's confidential records, and not only had the university failed to request Breeden's permission to access these, they had also refrained from notifying the union they would be using them in the hearings. The union's lawyer objected, and the hearings were suspended for a month while the administrative law judge considered whether such documents were to be admissible. In the end, the judge granted the university's right to employ student records, but only after certain documents, such as grades and financial records, were first removed. The overall implication? One lawyer or judge's interest trumps the rights of thousands of employees. Better those employees trust one another to act in their common interest, than trust the law to have their best interests in mind.

Ultimately, the hearings produced 103 exhibits totaling about 5,000 pages, and another 1,528 pages of testimony from thirty-two witnesses. Briefs from each side were submitted in March 1997. The university's argument largely followed the contours of its earlier Motion to Dismiss. "Notwithstanding the volume of evidence presented at the hearing," they argued,

> this is a simple and straightforward case.... Assistantships are necessarily subordinate to a person's enrollment and pursuit of a graduate program. Stipends and tuition waivers received by an assistant are forms of financial aid, along with fellowships, loans, etc. Faculty serve as advisors and mentors, not employers. Students serving as assistants have an "educational" relationship, not an employment relationship with the University. Assistants are learning through actual work experience to be teachers and researchers, which is the essence of graduate education. (University's Post-Hearing Brief, 2–3)[6]

The university then set out to refute the testimony of union witnesses. "The thrust of the union's case," according to UIUC, "seems to be that assistants are providing services to the University and that therefore they are employees eligible to form a bargaining unit. This argument ignores the fact that teaching experience gained through assistantships prepares students for professional careers. Assistantships are part of an *educational process*, not the end product" (University's Post-Hearing Brief, 27, emphasis in original). In general, the university held that anything an assistant does somehow constitutes "training" for a subsequent job; and that, because to do anything at UIUC, graduate employees need to first maintain student status, such status renders their employment *indicia incidental*, most crucially with regard to the student exclusion of the IELRA. Needless to say, the university hardly needed evidentiary hearings in order to make this latter claim. (As it turned out, neither would the hearing officer, to concur with it.)

In its brief, the union also restated much that it argued when contesting the university's Motion to Dismiss. Claiming "Assistants are plainly employees of the University" (Post-Hearing Brief of GEO, 6), the union argued that the real question was whether their concurrent status as students "excludes them from coverage as 'educational employees' despite the employment relationship" (Post-Hearing Brief of GEO, 6–7). They cited employment criteria such as being paid for services, having taxes withheld from pay, having appointments and pay "based on a 40-hour work week," being covered under workers' compensation law, having staff ID cards, and receiving benefits regarding death, plus "dental insurance, sick days, and vacation days by virtue of their employment" (Post-Hearing Brief of GEO, 7).[7] They further cited multiple exhibits wherein the university's own language acknowledges the employment status of graduate assistants. In addition, the union proposed "it would be consistent with the Act's stated purposes to interpret [that] exclusion to exclude from coverage only those students who are performing work as an integral part of their formal education or defined program of study, i.e. for the purpose of completing educational degree or credit requirements" (Post-Hearing Brief of GEO, 15).

The union also engaged the matter of why UIUC needed so many teaching assistants in the first place. They cited statistics from departments such as English and philosophy, where faculty lines have eroded over the past thirty years, as graduate assistants have come to teach close to two-thirds and half of their instructional units, respectively. Provost Larry Faulkner, a witness for the university, is quoted acknowledging that UIUC uses so many graduate assistants largely because it is located in a rural area, such that it is otherwise unable "'to attract professionally qualified individuals to teach some fraction of the things [they] would teach with assistants'" (Post-Hearing Brief of GEO, 33). The union also disputed the university's accounts of how faculty supposedly mentored graduate employees—an argument around which much of the university's brief was organized. Of one such example of mentoring, articulated by a professor of educational psychology, the union proposed that it "offered nothing concrete to show that Assistants' learning experiences were anything beyond any other learning experience one would obtain from a job, or life in general" (Post-Hearing Brief of GEO, 38).

The administrative law judge's decision came in April 1997, a year and a week after the union originally petitioned for an election, and just days after they had won an independently run contest by a two-to-one margin. If one word—*student*—had been enough to precipitate the legal battle, four others were enough to end this stage of it: "The petition," the judge wrote, "is dismissed" (Administrative Law Judge's Decision, 20). She was "unpersuaded that the term 'student' is ambiguous"; furthermore, she held that "a search of the legislative history of the Act fails to suggest that the statutory term 'student' should be given any meaning other than its plain and ordinary one" (Administrative Law Judge's Decision, 11). Thus, "absent a statutory definition indicating a different legislative intent, the words used in a statute are intended to have their ordinary and popularly understood meanings," and "any other finding would defy the apparent legislative intent in including the unqualified term 'student' within the statute" (Administrative Law Judge's Decision, 12). Finding "fatally arbitrary" the union's alternative readings of the act, she then proffered some slippery exegeses of her own. "It should be noted," she wrote,

that the drafters of this particular section of the Act were not particularly consistent in the use of nouns versus adjectives, so the inconsistency between singular and plural is not surprising or particularly significant in this context. For example, "supervisors" and "student" are used as nouns, yet "managerial," "confidential," "short-term" are adjectives modifying the noun "employees." Therefore, the fact that the word "student" is the only noun in singular form does not appear to change the meaning of the word. (Administrative Law Judge's Decision, 15)

A meaning, we may recall, alleged to be plain and ordinary!

Needless to say, the union retained its own definitions of the plain and ordinary and promulgated these in arenas outside of the hearing room. In the wake of the election—held on April 15–16, 1997, and won by a margin of 1,633 to 906—the union staged a series of "invitations to bargain," by making itself publicly available to a number of UIUC administrators. After all, the GEO's members had twice authorized the union to bargain a contract on their behalf. The university, of course, refused to enter into negotiations, but their visible reluctance was framed by the union as being consistent with a pattern of undemocratic practice—a public relations point the GEO was to recycle repeatedly in appealing to other audiences.

Indeed, whether it was the invitations to bargain, general meetings and rallies, or the subsequent work-ins held in 1999 and 2000, the union strove to incorporate in their events representatives from all sectors of the campus and community. Such coalition building speaks to a further evolution of the union-inflected academic identity. Many unions on campus—representing firefighters, clerical workers, custodial staff, and others—had their own fractious relations with UIUC's administration. GEO members attended their events and supported their efforts, while other unions' members turned out for graduate employee functions.[8] By the same token, graduate employees came to see their struggle to achieve basic health care rights as part of a larger, countywide problem in this area. Many of us were active in local political efforts both to fund facilities and elect candidates who ran on this issue—candidates who also often endorsed the union's cause. Here as well, the union's work clarified identities its members had always had. Graduate students may spend as much as a decade or more in the communities where their schools are located; they should think of themselves as residents with a stake in those communities.

Organizing as always in offices and labs across campus, the union also took its case directly to the school's Board of Trustees, to undergraduates and professors, to the public at large, and to the state legislature. Through petitions, referenda, demonstrations, work-ins, press releases, and lobbying campaigns, the union remained active in the midst of an otherwise abstract legal dispute. In some cases, they hoped to influence the Board of Trustees by showing that students and professors respected at least the right of graduate employees to organize. To that end, in the spring of 2000, the union collaborated with a slate of undergraduate candidates to sponsor a referendum in the Illinois Student Government Elections. One slogan used in the context of the referendum campaign demonstrates how the union sought to illuminate solidarity: "Our working conditions," the GEO said, "are your learning conditions." In addition to the support of sympathetic candidates, the union also secured endorsements from the student newspaper and some of its columnists. In the end, 77 percent of voters that spring said "yes" to the right of graduate employees to choose union representation. Although this resolution was nonbinding, it did secure considerable public relations value, as well as the prospect of future such support, rhetorical and otherwise. Faculty endorsements have been more limited, but by the summer of 2000 several departments in the humanities had passed resolutions supporting the union, and individual professors had helped in myriad ways, from donating funds, to writing letters on behalf of the union to local newspapers, to bringing food to unionists who occupied the office of the Board of Trustees in the spring of 2000. Lobbying efforts have been only partially successful. While the union was able to win bipartisan support in the Illinois House for a bill that would revise the IELRA to remove the student exclusion, the same bill died in the Senate, largely due to the efforts of that chamber's chair of the Rules Committee, who just happened to represent the district encompassing UIUC. Even after a substantial petition drive and phone effort, the chair refused to let the bill out of committee to be voted on by the full Senate.

It took two years, from 1993 to 1995, for the union to garner 500 members and succeed in affiliating with the Illinois Federation of Teachers-AFT/AFL-CIO. It took six months, from the fall of 1995 to the spring of 1996, to gather 3,226 signatures for the purposes of setting an election. The election that did take place, though not occurring under the aegis of state law, required another year's work. But even counting that entire four years from conception to election, the time entailed by the original organizing drive of the GEO has now been exceeded by the duration of the legal case. The original decision was appealed by the union to the full IELRB, and in April 1998, the board upheld it. The union then appealed the board's ruling to the Illinois Appellate Court that May. Finally, in June 2000, the Appellate Court overturned the board's decision from two years earlier, remanding the case to the board with the following directions: that a bargaining unit be determined by applying a test for "significant connection," whereby only those employees would be excluded whose work was so related to their academic roles that bargaining collectively would impair the process of education. (In reaching this unanimous decision, the Appellate Court rejected earlier definitions of *student*—offered by the university and accepted by the board—which presumed assistantships to be a form of financial aid.) Though the state Supreme Court refused to hear the university's appeal of this ruling, the matter of "significant connection" remained a potential stumbling block for organizing efforts at UIUC.

Essentially, the two sides were still arguing about what it means to be a student, when someone is both a student and an employee. While the Appellate Court's ruling made possible some kind of bargaining unit, it wound up authorizing, through the board, a unit comprising only assistants who taught outside of their degree-granting departments, or who performed clerical work too generic to be meaningfully connected to their field of study. When such a unit was broached in 2001, five years of back-and-forth legal skirmishing—roughly fifty distinct petitions, motions, responses, briefs, decisions, and appeals—resulted in a proposed bargaining unit that contained about four percent of the originally petitioned for fifty-six hundred graduate assistants.

Facing the prospect of such a decimated unit, the GEO retained the same basic options it had always confronted: rewriting state labor law through lobbying the legislature and governor and/or compelling recognition for whatever unit it chose to represent. Already by the winter of 2000, the shape of the bargaining unit had indeed evolved, as the union opted to no longer represent research assistants whose work more or less equaled their dissertations—a class typically absent or excluded from the formally recognized graduate employee unions across the country.

Finally, more than six years after petitioning for an election through formal channels, the union achieved a concession that may indeed result in its being voluntarily recognized by UIUC. Following further acts of civil disobedience on the campus, including a sit-in at one of the administration buildings, the union and UIUC in the spring of 2002 "reached an agreement about the composition of an electorate" (Joint Statement from Graduate Employees' Organization and University of Illinois at Urbana-Champaign). The new, prospective unit included most employees classified as teaching or graduate assistants, a population that would "represent an increase of approximately 800 percent from the initial ruling made by the Labor Board" the previous spring (GEO and Administration Announce Agreement). Assuming the board signs off on this agreement, graduate employees at UIUC will be eligible to vote for and achieve union representation.

This agreement remains a partial victory, of course. The GEO's fight is just beginning, which is perhaps only proper. Winning one election secures merely the right to representation—not that a certain contract is guaranteed or that the union no longer has to organize. The GEO kept organizing throughout the legal dispute, which is why they were able to steer their employer toward influencing the labor board. Along the way, the union accomplished a great deal. Grassroots union organizing has already brought better and more health care options and more competitive salaries to UIUC graduate employees. In addition, that on-the-ground organizing has brought about a sense of connection across the campus as academic workers collaborate through professional responsibility, union solidarity, and community spirit. None of this required a courtroom victory. The effort, at Illinois and elsewhere, is just, even when the law fails to see that. Organize first and let the law catch up.

So that is one lesson—the same with which I opened. I will conclude with one more. Most graduate employee unions are more or less TA unions. If you are a TA, in any field—help your students improve their writing, including spelling, punctuation, and grammar. You never know: some of them may grow up to be lawmakers.

NOTES

1. Throughout this account, I intend the word *formal* to more or less mean "according to Illinois state labor law" or, with regard to union-building issues, the state of being affiliated rather than not. In the first instance, the distinction matters insofar as formal recognition or bargaining rights must be honored by the employer, whereas an employer's consent to informally achieved such conditions may always be withdrawn. In fact, the earliest graduate employee union, at the University of Wisconsin, Madison, first achieved informal recognition in the 1970s, and later secured the formal variety more than a decade later, after the university withdrew its recognition. While acknowledging that formal recognition is always a more secure state for a union, it should be pointed out that (1) unions often achieve significant benefits for their members without it; and (2) the inherently transient nature of graduate employee bargaining units—that is, people are always graduating or moving on—means that a union of such individuals, even one that enjoys formal recognition, is always, of a necessity, organizing. (Arguably, the healthiest unions are the ones that never stop organizing; the postwar decline of the American labor movement in part reflected its failure to appreciate that.) Regarding my second use of *formal*, I would simply suggest that every graduate employee union should affiliate, so long as this is an option. The internationals with which one affiliates can provide the expertise and funding necessary for successful campaigns. Lest my advice here appear contradictory—U.S. unions do not organize; trust your affiliate to help you organize—let me just say that one important and undeniable contribution made by the graduate employee labor movement is to revivify the organizing mentality of labor in general.

2. For example, teaching assistants in the humanities, who think of themselves as training to be academics, are oriented differently toward their work than are engineering students, who are more likely to be headed into private industry. Graduate students in the sciences tend to be more like humanities colleagues in terms of overall orientation but differ in the kinds of assistantships they hold—such as research positions or grader/lab director appointments, rather than teaching positions in which they are the sole instructors for a course. Nevertheless, their overall academic job prospects resemble those of humanities students. Given this range of self-understandings, one has to organize around concerns specific to each circumstance, all the while recognizing that to achieve any goal on behalf of these populations, the solution is necessarily collective—that is, they can all benefit from a union, though the specific benefits may differ for each group.

3. For a more detailed account of this process, see Vaughn (1999, 41–43).

4. The union opted to participate in an election, even though it was not held under state labor law, for three reasons. First, to further facilitate the possibility of voluntary recognition. Although is has always been unlikely that the university would choose to recognize the GEO were it not legally obligated to, the union has repeatedly (and sincerely) invited the school to do just this. An election victory by the union, in this context, would simply be further proof that the university would be heeding the wishes of the majority. Second, an election was the inevitable next step: employees had overwhelmingly authorized one, and it was crucial, for purposes of momentum, that the union continue to advance its case. (And at this stage of the process, an election was far less controversial than, say, a work stoppage.) Third, an election victory, even one outside the formal framework of state law, could constitute a major public relations coup.

5. The comedic high points of the hearing were provided by philosophy professor Richard Schacht, who happened to serve on Breeden's committee. Schacht made various

claims about the importance of a teaching background for philosophy PhDs, and the relevancy of Breeden's laboratory directorship to his dissertation. In cross-examining him, the union's lawyer, Gil Cornfield, first got Schacht to acknowledge he was married to Judith Rowan, an associate chancellor. (Schacht, in other words, was no disinterested participant in these hearings.) Cornfield subsequently asked why, if a teaching background were so crucial, the Department of Philosophy requires no assistantship for the degree. Schacht could only respond that they strongly "encouraged" such an appointment. Then, after verifying where Schacht earned his PhD, Cornfield inquired about his graduate teaching background. "And at Princeton," he asked, " ... did you have a TAship?" Schacht: "I did not." "Did you," Cornfield continued, "have an RAship?" "No," Schacht replied, "I did not" (Richard Schacht's Transcript, 1513). Finally, Cornfield pressed him on earlier remarks regarding the relevancy of Breeden's work in Chemistry to the dissertation Schacht was overseeing. "Do you have any knowledge of what Dave Breeden has done in the isotope lab?" Cornfield asked. Schacht: "Not other than the—no, I have—I have very little knowledge of that" (Richard Schacht's Transcript, 1514).

6. Significantly, the university buttressed its argument with evidence from units such as psychology, speech communications, library and information science, accountancy, chemistry, crop sciences, and engineering, few of which employ many TAs, the category of assistant most commonly represented by graduate employee unions. "It is important to note," the university argued, "the distinction between 'mentoring' relationships in graduate education, as opposed to supervisory-subordinate employment relationship and the 'exclusive representative' principle embodied in collective bargaining" (University's Post-Hearing Brief, 19). Such a claim falls flat, though, when applied to a department such as English, where TAs, if they experience any "mentoring" at all, are most likely to receive it from peer advisers, rather than from professors.

7. In constructing this list, the union included some items that preceded their drive—for example, sick and vacation days—and some that coincided with and, in their opinion, resulted from it, such as the dental benefits. When these latter benefits were announced in the fall of 1996, they were granted only to graduate students who held assistantships, rather than to graduate students in general. The union felt it was significant that even in the midst of a struggle to assert and codify employee status for graduate assistants, an administration that vigorously opposed that effort would choose to offer it only to students who also worked.

8. Such reciprocation extended beyond the university as well. We often participated in other union pickets and demonstrations in the local community—for example, carpenters protesting nonunion work sites, or municipal workers engaged in a contract dispute—and beyond—the early years of the GEO coincided with some of the bitterest labor struggles in the country, three of which, involving A.E. Staley, Bridgestone/Firestone, and Caterpillar, were also occurring in central Illinois.

REFERENCES

Most of the documents below pertain to the Matter of Board of Trustees/University of Illinois at Urbana-Champaign, Employer, and Graduate Employees Organization, Petitioner, and Illinois Education Association, NEA, Interested Party, and Illinois AFL-CIO, Interested Party, before the State of Illinois Educational Labor Relations Board.

Administrative Law Judge's Recommended Decision and Order. 1997. Case No. 96-RC-0013-S. (23 April).

GEO and Administration Announce Agreement. 2002. Electronic memo (6 June).

Graduate Employees Organization. 1996a. Response to Employer's Motion to Dismiss. Case No. 96-RC-0013-S. (20 May).

Graduate Employees Organization. 1996b. Sur-Reply on Employer's Motion to Dismiss. Case No. 96-RC-0013-S. (7 June).

Illinois Educational Labor Relations Board. 1990. The Educational Labor Relations Act and The Rules and Regulations. (revised).

Illinois Educational Labor Relations Board (IELRB). 1996. Executive Director Decision on Motion to Dismiss. Case No. 96-RC-0013-S. (8 July).

Joint Statement from Graduate Employee's Organization and University of Illinois at Urbana-Champaign. 2002. <http://www.shout.net/~geo> (6 June).

Motion to Dismiss or, in the Alternative, for an order to show cause. 1996. Case No. 96-RC-0013-S. (2 May).

Post-Hearing Brief of the Graduate Employees Organization. 1997. Case No. 96-RC-0013-S. (4 March).

Reply Brief in Support of Motion to Dismiss or, in the alternative, for an order to show cause. 1996 Case No. 96-RC-0013-S. (31 May).

Richard Schacht's transcript. 1996. Case No. 96-RC-0013-S. 11 (December).

Testimony of Dave Breeden. 1996. Case No. 96-RC-0013-S. (17 September).

University's Post-Hearing Brief. 1997. Case No. 96-RC-0013-S. (4 March).

Vaughn, William. 1999. From sociality to responsibility: Grad employee unions and the meaning of the university. *Perspectives* 37 (November): 41–43.

Chapter 9

The Politics of Constructing Dissent:
The Rhetorical Construction
of Faculty Union Membership

Darla S. Williams

There is one reliable conclusion to be reached about American university and college faculty: They are masters of gallows humor. At conferences they make jokes about their laughable salaries, corporate-minded deans, and fund-raising presidents. They shake their heads over the legislators and the public who prioritize cost-saving initiatives over academically sound institutions. They express frustration and dismay over the breach between the intellectual life they anticipated during their graduate schooling and the reality they live today. They share their complaints and then retreat to their individualized research and teaching schedules, convinced that they can do little to change their organizations.

The purpose of this chapter is to understand the means by which employee resistance to dominant organizational practices is cultivated. This is accomplished through the discursive examination of identity construction by a faculty union during an organizational crisis. Promoting resistant attitudes and actions in an organizational context is inherently difficult. Employees must first recognize the degree to which the "natural" organizational order is in fact constructed according to a specific set of dominant interests and values. Following that, employees have to recognize their stake in questioning the established order and to envisage strategies for enacting resistance. Employees must re-vision their institutions; they have to conceive of an organization structured around a wide array of interests, not just those of the dominant group. Lastly, employees must be willing to sacrifice any current benefits they derive from the system (such as predictability, a paycheck, or upward mobility) for possible future benefits. Throughout the whole process, employees must be willing to confront the established order and to risk their current organizational status, even to the point of losing their jobs. Against the background of these material and symbolic difficulties, how does a faculty union cultivate the collective will to strike?

FACULTY IDENTITIES AND FACULTY UNIONS

There are several identity dilemmas for faculty unions: individualized socialization, conflicting allegiances, and cultivating risk-taking. First, socialization into an academic career does not prepare faculty for collective action. Academics become expert in their disciplines and subdisciplines through separation and specialization. In virtually all fields, one's approach to one's subdiscipline situates professional identity. Graduate school teaches prospective faculty that individual achievement and recognition are the keys to academic success. One must differentiate one's work and ideas from those of others, or it has no value. Scholars must accurately attribute ideas to their intellectual sources, so they will not claim credit for words or notions that are not their own. New assistant professors are advised to build their publication records in order to succeed.

The faculty union must compete with professors' various sources of identity. Socialization research suggests that professional employees, such as university faculty, identify primarily with the values of their professions. Medical doctors adhere to a code of ethics that transcends employment in any individual practice, while lawyers align their actions and values with their professional code, regardless of the firms in which they may be working. Academics identify with ethical values relevant to their research and to their teaching. Primary identification with a professional ethic means that university professors identify secondarily with their institutions. Therefore, the faculty union must compete for allegiance and attention with professional and institutional identities. Historically, unions have represented blue-collar workers whose collective interests were perhaps easier to define. These unions emphasize collectivity, identical treatment, promotion through seniority, and a leveling out of the differences among workers. Unionized intellectual workers are employees with conflicting allegiances. Their collective interests are not so easily defined, and their identification is less easily secured.

Lastly, the union must convince faculty to sacrifice their individual interests and to take risks for the sake of the group. This is an inherently difficult task, as detailed earlier, but for university faculty, there are the additional challenges of an individualized orientation to the profession and the arduous process of both graduate training and tenure. Professors invest a great deal of time and effort in attaining a tenured position at a college or university. Tenure-track university positions are increasingly difficult to obtain in many disciplines. The difficulty of securing a tenured position is a real obstacle to persuading professors to take risks.

Therefore, the task of the faculty union is to construct a compelling identity for its members: the activist academic. In order to counter those trends and practices that work against collective, resistant action, the faculty union must persuade its membership to adopt (at least partially and temporarily) this new identity. There are several steps to successfully constructing an activist identity for faculty: (1) critical evaluation of the status quo and the faculty member's role in the established order; (2) recognition of the faculty member's stake in questioning the institution; (3) visualization of a reorganized institution and reconstructed faculty roles; and (4) willingness to sacrifice for a "better" institution.

The purpose of this chapter is to examine the member identity, or identities, constructed in the messages from the Association of Pennsylvania State College and University Faculties (APSCUF) to university faculty during contract negotiations. I am a faculty member in the Department of Communication and Theatre at Millersville University, Millersville, Pennsylvania, one of the sister schools participating in the State System of Higher Education (SSHE). Organizational scholars have studied the construction of identity and membership by employing institutions, but few have examined the construction of identity by a secondary entity in the face of individualized socialization, conflicting allegiances, and aversion to risk.

First, I will employ research in the area of organizational identification to identify the rhetorical strategies employed in APSCUF's messages. Next, I will describe the identity (or identities) constructed in those messages and the values and practices associated with the activist identity. APSCUF's task involves critical evaluation of the organization and development of a critical awareness of faculty interests in the State System of Higher Education. Following that, I will employ critical organizational research to evaluate the political potential of APSCUF's communication with members. I will evaluate APSCUF's attempts to promote a critical reading of the organizational environment and to encourage a radical consciousness among members. APSCUF's focus on benefits for junior and adjunct faculty were valuable foci for advancing critical awareness. Finally, I will evaluate APSCUF's attempts to encourage resistance and construct an alternative identity and organizational vision.

LITERATURE REVIEW

Organizational Identification

In communication research, we often ask questions about the symbolic interpretation of language-in-use. Organizational communication scholars are particularly concerned with the potential of symbols for constructing identities and relationships in the workplace. The relationship between employee behaviors and organizational outcomes is one of the more basic concerns of organizational researchers (van Knippenberg and van Schie 2000; Scott 1997; Scott 2000). As a result, organizational identification has long been a concern of organizational scholars (Hall and Schneider 1972; Kaufman 1960; Lee 1969, 1971; Mael and

Tetrick 1992; Rotondi 1975a, 1975b). Identification may loosely be defined as the individual's sense of belonging to a group (Russo 1998). Organizational identification is a psychological and symbolic rapport between the individual and the organization (Cheney and Tompkins 1987; Russo 1998). The process of identification does not stop at the symbolic level; identification has behavioral implications. Employees who identify with their organization's values and interests are most likely to act in its best interests (Scott 1997). Organizational identification manifests itself as organizational commitment. Organizational commitment is distinct from but related to organizational identification (Mael and Tetrick 1992; Russo 1998). "Identification is considered the substance of the relationship; commitment is the form" (Russo 1998, 77). Both social identity theory (Mael and Tetrick 1992) and rhetorical theory (Cheney 1983a, 1983b; Cheney and Tompkins 1987; Tompkins and Cheney 1983; Tompkins, Fisher, Infante and Tompkins 1975) have been used to study organizational identification.

This chapter is primarily concerned with overt rhetorical attempts to encourage identification and subsequent action. Specifically, Cheney and Tompkins (1987) argue that organizational identification is both process and product, based in the communication of organizational interests to employees. They define identification as "the development and maintenance of an individual's or a group's 'sameness' or 'substance' against a backdrop of change and 'outside' elements" (5). The member feels that she or he is an agent of the organization, an extension of its purpose and values. Prominent unifying symbols and practices foster clear boundaries for membership (Bullis and Tompkins 1989) and a source of common identity. An individual identifies with an organization when she or he makes decisions that implement the factual and value premises of the organization (Cheney 1983a, 1983b; Tompkins and Cheney 1983). Tompkins and Cheney (1983) argue that most employees are socialized to varying degrees within an organization. "If the same individual then makes decisions with the consequences of particular choices for the organization uppermost in mind, then he or she also is identifying with the organization" (127). Finally, the most powerful context for identification is the enthymematic situation. Briefly, as developed by Tompkins and Cheney (1985), the enthymeme is a decision-making situation in which the organizational member provides the premise(s) for reaching a conclusion. When a member can automatically supply premises preferred by the organization without having to be prompted, she or he is participating in using those assumptions or premises to act. Therefore, due to its participatory nature, the enthymeme is a powerful identification context.

Modes of Control

As developed in the field of communication, organizational identification may function as a means of socializing members (Cheney 1983b; Tompkins and Cheney 1983), ensuring that organizational interests are served by individual decisions and as means of unobtrusive or concertive control (Bullis and Tompkins

1989; Cheney and Tompkins 1987). Modes of control range along a continuum, from more overt means of control, such as physical coercion or technological pacing and surveillance, to less obvious control forms, such as bureaucratic procedures or the internalization of organizational interests (that is, organizational identification) (Bullis and Tompkins 1989; Tompkins and Cheney 1985). Bullis and Tompkins (1989) describe the convergence of concertive control and organizational identification as a participatory process in which the individual begins to define his or her own values and the organization's values as increasingly similar. Members internalize the organization's values, making decisions according to organizational premises, and begin to "think in organizational terms and act as agents of these juristic persons [organizations], experiencing autonomy while making organizationally preferred decisions. Beliefs, values, and symbols direct behavior indirectly" (289). As is obvious from the definition and description of organizational identification, this process reproduces dominant organizational interests in the individual actions taken by employees. This is not to say that organizational identification controls perfectly or completely, but that the main outcome of the process is the furthering of organizational interests.

Some of the overt control strategies described by organizational scholars may also be relevant to understanding the means by which the faculty union encouraged identification in this study. One means of encouraging organizationally consistent action is the threat of sanction. Employees may receive clear, unmistakable orders from their employers, either directly (simple controls) or through technological routines (technological controls) (Bullis and Tompkins 1989; Tompkins and Cheney 1985). Bureaucratic controls are more unobtrusive and function by embedding compliance in organizational routines and practices (Bullis and Tompkins 1989; Tompkins and Cheney 1985). In their review of bureaucratic controls in the United States Forest Service, Bullis and Tompkins (1989) found that manuals and centralized planning had eclipsed earlier unifying symbols in the organization. Correcting deviation was almost automated under such a system of consulting the manual for decision making. In the faculty union under study, the possibility for explicit sanctions provided a possibility of overt control, and it may be expected that messages to members reference such sanctions. Faculty members who intended to cross any picket lines were facing the threats of name calling, being ostracized by colleagues, and possible retribution from colleagues. Faculty who intended to strike faced threats from the direction of their employing organization, although most likely threats seemed to originate with higher levels of command. Faculty were concerned about future retribution from administrators and colleagues. For both groups, overt controls would seem to be operative and relevant.

Shifting Allegiances

Identification is neither singular nor static. Organizational tenure, competing allegiances, and changing personal circumstances may impact organizational identification. Several studies have suggested that an employee may identify with multiple targets within or beyond an organization (Russo 1998; Scott 1997; see also Barker and Tompkins 1994; Cheney 1991; Tompkins and Cheney 1983). For professional employees, identification with one's occupation may be especially strong, given the amount of time and education invested in preparing for that profession (Russo 1998). Such identification may be variable, however, with tenure, geographical separation (Scott 1997), and institutional particularities. Russo's study (1998) also demonstrated that for the journalists with long tenure in an organization or with outside family commitments, their primary identification tended to rest with their employer and with their colleagues.

University professors at different stages of their career may experience varying levels of commitment to their employing institutions. Younger professors whose graduate school training is more recent may identify more closely with their disciplines. It is not uncommon for younger professors to change jobs before they get tenured, depending on the availability of tenure-track jobs in their disciplines. Professors with longer tenure in a particular institution may be expected to have stronger identification with that organization. Across the SSHE system, organizational cultures at individual universities naturally varied. Some schools had reputations for antagonistic relationships between faculty and administrators, while other schools were noted for having mostly harmonious relationships between faculty and administration. Different faculty had different relationships with the individual university and with the faculty union. Female, junior, and adjunct faculty members (who were eligible to join APSCUF) may be expected to relate differently both to the institution and to the faculty union, given their sometimes divergent interests. That is, not every contract negotiation equitably represents the interests of all faculty members. Some members will feel better served by the union than will others; therefore, it is reasonable to expect different, dynamic levels of identification with APSCUF by faculty. A brief review of the situation under study is relevant to understand institutional arrangements and organizational processes. Overlapping bureaucracies complicated the contract negotiation process, and the faculty union was contending with evasive negotiators and bad publicity.

THE PENNSYLVANIA CONTEXT

A faculty strike that would have displaced approximately 95,000 Pennsylvania university students was narrowly averted during the recent contract negotiations between the Board of Governors of the SSHE of Pennsylvania and APSCUF, the faculty union representing full-time and part-time faculty in the SSHE universities. APSCUF is a single statewide union with local chapters on each of the fourteen SSHE campuses. There is both a statewide APSCUF president and a local APSCUF president, as well as officers at both state and local levels. Officials at each of these levels have different responsibilities and different levels of authority, but the state APSCUF generally supervises the activities of local APSCUF chapters. The state APSCUF president during the negotiation under study was Dr. William Fulmer, and the Millersville APSCUF chapter president was Dr. Steve Centola. Throughout the negotiations, APSCUF union officials met repeatedly with faculty at the fourteen SSHE universities around the state to enlist their continued support of a bargaining stance that had the potential to result in a faculty strike. The climate for SSHE faculty was relatively hostile. Conservative political rhetoric dominated the news coverage of the negotiations. Governor Tom Ridge and the faculty union had an ongoing antagonistic relationship. Rumors circulated among faculty that the governor was bent on breaking the faculty union and that the future health of the SSHE system was at stake. Public opinion was not especially supportive toward faculty; the faculty's perception was that the public would ultimately be unsupportive of a strike.

Much of the internal communication from the state union president was pessimistic about the possibility of reaching agreement and avoiding a strike. There was no strike fund to support union members, so faculty would receive no pay and would have no health coverage during a strike. Lastly, faculty were divided as to whether striking would be beneficial or detrimental. The large majority of faculty voted for an authorization to strike, but the resolve of the majority was still untested.

For clarity, background information about the two parties involved in the contract negotiations is necessary. First, the State System of Higher Education (SSHE) consists of fourteen sister universities, each named after the town in which it is located, across the state of Pennsylvania. Before the sister universities belonged to a single system, they constituted a series of separate state teaching colleges. In 1982, Pennsylvania Act 188 created the SSHE system (Mercer 1993). The universities are publicly owned and moderately sized, consisting of a few thousand students each. For example, Millersville University enrolls approximately 7,500 full-time graduate and undergraduate students a year. Approximately 5,500 faculty are employed in the SSHE system. The APSCUF website states that one in thirty-four Pennsylvanians is attending or has graduated from a SSHE university. Over half of SSHE alumni (72%) report staying in Pennsylvania after graduation, according to APSCUF. The Pennsylvania State University (PSU) system provides the major in-state competition to the SSHE system. In addition to its massive main campus, PSU has satellite campuses around the state that compete for state funding and for students. One of the critical selling points of the SSHE system is that only professors teach the courses at SSHE schools. No graduate teaching assistant is allowed to teach a course, as they do in the PSU system. For students and parents concerned about the staffing of undergraduate courses, this is a distinct attraction.

APSCUF began in 1937 as a professional organization for faculty teaching in Pennsylvania teacher colleges. Membership in APSCUF is voluntary, and the union currently represents approximately 90 percent of the 5,500 full-time and part-time faculty members teaching in SSHE universities. Pennsylvania is a right-to-work state. That is, workers are not compelled to join the union that negotiates their contract (Delaney 1998). APSCUF has negotiated a collective bargaining agreement with Pennsylvania since 1972 (before the creation of the SSHE system). According to its website, APSCUF was crucial in the creation of SSHE through the passage of Act 188. Faculty at all fourteen SSHE universities constitute a single bargaining entity. APSCUF consists of both state officers and local chapter (campus) officers. On a campus, each department has representatives that sit on a council that meets regularly with the campus officers. Each campus elects delegates that represent it at the state level. At the state level, there are elected executive officers, professional staff, and decision-making bodies. The organization has multiple layers at both the fourteen campuses and at the state level.

APSCUF is concerned with salary, benefits, faculty governance, tenure, promotion, academic freedom, and other professional issues. On its website, APSCUF characterizes itself as follows:

APSCUF is concerned about more than just wages, hours and conditions of employment. We are vitally concerned about the quality of academic life in the SSHE. The pursuit of excellence in teaching and expanding our research potential are high priorities for the organization. We are at the forefront of encouraging administrations to involve their faculty in the governance of universities. <http://www.apscuf.com>

The current state president, William Fulmer, defines APSCUF as "the sole voice for protecting the rights faculty have won ... ours is the strongest voice raised in defense of maintaining the academic excellence of our institutions" <http://www.apscuf.com>. In the latest contract negotiations, the union placed special emphasis on working conditions and benefits for junior and adjunct faculty. In their literature and in meetings, APSCUF emphasized the fact that women and minorities were most affected by this particular bargaining position. The racial and gender equity values associated with this emphasis suggest an inclusive focus for the organization. APSCUF's motto, emblazoned over a symbol of a lighted torch, is "We deliver on the promise of higher education." In sum, APSCUF concerns itself with a broad range of issues and identifies faculty interests and vitality with those of the SSHE.

LAYING THE GROUNDWORK FOR RESISTANCE

In this case, identification proceeded through a series of providing explicit fact and value premises for APSCUF members and nonmembers. APSCUF literature was addressed to faculty who had already joined the union and to faculty who had elected not to join the union but who were covered by the contract under negotiation. Establishing facts and their significance was an important part of some of the literature that preceded the strike authorization vote that took place later in the fall 1999 semester. There were many complex issues on the table and facts were in dispute. Some of the factual arguments APSCUF made were in response to factual arguments made by the SSHE state administrators in press releases and advertising around the APSCUF contract negations. In order to build support for the difficult choice to strike—a choice that entailed risk, sanctions, and financial loss—APSCUF made communicating reasons, or premises, to its members. It may be the case that many faculty members had never faced a possible strike, and such reasons were not obvious to them. Additionally, the communication of these premises would build support among those faculty inclined to adopt them (Cheney 1983a). Factual premises were primarily concerned with financial reasons for resistance, while value premises were connected by a more abstract concept: Faculty were portrayed as the protectors of "quality" education in the SSHE.

The Union Reframes the Debate

There were four main points made by much of the text concerned with factual premises: (1) faculty had made financial sacrifices for SSHE; (2) the current SSHE proposal was financially detrimental to women and minorities; (3) faculty salaries were not responsible for increases in student tuition; (4) other parties, such as competing unions, administrators, and the state budget, were flourishing financially. First, APSCUF described the sacrifices made by faculty in the previous contract negotiation. In an APSCUF document promoting a strike authorization vote, APSCUF mentioned three items on which faculty sacrificed in their previous contract: health care benefits, raises in the last contract, and summer school pay (APSCUF September 2, 1999c). The message detailed facts from the last contract that document the sacrifices that faculty have made to SSHE. For example, in detailing the benefit sacrifices, APSCUF argued, "The system claims that their offer has no reduction in healthcare [sic] benefits. However the system's refusal to raise the contribution level to our health welfare fund is a reduction in your benefits. Why? The contribution level is the same today as it was in 1993!" (APSCUF September 2, 1999c). The same memo pointed out that faculty raises for the last contract were 0 percent, 2 percent, and 3 percent, and that for some faculty who received no step raises, their total accumulation over the life of the contract was less than cost of living increases for that period (APSCUF September 2, 1999c). Additionally, this same text points out that summer and overload pay was frozen at 1995 rates.

Attached to the same packet of information was a critical factual analysis of SSHE claims about faculty salary and benefits. This analysis pointed out that according to faculty reports of per weekly working hours "faculty report an average workweek of 55.3 hours. Nine months of 55.3 hours per week is equal to just over twelve months of 40 hours per week. The State System considers 35 hours as a standard work week" (APSCUF September 2, 1999a). Finally, in answer to SSHE claims that APSCUF faculty are paid in the 90th percentile nationally, APSCUF argued that, in fact, the faculty are paid in the 70th percentile.

APSCUF supported this assertion by citing the statistic provided by most recent national data supplied by the American Association of University Professors (AAUP) and published in *Academe* magazine in 1999. State APSCUF said that the SSHE continued to cite an old statistic, although APSCUF informed them of their error. APSCUF also cited the deleterious effects of the previous three-year APSCUF contract on professors' salaries. The minimal raises in the previous contract combined with reduced benefits actually led to a 0.54 percent decrease in faculty salaries (APSCUF July 8, 1999).

One of the factual premises made repeatedly by APSCUF in their messages was that they were asking for a contract that was equitable to women and to minority faculty, while SSHE was asking for a contract that would discriminate against those groups. In a letter addressed to the faculty, the state APSCUF president characterized the SSHE contract proposal as "a transparent attempt to divide the faculty" (Fulmer August 2, 1999). The SSHE proposal put forward a cut in the amount of money awarded to faculty members who went up a step within their rank—each rank has several steps, up to an ultimate level "Z," at which the automatic advances stop. Fulmer said, "Acceptance of such a proposal would hurt our newer faculty (a disproportionate number of whom are women), it would irretrievably fracture our union, and it would decimate our efforts in all future negotiations" (August 2, 1999). Another bulletin from APSCUF highlighted the long-term negative impact of such a divisive policy on the future recruitment of female and minority faculty (APSCUF September 2, 1999c).

In order to counter possible public perceptions that faculty were simply greedy and willing to sacrifice student well-being for their own financial benefit, APSCUF publicized a bar graph produced by one of the local APSCUF chapters. The flier had a heading that stated, "Members of the State System of Higher Education Board of Governors should take a MATH COURSE at one of our 14 state-owned universities." The bar graph was a quick, clear presentation of the breakdown of budget increases in the SSHE. Management payroll accounted for the largest amount of increase (24.7%), and faculty payroll accounted for the smallest increase (7.5%). The flier was a reaction to SSHE advertisements that argued faculty salaries were causing tuition to become too high at state schools. The text accompanying the graph criticized the figures used by SSHE, calling them "selected facts" (APSCUF September 2, 1999b). Additionally, the bulletin drew out relationships among statistics, enhancing their explanatory power. Management personnel increased by 8 percent over the four-year period covered, while management pay raises amounted to about 25 percent over that same period, "three times greater than increases in faculty payroll" (APSCUF September 2, 1999b). Finally, the flier cited outside support for their assertion that administrators, not faculty were the cause for increases in tuition. Beneath a bold headline that asks, "Wonder where the State System of Higher Education Board puts its priorities?" the text reports findings from an independent commission that each university in the state system was overspending on administration costs by between $3.9 to $6.4 million (APSCUF September 2, 1999b).

Finally, throughout the APSCUF literature, it was noted that other SSHE unions had negotiated better contracts at a time that APSCUF was making sacrifices (Fulmer August 2, 1999). APSCUF argued that the Commonwealth of Pennsylvania and SSHE (Fulmer September 16, 1999) had surpluses that made cuts in SSHE unnecessary and that too much of SSHE's resources went to management (APSCUF September 2, 1999b; APSCUF September 2, 1999c). The messages across the literature were fairly consistent, reinforcing the facts and the contexts for those facts with similar language.

Casting Symbols: Risk Becomes Heroic

In each case involving factual premises, APSCUF provided statistics, wherever possible, to substantiate claims and/or enhance credibility. In many cases, APSCUF was responding to SSHE factual claims about faculty salaries and benefits and providing an alternative analysis and "good reasons" for resisting the employing organization. In other words, APSCUF was providing a competing set of facts; it is important to note that these facts are not baldly stated. Rather, they were surrounded by a few unifying symbols and by value premises, the most important of which was "quality." APSCUF tried to provide an interpretive context for both understanding those facts and for integrating those facts into decision making. APSCUF's president, William Fulmer, explicitly defined interpretive context in one letter to members. This letter responded to a letter all SSHE faculty had received from the chancellor of the system. The letter was a presentation of SSHE's case for faculty accepting the contract proposal SSHE had made. Faculty had evidently complained about the tone and the content of the letter. Fulmer responded, "Many of our colleagues expressed anger and dismay with Chancellor McCormick's letter to the faculty ... [this] letter certainly portrayed management's position well. It suggested that management is reasonable, and that the Board of Governors proposals are legitimate. With his letter we get to see, firsthand, how masterful 'spin doctors' can be" (September 2, 1999).

The interpretive context for facts is a very important component for reaching and persuading faculty. Contract negotiations are complex, involving many issues and facts that are beyond the knowledge base of faculty. Furthermore, some information must necessarily be kept confidential during a contract negotiation, so not all facts can be disseminated among the membership, as it undermines the bargainers' position. Lastly, faculty members are both geographically and culturally dispersed. That is, SSHE schools are all over the state of Pennsylvania. Although the universities are linked through the SSHE, each is an independently operating institution. Finally, campus cultures and relations between faculty and local administrators vary widely. While relations between administration and faculty were relatively harmonious at Millersville University, for example, other campuses were rumored to have much more antagonistic histories. Therefore, providing a common context for situating facts and for making decisions was immensely helpful in fostering identification with one's geographically dispersed colleagues and head office (state APSCUF). Additionally, unifying symbols, common to all APSCUF members, were visual reminders of solidarity.

APSCUF letterhead contained the following recognizable symbols: a torch next to the bolded acronym for the union and, underneath, a listing of the fourteen sister schools who are part of the SSHE and whose faculty are represented by APSCUF. Additionally, during the contract negotiations, local chapters produced other unifying symbols for their members. The Millersville chapter distributed buttons with messages such as "Save Our System," "Students Pay for Quality, Not Shortcuts," "APSCUF Quality Faculty = Quality Education," and "APSCUF Stands for Quality." The accompanying memo asked the faculty members to wear their buttons in visible show of their solidarity. The theme that unified many of the value appeals was that of "quality." More specifically, faculty were presented as heroic figures, willing to take risks for the benefit of their students and their institutions. They were portrayed as the guardians of quality; the last line of defense against administrators and legislators who would undermine the quality of the SSHE system. In developing the values and roles communicated by the APSCUF literature, the roles of faculty, the SSHE administration, and the abstract principle of "quality" were the central elements of the texts.

Quality, Heroes, and Villains

In his critique of the contemporary university, Readings (1996) attacked the use of feel-good terms such as "excellence" and "quality" to represent absolutely nothing, while allowing institutions to undermine real efforts toward intellectual excellence or institutional quality. In this case, APSCUF may have used the term "quality," but certainly with a different end. Rather than distract students and faculty from attempts to erode programs and undermine academics, APSCUF was using "quality" as a term that supported their point of view. Quality was strategically ambiguous (Eisenberg 1984) and abstract enough to represent faculty across a number of disciplines. The use of an abstract principle to unite faculty is useful, but not without translation into specific behaviors and attitudes. Finally, the notion of aspiring to something greater than oneself or one's current situation plays into the academic culture.

Earlier in the negotiations, quality emerged from the maintenance of a stance consistent with that advocated by APSCUF. Quality was used in some of these messages as a means of distinguishing between targets of identification; APSCUF stood for quality, SSHE negotiators did not. In some of the APSCUF rhetoric, however, quality became a basis for settling terms between the SSHE Board of Governors and APSCUF. That is, the two sides could come together and both support the issue of quality, if only the SSHE governors would support AP-SCUF. As the negotiation process threatened to break off, specification of behaviors that supported quality and organizational commitment became more specific. Strike plans issued by APSCUF contained very concrete sets of instructions for supporting the organization.

Quality was the ultimate rationale for identification and resistance in the APSCUF literature. The sheer repetition of the term made it the most important feature of the value rhetoric directed toward members. Quality was characterized as an honorable, high-minded reason, beyond the reach of self-interest. Those who acted in the interest of quality were acting heroically. Those who did not serve quality were villains. Quality was consistently aligned with APSCUF's actions and motives in its literature. For example, in a characterization of the APSCUF negotiatiors' strategies, Fulmer (September 2, 1999) said, "The focus of our team has been to preserve the quality and integrity of our livelihoods, the proper education of our students, and the quality and fairness of the System." In response to statistics publicized by the SSHE Board of Governors, ASPCUF responded, "Our APSCUF professors must take a stand to protect the quality of education for our students" (APSCUF September 2, 1999b).

Furthermore, quality was used to define heroes and villains in the negotiations. Professors were portrayed as guardians of quality, willing to make personal sacrifices for their students' educations. For example, "We, the faculty must prevail as we continue to serve as the guardians of the State System of Higher Education. In solidarity we will do so." (Fulmer September 2, 1999). In a press release, APSCUF president Fulmer explicitly linked professors to the health of the universities. He argued, "The Faculty is the guardian of the State System, and we believe it's our responsibility to stand up for quality" (APSCUF August 11, 1999, 2). Finally, Fulmer alluded to the sacrifices that APSCUF members made by observing, "Despite severe provocation our team has managed to keep its perspective and to present rational arguments with supportive data for our positions and proposals" (Fulmer September 2, 1999).

In contrast, SSHE's antagonistic relationship to quality, as it was defined by APSCUF, was the basis for portraying SSHE negotiators and administrators as the enemies of students in state system universities. In one letter, Fulmer charged some of the Board of Governors members with outright opposition to academics. He said, "But certain members of the Board of Governors have systematically orchestrated a campaign against public higher education" (APSCUF September 2, 1999b). In other literature, Fulmer contrasted the roles of APSCUF with that of SSHE administrators in relation to quality. In reaction to a letter sent by the chancellor to the students, Fulmer argued,

Moreover we deeply resent the Chancellor's effort to use students as a weapon in these negotiations. He and his managers seem to see students only as numbers or as dollar signs. We, their faculty, see their faces, know their names. We interact with them every day, we come to know them closely, and we care for them. We would not be in this profession if we did not. It is heartrending for us to consider striking and interrupting their education, their plans, and their dreams. We could and would never do so unless there were strong principles involved, as there clearly are in this case. (September 16, 1999, 2)

Fulmer compared the caring, sacrificial attitude of faculty with an instrumental approach practiced by the chancellor and the Board of Governors. The high contrast between the two positions revolved around the question of commitment to quality in the APSCUF rhetoric. Quality was used divisively, but it was also stretched to invite participation.

Quality was extended as a possible symbolic basis for finding common ground between APSCUF and SSHE negotiators. In an APSCUF press release, quality was used in the headline: "APSCUF calls on State System to negotiate an agreement that focuses on quality education" (APSCUF August 11, 1999, 1). In this same press release, "quality" was used repeatedly as a rationale and a rallying cry. In the press release, APSCUF president Fulmer was quoted as saying, "A well compensated faculty is necessary to maintain and enhance the quality of instruction we provide to our students. We will not sacrifice the quality our students deserve.... Cutting corners at the expense of quality is not an acceptable option, and it's time that State System management stands up for quality and breaks this negotiations logjam" (APSCUF August 11, 1999, 1). APSCUF rhetoric incorporated quality, a previously divisive appeal, as a possibility for agreement. In other words, if SSHE state administrators were also interested in quality, they could show that commitment.

This rhetorical choice between heroic sacrificial support of quality and villainous rejection of academic excellence would seem to be very persuasive, although it may not necessarily indicate high identification with APSCUF (Tompkins and Cheney 1985). By training and probably through self-selection, most academics are socialized to have "high standards," although the content of those standards may often be under debate. One person's high standard is another person's minimum level of acceptability. However, we are taught through our professional training to think of ourselves as noble idealists who value the pursuit of knowledge above expediency and wealth. Obviously, we do not always practice noble idealism, but academics are taught to value high standards. The other underlying issue consists of the long-term effects on the reputation of the institutions in the SSHE system. Factual appeals and value appeals combined speak to the concern for undermining the current reputation and working conditions of the institutions and the difficulties of attracting good colleagues and students in future years. These concerns were not idealistic but very material in some ways. Behind the fairly ambiguous and pervasive symbol, "quality," were real concerns about the future desirability of teaching in a SSHE institution. Such concerns may have seemed selfish on an individual level, but loftier when cast as a systemic issue that affected students and the trajectory of several institutions. In other words, for those inclined to identify with APSCUF, the union provided principles and a role for resistant faculty. Furthermore, the rhetoric contrasted that role with the unseemly position of the villain or the scab.

Preparing to Strike

The last section of this analysis demonstrates the concrete instructions sent to APSCUF chapters for strike behavior. APSCUF faculty never struck during this negotiation, but they were prepared to. In our local chapter, faculty volunteered to chair ad hoc committees relevant to the strike, they volunteered for picket duty, and arrangements had been made for complete relocation of our local APSCUF chapter office: our strike headquarters. These strike directives were not disseminated widely to all faculty, but they would have been had we struck. The complications of striking, however, were widely known among faculty and have been included in this analysis because they clarify what was entailed in organizational commitment to APSCUF.

Following a strongly supported strike authorization vote and the floundering of negotiations, APSCUF began sending messages to chapters about the specifics of striking and picketing. The following information was widely distributed to faculty. Any faculty member who struck would not receive a paycheck. Any faculty member who struck while on sabbatical, maternity, or sick leave would lose her or his leave. Faculty members were advised to refill prescriptions and schedule doctor appointments prior to the strike due to uncertainties about reimbursement. Should a strike go on for any length of time, faculty would have to pay for their own health benefits. Faculty were advised that their e-mail accounts would probably be inaccessible. They were asked to remove their teaching materials from their offices so no substitute faculty could be brought in to teach their classes. Faculty were asked to return any items that belonged to the university, such as laptop computers, prior to the strike. They were asked not to return to their offices during the strike, but if absolutely necessary, they were to do so at night or at another time when there were no pickets. They were instructed not to cross or give the appearance of crossing a picket line at any time. Faculty were asked not to conduct their classes in off-campus locations during the strike.

An information packet was sent to APSCUF chapter presidents for answering faculty questions and for conducting the strike, should it happen. This information was published in the Millersville APSCUF newsletter, although it may not have been that widely shared on other campuses. Some sample instructions included the definition for striking, "It means withholding services—all services. That means that you do not go to work, teach off campus, assign work to students, or do anything to help management cover your classes" (APSCUF October 5, 1999, 2). APSCUF defined the campuses as public places, where picketing was possible. APSCUF advised picketers against some behaviors. The memo advised, "Picketers should not block entrances to buildings and parking lots and they should not bar people from using such entrances.... Menacing or threatening talk or actions as well as actual physical assault can constitute unprotected or unlawful employee activity" (APSCUF October 5, 1999, 4). Instructions advised picketers not to bring weapons to the line and to wear comfortable shoes

(APSCUF October 5, 1999). Finally, the Millersville APSCUF newsletter from Steve Centola, the local president, reinforced the definition of behaviors that demonstrated commitment—supporting the strike in spirit and in practice. Centola (1999) said, "As we prepare for the unpleasant tasks we might have to carry out, it is important that we approach the strike with resolve.... Please ask your colleagues not to cross the picket lines. We should not teach our classes or perform any of our other professorial responsibilities." Centola also reiterated value premises with these specific suggestions. He reminded faculty, "If anyone is wavering and has lost the resolve to strike, that person should remember that the issues that divide us affect both the quality of education and the equity of compensation" (Centola 1999, 1). Messages to members situated concrete instructions within a context of reasons, much the way factual and value premises were combined in earlier messages from APSCUF.

Messages in preparation for the strike were concrete, specific, and reminded members why they were striking. These texts clarified those acts that constituted organizational commitment. Such messages were necessary at the time. APSCUF faculty had never struck. It is likely that most faculty had never been involved in a strike, and simple confusion necessitated the concrete instructions. Additionally, these memos and letters reinforced resolve and created a clear path for committing to the strike.

CONCLUSIONS: MOVING FROM ALLEGIANCE TO RESISTANCE

In this case of competing organizational allegiances, APSCUF did not force its members to choose between their institutions and their professional identities. In this case, resistance, in the form of supporting APSCUF negotiators and supporting the strike, should it have become necessary, was portrayed as a form of institutional patriotism. That is, by refusing to sell out the quality of education in their institutions, professors would be acting heroically rather than radically. They had a noble cause that justified their resistance. Rather than asking for dedication strictly to APSCUF, the faculty union asked professors for institutional loyalty through a prescribed set of practices. This rhetorical move is safer, not pitting local institutions against the union, but creating a common interest between union and institution. In this case, striking would not have constituted rejection of the institution; rather striking was the ultimate act of loyalty.

Resistance was promoted through the provision of persuasive financial facts and an abstract value at the beginning of the negotiations breakdown. APSCUF guided members as to which facts they should adopt as a basis for their decision making. Repeated calls for quality and the identification of a heroic role were fairly abstract. Identification was built around fairly undemanding and probably already-existing principles. As the strike became a more compelling reality, APSCUF's messages to members shifted to very concrete instructions for carrying out organizational commitment. These directions were contextualized by reinforcement of the primary value appeal—quality. That is, as the need for resistance became more compelling, the rhetoric became more focused. Taken as a whole, the early messages to members were necessary for the favorable reception of later messages. Professors who did not have "good reasons" to strike would have been far less likely to strike. Those who felt that there were solid financial reasons and principles at stake were more likely to take the next step and to strike.

Throughout, the SSHE Board of Governors, the chancellor, and the SSHE negotiators were portrayed as treasonous, opposed to the best interests of students and the long-term health of the system. This identification by antithesis (Burke 1969) can be a very powerful unifying strategy. If only they cared about quality, went the APSCUF argument, they would join us in working for an equitable, adequately-resourced faculty. In their factual documentation, APSCUF described SSHE's bad-faith publication of erroneous figures and SSHE's faulty arguments about the role of faculty salaries in increasing tuition.

Due to the eventual contract agreement reached between the APSCUF and SSHE negotiators, the effectiveness of APSCUF's rhetoric was never subjected to its ultimate test. However, there are some indications that faculty were overwhelmingly willing to strike. Strike authorization statistics indicated that the large majority of faculty supported a strike. Approximately 92 percent of voting APSCUF faculty supported a strike authorization (90 percent of the total APSCUF faculty voted in this referendum). While this study examined messages directed at members, there are a number of publics affected by contract negotiations at educational institutions. Students, parents, lawmakers, university coworkers, and local residents in the university towns are all potentially affected by the strike. This study does not determine the content of messages directed toward those groups or the effectiveness of those messages. Insight into fostering resistance would be enhanced by studying these groups. Public support is very important to the success of a job action by state employees. Such a wholistic understanding of resistance rhetorics and the affected publics would be a daunting, but valuable project.

There are several directions that research in resistance rhetoric should continue to follow. What does other resistance rhetoric look like? Do messages build toward a specific event in the way they did in this study? What are member reactions to the union messages? How do members perceive abstract value premises? How clearly do members grasp financial data? This study represents an attempt to understand an organization not as a singular entity with a monolithic membership. Rather, this study treats the organization as a collection of memberships with contrasting, even conflicting, goals, values, and data. Renegotiating the terms of a relationship between two entities reveals those conflicts and encourages the groups to articulate their identities and ideologies. This analysis provides an opportunity to conceptualize the organization as a multilayered, complex, and human enterprise.

NOTE

An earlier version of this chapter was presented at the 2000 Canadian Society for the Study of Rhetoric conference in Edmonton, Alberta. The author wishes to thank the Faculty Grants Committee of Millersville University for supporting her research.

REFERENCES

Association of Pennsylvania State College and University Faculties. July 8, 1999. SSHE managers—The spin doctors. Duplicated.

———. August 11, 1999. APSCUF calls on State System to negotiate an agreement that focuses on quality education. Duplicated.

———. September 2, 1999a. A dissection of recent State System propaganda. Duplicated.

———. September 2, 1999b. Members of the State System of Higher Education Board of Governors should take a math course at one of our 14 state-owned universities. Duplicated.

———. September 2, 1999c. Top ten reasons to vote "yes" for strike authorization. Duplicated.

———. October 5, 1999. Picketing on campus. Duplicated.

Barker, J.R., and P.K. Tompkins. 1994. Identification in the self-managing organization: Characteristics of target and tenure. *Human Communication Research* 21: 223–240.

Bullis, C.A., and P.K. Tompkins. 1989. The forest ranger revisited: A study of control practices and identification. *Communication Monographs* 56:287–306.

Burke, K. 1969. *A rhetoric of motives*. Berkeley: University of California Press.

Centola, S. 1999. President Centola urges faculty to honor strike. *APSCUF-Millersville Newsletter* 19(1):1.

Cheney, G. 1983a. On the various and changing meanings of organizational membership: A field study of organizational identification. *Communication Monographs* 50:342–362.

———. 1983b. The rhetoric of identification and the study of organizational communication. *Quarterly Journal of Speech* 69:143–158.

———. 1991. *Rhetoric in an organizational society: Managing multiple identities*. Columbia: University of South Carolina Press.

Cheney, G., and P.K. Tompkins. 1987. Coming to terms with organizational identification and commitment. *Central States Speech Journal* 38:1–15.

Delaney, J.T. 1998. Redefining the right-to-work debate: Unions and the dilemma of free choice. *Journal of Labor Research* 19:425–442.

Eisenberg, E. 1984. Ambiguity as strategy in organizational communication. *Communication Monographs* 51:227–242.

Fulmer, W.E. August 2, 1999. APSCUF President's letter. Duplicated.

———. September 2, 1999. APSCUF President's letter. Duplicated.

———. September 16, 1999. State System students do deserve to be in class. Duplicated.

Hall, D. T., and B. Schneider. 1972. Correlates of organizational identification as a function of career pattern and organizational type. *Administrative Science Quarterly* 17:176–189.

Kaufman, H. 1960. *The forest ranger: A study in administration behavior.* Baltimore, MD: Johns Hopkins University Press.

Lee, S.M. 1971. An empirical analysis of organizational identification. *Academy of Management Journal* 14:213–226.

———. 1969. Organizational identification of scientists. *Academy of Management Journal* 12:327–337.

Mael, F.A., and L.E. Tetrick. 1992. Identifying organizational identification. *Educational and Psychological Measurement* 52:813–825.

Mercer , J. 1993. Campuses that stress teaching and community. *The Chronicle of Higher Education,* October 20, A44.

Readings, B. 1996. *The ruins of the university.* Cambridge: Harvard University Press.

Rotondi, T. 1975a. Organizational identification and group involvement. *Academy of Management Journal* 4:892–896.

———. 1975b. Organizational identification: Issues and implications. *Organizational Behavior and Human Performance* 13:95–109.

Russo, T.C. 1998. Organizational and professional identification: A case of newspaper journalists. *Management Communication Journal* 12:72–111.

Scott, C. 1997. Identification with multiple targets in a geographically dispersed organization. *Management Communication Quarterly* 10:491–522.

Scott, S. 2000. Identifying organizational identification. *Academy of Management Review* 25: 43–62.

Tompkins, P.K., and G. Cheney. 1983. Account analysis of organizations: Decision making and identification. In *Communication and organizations: An interpretive approach,* ed. L.L. Putnam and M. Pacanowsky, 123–146. Beverly Hills, CA: Sage.

———. 1985. Communication and unobtrusive control in organizations. In *Organizational communication: Traditional themes and new directions,* ed. R D. McPhee and P.K. Tompkins, 179–210. Beverly Hills, CA: Sage.

Tompkins, P.K., J.Y. Fisher, D.A. Infante, and E.L. Tompkins. 1975. Kenneth Burke and the inherent characteristics of formal organizations: A field study. *Speech Monographs* 42:135–142.

Van Knippenberg, D., and E.C.M. van Schie. 2000. Foci and correlates of organizational identification. *Journal of Occupational and Organizational Psychology* 73:137–148.

Afterword: Classroom, Lab, Factory Floor: Common Labor Struggles

Carl Rosen

Academic workers are not a world unto themselves, facing problems and in need of solutions unlike any other segment of the workforce. Nor are academic workers exactly the same as workers in any other particular industry. Instead, they prove the rule that every industry, workplace, and workforce has a set of unique characteristics that shape how the workers will respond to unionization and how they can best take on their employer to defend and advance their interests. Such factors as the relationship to immediate supervisors and upper management; the ability to choke off key activity; whether employment is permanent and full-time; the pay and benefits of the job; how regimented the work is; the sense of fair treatment; the opportunities for advancement; the surrounding political climate and the legal regulations for unionization; and the previous experiences of the workers come into play in every union organizing campaign. While academic workers may currently face a set of circumstances that taken together make their particular barriers to unionization appear somewhat different than those faced by most American workers, the same basic factors that apply in all situations must be taken into account. At most, what sets apart academic workers is their increased ability, by virtue of their training, to put their thoughts about their situation into writing. But even here, it is only at a written level, not a verbal level, that they may hold an advantage on self-analysis, for all workers facing the questions of unionization and confrontation with their employer evaluate the same factors from their personal perspective, consciously or unconsciously, and then verbalize and act on their analysis in one form or another.

Both the chapters in this book and the experience of my union bear out this view of academic workers. The United Electrical, Radio and Machine Workers of America (UE) was originally a union of factory workers, with a proud heritage as an original CIO (Congress of Industrial Organizations) union from the 1930s. UE successfully took on the task to organize such industrial behemoths as GE, Westinghouse, and RCA. But it is not this factory union background that colors our viewpoint—it is our approach to trade unionism. UE believes in democratic rank-and-file control of the union's affairs, at all levels: in maximizing the education and involvement of the membership; in militant struggle to defend the interests of the workers against those of the employers; and in seeing the union as part of a broader social movement for justice for working people. While practice is rarely as perfect as preaching, this spirit does pervade the union. This democratic and social justice approach to unionism is perhaps what allowed the organization and consolidation of UE Local 896-COGS at the University of Iowa the space and tools to work out their issues internally based on their own experiences and needs and, over time, to gain a clear sense that the workplace problems they confront do fit within the general pattern of conflicts between employers and employees that all of our members face.

The chapters in this book raise many questions about how academic workers fit into the labor movement. The primary question involves identity: Are graduate employees and other faculty workers or, more broadly, a genuine part of the working class? Once this central identity question is dealt with, the issues of uniqueness raised in some chapters of this book can be seen as simply specific characteristics regarding the academic workforce and workplace that need to be evaluated in the context of the factors affecting unionization in every workplace. Similarly, the structural union problems raised in this book can be seen as part and parcel of the issues confronting labor unions in general. Lastly, all of this plays out in the context of an academic industry undergoing major structural changes itself.

IDENTITY AS WORKERS

Of course, graduate employees and faculty—of all types—are workers and part of the working class: They receive a paycheck from an employer and the employer can make the rules for their work and decide to terminate their jobs,[1] and their pay, independent of the individual desire of the worker. As such, they also need and deserve unions. This is the working-class UE perspective on who is a worker and who needs a union. It is one that has stood the test of time, regardless of industry.

Just because academic workers have many years of higher education under their belts does not change their position as part of the working class. Even medical doctors, especially those who receive a salary from hospitals or HMOs, are increasingly recognizing their employer-employee relationship and responding with true unionization; they are coming to realize that their traditional professional organizations were designed more to limit competition than to protect their interests against a corporatized, profit-driven employer. The argument some universities make—that graduate employees are apprentices and therefore not eligible for unions—has no merit: apprentices in the building trades are members of their unions and produce value for their employers during their apprenticeship. Those who toil in academia are paid by their employer so long as they do something of value for that employer and as such are workers, regardless of their degree status.

This does not mean that academic workers automatically sense this; their viewpoint is shaped by their experiences. It is the union's job to put those experiences in perspective so that they can see their common bonds and decide to take action. Identity becomes a question of class consciousness: Academic workers are part of the working class, but are they conscious of that fact? But again, the struggle for identity and consciousness is not unique to academia. This struggle for identity is played out in every workplace. In factories, bosses try get the workers to identify with the employer through teamwork schemes, fear of competitors, bonus plans, and other means. The appeal for "collegiality" in a university setting is the academic version of this propaganda war. In the end, it is experience that teaches workers which side they are on, and it is probably generally true that the lessons are harsher in industrial plants than on academic campuses. But the underlying reality is always there and eventually comes to the surface. Part of the task of the union leadership is to help their fellow workers see through the various veils that management uses to disguise the real differences of interests that exist between "them" and "us."

FACTORS IN UNIONIZATION

So if academic workers are indeed workers, are there still special qualities about either themselves or the work they do that makes them less prone to union organization? I would argue that essentially every concern raised in this book can be shown to be an issue that confronts unions engaged in organizing workers in other industries also.

Weighing heavily in the decision of any worker as he or she decides whether to fight to make his or her job better is the importance of the job and how long he or she expects to be there. A worker moonlighting on a second job part-time is not as likely to be committed to a battle to increase the hourly wage as is a worker for whom the job provides his or her entire income. This is similarly true for a worker who expects to leave a job soon either due to quitting the workforce entirely or because he or she may be promoted to management or some other higher-paid position.

These effects are well known to union organizers in any industry—they clearly impact the academic workplace as well. Graduate employees and contingent faculty may be temporary and part-time employees, but when the work provides the main source of income and there does not appear to be a rosy employment picture ahead for them in their discipline, these workers may make the commitment to stand and fight. This might partially explain the general impression that teaching assistants, clustered in the humanities and social sciences where future teaching prospects are limited, are easier to organize into graduate employee unions than are research assistants, who are more likely to be in the hard sciences where they can hope for a more lucrative future in the private sector. Research assistants are also more likely to have their future career prospects tied closely to their research project and therefore to the professor for whom they are working. Joining a union can be viewed as a challenge to that professor and therefore as detrimental to the graduate employee's chances at success in their field. This effect is certainly not absolute, however. Relationships with active union supporters can overcome these concerns in many cases. In addition, as corporate control of research funding becomes ever greater, one likely result is that university research work will become more regimented and leave research assistants feeling more exploited, creating the conditions for an even stronger pro-union sentiment than currently exists within the ranks of teaching assistants.

Management schemes to divide the workforce can also have the same effects in an academic workplace as elsewhere in industry. Two-tier pay and benefit schemes, merit pay systems, and lean employment structures are designed to get more work out of employees for less money, while simultaneously reducing the chances of solidarity between workers by making them think that their fellow-workers are either competitors or a drag on their pay. To the extent that these approaches are imposed in an academic setting, they can provide additional barriers to unionization. But just as factory workers have learned to see through the schemes and overcome them, so can academic workers when the chips are down.

Similarly, fear of privatization or outsourcing of bargaining unit work can have a chilling effect on workers' desire for unionization. But it can also be a strong motivator, as workers strive to get contractual job security protections. The fact that these pressures have generally come more slowly to academic workplaces than to other industries does not change the dynamic in any meaningful way.

How workers view their work can also shape their reaction to union drives, especially when they are led to believe they have a special status within society. That is why, particularly in response to many of the recent changes in academia, it is has been natural for union supporters to make the argument that unionization is necessary to fight for maintaining or restoring quality education in the institution. While this can be absolutely true, it is certainly not unique to educational settings. Craft unions in the skilled trades have played on this angle for decades, and more than one manufacturing union has made this claim. More recently, it has been at the core of health care union organizing drives that emphasize patient care. This appeal to the sense of commitment on the part of the worker can be very helpful with those who are not otherwise strong union supporters and may be especially necessary in a not-for-profit setting, but unions need to tread carefully here since it is essentially encouraging identification with the purported mission of the employing institution. Clever employers can sometimes find ways to co-opt these workers by manipulating these sentiments into identification with management itself, thus replacing the agenda set forth by the employees with that of the employer. While it is important to start a dialogue with workers where they are currently at (identification with mission), the union must move them beyond that to greater class-consciousness (identification as workers carrying out the mission with some interests not in common with management) or risk losing them in the end.

Fairness issues have always been key to union organizing drives. An organizing drive that focuses on money alone can frequently be defeated by a one-time wage increase granted by the employer. It is much more difficult for an employer to change a culture where workers feel they are treated unfairly, especially when that culture is how management has always exerted its control. This gives great power to union demands for seniority rights, grievance procedures, consistent rules, just cause for discipline, nondiscrimination, and other equalizers. Although academic institutions are famous for their political backbiting, the fairness issues that their employees face are part and parcel of those confronting all workers.

The various levels of legal protections for unions have no small impact on the ability of workers to organize themselves into effective unions. Public employees at the University of Michigan have the right to strike; those at the University of Iowa are forbidden to strike but are guaranteed a contract through a binding arbitration process. Their counterparts at the University of Florida have essentially no legally enforceable way to force a better contract out of their employer than it is willing to grant voluntarily. Some states allow union contracts to require that all workers contribute towards the cost of their representation; others forbid it. It is therefore not surprising that the relative strengths of unions facing these differing regulations are roughly proportional to the rights they have under the law. But these legal obstacles are by no means unique to academic workers. They are faced by millions of public and private sector workers across the country, in no small part because even the applicable law is rarely enforced to the benefit of workers. To overcome these obstacles today requires nothing less than solidarity, creative tactics, and tenacity—in other words, organize the workers and don't rely on the law, the explicit message of the University of Illinois experience described in this volume.

This leaves only the question of whether academic workers have a different response to unions due to their own advanced intellectual training. Certainly a portion of the workforce has an ideological education that allows them to make arguments for or against unions. These activists probably cancel each other out, leaving the rest of the workforce looking at unionization issues about the same way that most workers do, based on how they perceive it will affect their job situation. Unions probably find more advantage in the technical skills and organizational ability that are readily available in an academic workforce. This can allow the union leadership to more efficiently move the rest of the membership into action. Overall, though, the level of academic training does not significantly color the outlook of academic workers; it is their expectations and experiences on the job that matter the most.

In sum, while academic workers certainly face a unique set of circumstances, some for the worse (graduate employees have a high level of turnover built in to their jobs) and some for the better (racial divisions within an academic workplace are unlikely to be as viciously exploited as in a factory), the factors that go into determining whether a workforce is ready to unionize are no different than in any other industry.

UNION STRUCTURES WITHIN A DEMOCRATIC APPROACH

The organizing drives reported in this book have caused many campus-based union activists to confront head-on some of the shortcomings in the U.S. labor movement. Workers in this country have been ill-served by the descent into corrupt, business unionism or service unionism that befell many unions beginning with the McCarthy-period attacks on those most committed to an aggressive, rank-and-file based, organizing approach to union activity for both organized and unorganized workers. Fortunately, some unions have been working hard to reverse these trends in the past decade, and newly organized workers, including academic workers, have an opportunity to both benefit from and contribute to this rebirth within the labor movement. But this does not mean that every criticism of perceived union failings is well placed, nor that those in the vanguard of organizing on a campus have all the answers. The passion of the newest union members needs to complement the experience of those who have been in the trenches for the long haul—the union movement cannot prosper without both. Unions must provide the tools and structures to allow their members to fight on their own behalf; union members must understand that some level of internal discipline is needed to combat employers who oppose the demands of the workers.

The core issue here is democracy. Democracy is messy, but it remains the only method to keep workers engaged in their union and minimize the chances of corruption or laziness on the part of the leadership. Democracy requires a major investment in education and a willingness to watch as members make mistakes and learn from them. Fundamentally, democracy requires a belief that union members will make the right decisions in the long run. Unions that do not practice this are always vulnerable to rot from the inside and attacks from the outside.

However, democratic, rank-and-file controlled unionism should not be confused with an absence of leadership. Elected officers, of course, are required to make sure the decisions of the membership are carried out and to represent the union in dealing with the employer. But they must also give leadership to the union. They are the most involved in the day-to-day struggles of the union and have generally received the most union education. At difficult junctures, they have a responsibility to not only explain the entire situation to the membership but also to offer a recommendation based on their knowledge and experience. It is then up to the membership to vote on whether or not to follow the recommendation. Failure to offer guidance is not promotion of democracy—it is an abdication of duty, often driven by fear of having to say things that the members may not want to hear.

At the local level, structure must accommodate a wide range of perspectives. An old belief in UE is that in any given workplace about 20 percent of the workers can be counted on from the start to be ideologically committed to unionism; about 10 percent will ally themselves with management; and the remaining 70 percent can be swayed to either side based on their assessment of the available information, past history, and the probable outcomes. It is the task of the 20 percent to provide the leadership to keep that 70 percent committed to a union point of view. But the 70 percent also serve as a stabilizing force that keeps the 20 percent from veering off into naïve, overly idealistic, or just plain reckless adventurism. Some of the examples in this book imply that substantially less than a majority of the workforce is involved in the union, generally due to open-shop laws. This can be a grave danger if it results in the actions of the committed minority being unchecked by the less ideological majority. Under the oppressive conditions faced by labor today and in a union structure that is not fully committed to widespread education and organizing, that minority of activists can rapidly become isolated from the bulk of the employees. If this happens, the union loses its strength. Democratic votes in which only a minority participate is not the kind of democracy that builds the union. The union cannot afford to become seen as an organization that only those in certain political or social circles join. While the ideologically committed are needed, and it is reasonable to use social activities as a recruiting tool, the bulk of the workforce needs to participate in the union because they see it primarily as a means to make gains and defend their interests.

Democracy within union locals also needs to be structured to ensure that the work of the union gets done. For example, UE Local 896-COGS first tried a system of three co-presidents as a way of spreading out the work and also to ensure that no one person had too much power, given the very strong democratic impulses of the union activists. But this structural experiment failed, bogging the union down as it tried to move forward under a system in which neither responsibilities nor lines of authority were clearly defined. COGS ended up conferring with another large and diverse UE local with similar workplace issues: Local 1111 at the Allen Bradley factory in Milwaukee. COGS adopted a modified version of Local 1111's system that fit their own needs, including multiple area chief stewards reporting to one overall chief steward, a vice president whose primary responsibility is coordinating new employee organizing, and one president. While ultimate authority still rests with the membership, who can review all actions at monthly general meetings, the day-to-day work of the local can be completed within a well-defined structure. Between the executive board, monthly newsletter and regular e-mail communication, and general membership meetings, there are plenty of checks and balances on the power of any single individual. Finding structural practices that achieve the highest level of participation possible while not bogging all members down in genuine minutia is often difficult, but it can and must be done.

Multi-site or statewide bargaining units, often the case with public higher education unions, present a special challenge. The union has its strength greatly reduced if individual locals are going in different directions, either on goals or strategy. At a certain point, the will of the majority of the locals may have to overrule the wishes of some of the other locals, resulting in these locals feeling disempowered. The way to avoid this apparent clash between democracy and the need for unity is not to throw out democratic practices, nor to wander off into disunity, but instead to have a sound union education program in place from the start, put all of the information in front of all of the members, and maximize the possibilities of dialogue between the various locations. Having done that, the chances are very good that the workers at the various locations will draw the same conclusions together, with no single location feeling like something was forced on them unfairly.

The question of whether newly organized workers are members of the union deserving of full democratic rights has a similar answer. Unions have legitimate reasons not to grant full rights to those not yet under contract and paying dues. After all, the organizing drive itself is being financed by the dues money of those already in the union, and they have a right to say how it should be spent. Moreover, the depth of experience of newly organized workers with regards to organizing strategies is unlikely to match that of the officers and staff in an actively organizing union. However, unions cannot afford to let a situation develop to the point that the new union members feel they are being dictated to by the national union or the staff. Again, the best way to avoid that is by investing the time in education and discussion. Then, while the workers may not get to vote on every part of the strategy, they'll be far more likely to feel comfortable with it. This presupposes, of course, that many key decisions, such as initial contract demands, bargaining committee elections, and contract ratification are put to a democratic vote.

To the extent that unions organizing in the academic sector, or in any other industry, follow these practices, they will find a substantial contribution to their strength and vitality from their new members. To the extent that they don't, it is incumbent on the new union activists to find constructive means to bring about positive change within their unions, working to maximize unity with the rest of the membership. This may require the acceptance of less than ideal conditions in the short term while building for the long term. And it can only be done from a strong base of their own, a base established by taking care of the needs of their own local membership. In the process of doing this, they will probably find that not every idea and practice of those within the existing union structure is without merit. They may also find more than a few unionists sprinkled throughout the bureaucracy that are ready to move forward when they see the possibilities.

CHANGES IN THE ACADEMIC INDUSTRY

This book exists due to the upsurge in organizing on campuses in the 1990s. That upsurge can largely be traced to the changes being forced on many academic workers: As noted in these pages, colleges and universities are increasingly resorting to outsourcing, privatization, temporary and part-time work, and many of the other anti-worker practices that have been foisted on many workplaces for the past few decades. In addition, public employers, who at one time showed relatively little hostility to union organizing, have become much more antiunion.

These changes should not come as a great surprise since they fit into a general pattern of economic development being pushed throughout most of the world. The complete solutions to these problems will not be found simply by organizing individual workplaces, although this is a necessary start. A much higher level of solidarity, including currently banned practices like secondary boycotts and strikes, will be necessary to restore some balance to the labor-management power relationship. But beyond that, many of the problems workers face require solutions in the political sphere that will only come about when the labor movement is again seen as leading a social movement on behalf of all working people.

Meanwhile, the capitalist system is ruthlessly efficient at finding ways to rationalize anything it can get its hands on, and currently corporations see profit for the taking in the large amounts of money spent in education. Unions in academia must respond or employees will face ever-diminishing standards of life and work. Public sector unions in particular have to adjust their methods to fend off the same antiunion attacks that factory unions have suffered for decades. On the other hand, it is the very changes imposed by the corporate agenda that are driving many academic workers to unions for the first time. Capitalism at work is creating a working-class consciousness in academia.

NOTES

1. The tenure system is designed primarily to provide job security for faculty, being historically rooted in the desire to protect academic freedom in both the classroom and in research. However, academic institutions reserve the right to terminate even tenured professors if there is no longer a programmatic need for their services or in cases of "financial exigency." More commonly, colleges and universities find subtler means of

squeezing out tenured professors: Administrators may simply reduce a program's funding bit by bit over a period of years; or, entire departments can be eliminated by refusing to reauthorize tenure-line positions as older professors retire. As these tenure-line
positions are replaced by contingent faculty, who have no job security and are paid significantly less, a perhaps unintended, but far-reaching attack on academic freedom is implemented. For a discussion of program elimination and the attack on tenure in the 1980s
and 1990s, see, for example, Philo A. Hutcheson, *A professional professoriate: Unionization, bureaucratization, and the AAUP* (Nashville, TN: Vanderbilt University Press,
2000).

Index

Academe, 25

AFL-CIO, 65, 91

All-Campus Labor-Council, 149

Allen Bradley Factory, 197

American Association of University
Professors (AAUP), xix, 3–4, 14, 15,
16, 29, 180

American Council on Education, 67

American Federation of Labor (AFL), 3,
25

American Federation of State, County,
and Municipal Employees
(AFSCME), 74, 84; Local 12, 84

American Federation of Teachers (AFT),
xvii, 3, 11, 14–15, 72–79, 120, 128,
134, 154, 166; Local 1600, 61

Associated Student Employees (ASE),
96–103, 114

Association of Pennsylvania State College and University Faculty
(APSCUF), 13, 173, 176–187

Bennington College, 7

Bergman, Barbara, xiv

Bérubé, Michael: *The Employment of
English*, 14

Black Caucus, 132

Bourdieu, Pierre, 33–34, 36

Bradley, David, 31

Branch, Taylor, 81

Breeden, Dave, 162, 168–169

Bridges, Harry, 64

Bunn, Elizabeth, 91, 110

California Alliance of Unionized Student
Employees (CAUSE), 95, 98–105

Campaign to Organize Graduate Students (COGS), 8, 9, 11, 71–87, 192,
197

Campus Equity Week, 14, 68

Canadian Association of University
Teachers (CAUT), xix, 14, 45

Canadian Union of Public Employees
(CUPE), xix

Centola, Steve, 177, 186

Chalk Lines (Martin), 14

Chavez, Caesar, 64

Chicago City Colleges, 59, 61

City University of New York (CUNY), 6,
23, 31

Coalition of Contingent Academic Labor,
Boston, xvii

Coalition of Contingent Academic Labor,
Chicago, 68

Coalition of Graduate Employee Unions
    (CGEU), 121
Coleman, Mary Sue, 82
Columbia College, 66–77
Communications Workers of America
    (CWA), 74
Congress of Industrial Organizations
    (CIO), 65, 192
Cornell University, xvii
Cornfield, Gil, 169

Employment of English, The (Bérubé), 14

Faculty Staff Union, xvi
Faulkner, Larry, 164
Fédération des association québecoise de
    professeures et professeurs d'uni-
    versité (FAPUQ), xix
Fédération nationale des enseignantes et
    des enseignants du Québec
    (FNEEQ), xix
Florida Agricultural and Mechanical
    University (FAMU), 119–120, 122,
    126, 131
Florida Education Association (FEA),
    119–121, 123, 125, 128, 132
Frente Auténtico del Trabajo / Authentic
    Workers' Front (FAT), 86
Fulmer, William, 177, 178, 180–181,
    183–184

Gainesville Civic Media Center, 132
Gerhardt, Kenneth, 124
Graduate Assistants United (GAU), 11,
    127–134
Graduate Employees and Students Orga-
    nization (GESO), xvii, 148
Graduate Employees Organization
    (GEO): Illinois, 13, 154–169; Michi-
    gan, 12–13, 140–150
Graduate Student Caucus of the Modern
    Language Association, 14
Green Party, 86

Harold Washington College, 59–60
Harvard University, 9
Higher Education Employee Relations
    Act, California (HEERA), 94

Hotel Employees and Restaurant Em-
    ployees (HERE), 9
Huron Valley Labor Council, 149ZZ
Hutchinson, Bill, 65

Illinois Education Association (IEA),
    66–67
Illinois Educational Labor Relations Act
    (IELRA), 13, 156–161, 163–164, 166
Illinois Educational Labor Relations
    Board (IELRB), 156–158, 160–162,
    166
Illinois Federation of Teachers, 166
International Brotherhood of Electrical
    Workers, 65; Local 1634, 84
International Longshoremen's and
    Warehousemen's Union (ILWU),
    63–64
Iowa City Federation of Labor, 84
Iowa Public Employee Relations Act, 89
Iowa United Professionals (IUP) Local
    893, 86

Kerr, Howard, 46
Kingsley, Robert, 85

Lewis, John L., 65
Lutz, Richard, 124

Managed Professionals: Unionized
    Faculty and Restructuring Aca-
    demic Labor (Rhoades), 14
Manifesto of a Tenured Radical (Nel-
    son), 14
Martin, Randy: Chalk Lines, 14
Martin Luther King Day, 81–83
Marx, Karl, 63
Marxist Reading Group Conference, 131
Massenburg, Mary Ann, 98–105
McCarthyism, 74, 78, 85, 196
McGill University, xix
McGuire, Peter J., 65
Meany, George, 65
Menand, Louis, 23, 28, 32–33
Miami-Dade Community College, 128
Michigan State University, xvi
Millersville University, 173, 177,
    181–182, 185–186

Modern Language Association, 14
Montgomery, David, 91

Nader, Ralph, 86
National Education Association (NEA), xix, 3, 14, 15, 119, 120–121, 125, 128, 132
National Labor Party, 121
National Labor Relations Act (NLRA), 6, 14
National Labor Relations Board (NLRB), xvii-xviii, xx, 14, 66, 154; *v. Yeshiva University*, 6, 14, 31
National Organization for Women (NOW), 132
National Public Radio (NPR), 31
Nelson, Cary: *Will Teach for Food; Manifesto of a Tenured Radical*, 9, 14, 148
Newspaper Guild, 15
New York University, xvii, xx, 14, 139
North Central Florida Labor Council, 132, 134
Northern Illinois University (NIU), 158

Ontario Public Service Employees' Union, 56

Part-time Faculty Association, Columbia College (Pfac), 66–67
Pennsylvania Act, 177
Pennsylvania State University (PSU), 177
Public Employee Relations Board (PERB), 94, 95, 103

Reuther, Walter, 65
Rhoades, Gary: *Managed Professionals: Unionized Faculty and Restructuring Academic Labor*, 14, 43, 54
Ridge, Tom, 177
Rockwell-Collins International, 84
Roosevelt University, 59, 67
Roosevelt University Adjunct Faculty Organization (RAFO), 67
Rowan, Judith, 169
Ryerson Faculty Association (RFA), 10, 41, 44, 46–51, 53–56

Ryerson Polytechnic University, xix, 41, 44–56

San Francisco General Strike, 10, 63
Schacht, Richard, 168–169
Service Employees International Union (SEIU), 74–76, 78, 84; Local 150, 75; Local 199, 84
Simms, Leslie, 75–76, 79
Small, Mary Jo, 80
Stanford University, 35
State System of Higher Education, Pennsylvania (SSHE), 31, 173, 176–184, 187
State University of New York, 6
Students Against COGS (SAC), 80
Students Against Sweatshops (SAS), 9, 84
Students Tired of Propaganda (STOP), 75–76, 80
Sweeney, John, 91, 110
Syracuse University, xvii, xviii

Taft-Hartley Act, xvii
Teaching Assistants Association (TAA), 146
Teamsters, 66–67, 149
Temple University, xvi, 31–32

United Automobile Workers (UAW), xvii, xx, 9, 11, 65, 91–114; District 65, 94; Local 2865, 105–106
United Brotherhood of Carpenters and Joiners, 65
United Electrical, Radio and Machine Workers of America (UE), xv, 9, 71–72, 74, 76–81, 83–87, 191–192; Local 893–IUP (Iowa United Professionals), 78 86; Local 896–COGS, xv, 8, 9, 11, 71–87, 192, 197
United Faculty of Florida (UFF), 11, 119–121, 124–129, 132
United Farm Workers (UFW), 64
United Mine Workers of America, 65
United Parcel Service (UPS), 66–67
United Student Labor (USL), 103, 105
University of California (UC), xix, xx, 11, 35, 91, 93–98, 102–106, 109,

112; Berkeley, 94, 95, 105, 107, 109, 112, 113; Davis, 95, 107, 112, 113; Irvine, 113, 95; Los Angeles, 95, 113; Riverside, 94, 95, 107, 112, 113; Santa Barbara (UCSB), xiii, xx, 11, 91–113; Santa Cruz, 94, 95, 107, 112, 113; San Diego, 95, 113; San Francisco, 113

University of Florida (UF), 11, 117–134, 158, 195

University of Illinois, Urbana-Champaign (UIUC), xvi, 13, 154–160, 162–169, 195

University of Iowa, xiv-xvi, xix, xx, 8, 11, 12, 71–87, 192, 195; Hospitals and Clinics, 84; Student Federation of Teachers, 72

University of Massachusetts, xix

University of Massachusetts-Amherst, xvii, 112

University of Massachusetts-Boston, xvi-xvii

University of Michigan, 13, 140–150, 195

University of Minnesota, 7, 30–32

University of Phoenix, 67

University of South Florida (USF), 119–120, 122, 126

University of Wisconsin—Madison, 5, 72, 146, 168

Unusual and Unexpected Classroom Materials Policy, 7–8

Van Hise, Charles, 5

Vietnam War, 72

Wagner Act, xvii

Will Teach for Food (Nelson), 9, 14, 148

Wisconsin Idea, 5

Workplace, 14

Yale University, xvii, 35, 142, 148

Yeshiva decision, 6, 14, 31

York University, 46

About the Contributors

JOE BERRY has been a contingent history and labor studies teacher in three states. He has been, variously, an activist, part-time organizer, officer, and staff representative in both the AFT and NEA. He teaches at Chicago's Roosevelt University, Malcolm X College, and Indiana University–Northwest. He chairs the Member Organizing Committee for Roosevelt Adjunct Faculty Organization/IEA/NEA, and is pursuing a PhD on contingent faculty organizing strategies at The Union Institute.

SUSAN ROTH BREITZER is a PhD candidate in history at the University of Iowa. Her research and writing interests include United States labor, social, and political history. Her dissertation is entitled "Class, Ethnicity, and Community: The Jewish Working Class of Chicago, 1886–1928." She has written a book review for *American Jewish History;* and articles on Jewish, labor, social, and political history for *Jewish Women in America* (1997), *Historical Encyclopedia of U.S. Independent Counsel Investigations* (2000), *Encyclopedia of New England Culture* (in press), and the *Dictionary of American History* (in press). During the 1997–98 school year, she was chair of the Press and Publicity Committee of UE Local 896-COGS.

MIKE BURKE is an associate professor in the Department of Politics and School of Public Administration at Ryerson University. He recently co-edited a book with Colin Mooers and John Shields titled *Restructuring and Resistance: Canadian Public Policy in an Age of Global Capitalism* (Fernwood, 2000), in which he examined recent transformations in Canadian health-care policy and new trends in labor market inequality in Canada.

Susan Chimonas completed a PhD in sociology from the University of Michigan. Her dissertation research examined the allegations (now largely discounted) of mass, Satanic ritual abuse of children in day care during the 1980s. As a member of the Graduate Employees Organization, she served as department steward and publicity campaign manager during the 1998–99 contract negotiations. Dr. Chimonas lives in New York City and is a postdoctoral researcher at the Institute for Health, Health Care Policy, and Aging Research at Rutgers University.

Jonathan T. Church is assistant professor of anthropology and chair of the Department of Sociology and Anthropology at Arcadia University. He has published in the *International Journal of Qualitative Studies in Education*, the *Chronicle of Higher Education*, as well as *Anthropological Quarterly*. He is the ethnographer for the "Talking Towards Techno-Pedagogy" initiative sponsored by the Mellon Foundation. He has done research on the politics of identity in the Shetland Islands. Also, he has researched the negotiations of identity across race, gender, and sexual orientation for volunteer caregivers to persons living with AIDS in Philadelphia. His current research is studying how online game players establish notions of self and identity.

Eric Dirnbach completed a PhD in biophysics from the University of Michigan. While at Michigan, he was a member of the Graduate Employees Organization and served as department steward, a member of the Steering Committee, and as president during the 1998–99 contract negotiations. He has also been active in the antisweatshop movement, founding a student group at Michigan that has worked toward establishing requirements for its apparel manufacturers to end their sweatshop labor practices. Dr. Dirnbach now works in the labor movement on Special Projects with the Union of Needletrades, Industrial and Textile Employees (UNITE!) in New York City.

Deborah M. Herman received her BA and MA from the University of Northern Iowa in Spanish language and literature. She is currently an interdisciplinary doctoral candidate at the University of Iowa. Her recent publications include "Iowa College Students' Attitudes toward Official English Legislation" in *The Journal of Language, Identity and Education* and "'Our Patriotic Duty': Insights from Professional History, 1890–1920" (in Osborn 2002, Bergin & Garvey). She was president of UE Local 896-COGS at the University of Iowa from 1998 to 2000.

David Montgomery is the author of *Citizen Worker* (Cambridge University Press, 1993) and *The Fall of the House of Labor* (Cambridge University Press, 1989). He has been a machinist and union shop steward and later taught history at the University of Pittsburgh, Warwick University, Oxford University, and Campinas in Brazil. He has also served as president of the Organization of American Historians. Currently he is Farnam Professor of History Emeritus at Yale University.

JOANNE NAIMAN is a professor of sociology at Ryerson Polytechnic University in Toronto, Canada, where she has taught a variety of courses to undergraduates since 1971. The second edition of her book, *How Societies Work: Class, Power, and Change in a Canadian Context,* was recently published by Irwin. She has also been active for many years in social justice and social change issues and was vice president of her faculty association from 1998 to 2000.

CARL ROSEN is president of District Council 11 of the United Electrical, Radio and Machine Workers of America (UE). Before being elected to that post in 1994, he worked for thirteen years as a maintenance electrician. He has been an elected member of the national UE General Executive Board since 1990 and a general vice president of UE since 1994. He earned a bachelor's degree in applied mathematics from Harvard University in 1980, with economics as his field of application.

JULIE M. SCHMID received her PhD from the University of Iowa's Department of English in 2000. Her research interests include contemporary performance poetry, avant garde poetics, and critical higher education studies. She has presented on the academic labor movement at a number of conferences and has published essays on academic labor in the *MMLA Journal* and in *Workplace*. She served as a departmental steward (1996–1998) and vice president (1998–1999) of UE Local 896-COGS. She now works for the Department of Organizing and Services of the AAUP.

WESLEY SHUMAR is a cultural anthropologist at Drexel University whose research focuses on higher education, virtual community, ethnographic evaluation in education, the semiotics of mass culture, and the self in relation to contemporary personal and political issues of identity and globalization. He is also an ethnographic evaluator for the Math Forum, a virtual math education resource center. Dr. Shumar is author of *College for Sale: A Critique of the Commodification of Higher Education* (Falmer Press, 1997) and coauthor of the forthcoming *Culture, Subject, Psyche: Anthropology, Psychoanalysis and Social Theory* (Athlone Press and Wesleyan University Press). He is also co-editing a forthcoming volume entitled *Building Virtual Communities: Learning and Change in Cyberspace* (Cambridge University Press).

RICHARD SULLIVAN is a doctoral candidate in sociology at the University of California, Santa Barbara. His current research addresses the connection between labor organizing and American culture of capitalism. He is currently a member of UAW Local 2865. In addition to being an activist with ASE/UAW in Santa Barbara, he has also been a staff organizer for SHARE/AFSCME in Worchester,

Massachusetts, and a volunteer activist with MGAA/AFT at the University of Wisconsin, Milwaukee.

JAMES THOMPSON earned an MA in history from the University of Akron. He is currently a PhD candidate and teaching associate in the Department of History at the University of Florida. His dissertation, "Making Coffee: American Empire and Consumption before the Cold War," intersects the study of commodity culture with diplomatic and commercial history. He argues that a transnational regime of entrepreneurs, diplomats, and statesmen organized cultural production and commodity exchange to foment modernist state building and imperial expansion in the Americas. From 1999 to 2001, Thompson served as co-president for Graduate Assistants United (UFF-FEA/AFL-CIO) at the University of Florida and as chief negotiator during 2000–2001 contract bargaining with the Board of Regents. He is the recipient of the graduate student Award for Service to the Profession (2000) from Teachers for a Democratic Culture.

WILLIAM VAUGHN is an assistant professor of English and director of freshman composition at Central Missouri State University in Warrensburg. He is a founding member of the Graduate Employees' Organization, IFT-AFT/AFL-CIO, at the University of Illinois, Urbana-Champaign, and has published widely in areas such as early American literature, sublime theory, and academic activism.

DARLA S. WILLIAMS is an assistant professor of organizational communication at Millersville University. Her research interests center around identity and resistance, particularly as they relate to organizational phenomena and gender issues. She is currently involved in research projects studying identity and resistance in both educational institutions and on film. She teaches courses in organizational communication and gender and communication. She received her PhD in organizational communication from Purdue University.